The First Elections

The First Elections

The Rise of Electoral Democracy in the Early American Republic

Jay K. Dow

University Press of Kansas

Published by the University Press of Kansas (Lawrence, Kansas 66045), which was organized by the Kansas Board of Regents and is operated and funded by Emporia State University, Fort Hays State University, Kansas State University, Pittsburg State University, the University of Kansas, and Wichita State University.

Library of Congress Cataloging-in-Publication Data

ISBN 9780700641505 (cloth)
ISBN 9780700643882 (paper)
ISBN 9780700641512 (e-book)
LCCN 2025047003

British Library Cataloguing-in-Publication Data is available.

EU Authorised Representative Details: Easy Access System Europe
Mustamäe tee 50, 10621 Tallinn, Estonia | gpsr.requests@easproject.com

Cover art: *Election Day in Philadelphia* (detail), 1815, by John Lewis Krimmel, Winterthur Museum. Museum purchase with funds provided by Henry Francis du Pont.

This book will be made open access within three years of publication thanks to Path to Open, a program developed in partnership between JSTOR, the American Council of Learned Societies (ACLS), University of Michigan Press, and the University of North Carolina Press to bring about equitable access and impact for the entire scholarly community, including authors, researchers, libraries, and university presses around the world. Learn more at https://about.jstor.org/path-to-open/.

Electioneering Enthusiasm is evidently diffusing among Freemen, created, perhaps, by the ridiculous Insinuations of such as are neither well-born or well-bred: It is, however, presumed, that at this all-important Crisis, local interests, partial Opinions, nor political Frenzy, will influence the Freemen, at the approaching Election of Federal Delegates; for certainly every candid Mind, from the popular citizen to the obscure Villager, must be impressed with the serious, national Importance, of deputing the ableist, wisest and most approved statesmen . . . for on the Members FIRST *delegated, rests the Pillars of our rising Empire.*

Weekly Monitor, Litchfield, Connecticut, October 27, 1789

Contents

Tables and Figures

Tables

Figures

Preface and Acknowledgments

The genesis of this book owes to my affiliation in the University of Missouri's Kinder Institute on Constitutional Democracy (KICD). The institute houses political scientists, historians, and legal scholars with shared interests in American political thought, development, and the constitutional tradition. Most KICD faculty, myself included, focus on the early republic and the development and expansion of its ideas and institutions.

When I joined the KICD one of the first things that struck me was how the historians talked about early American elections. They described vibrant, participatory elections that were organized around the nascent parties and substantive political differences. This surprised me. I shared the received understanding that the early United States electoral universe was the province of "men in silk stockings" and that average men deferred to their social and economic superiors in political matters. I uncritically accepted the received narrative that it was not until the Age of Jackson that the United States developed recognizably modern elections. Institutionalized political parties, campaigning, position taking, and other familiar aspects of elections emerged in the Age of Jackson, not the Age of Jefferson. To be sure, some political scientists and historians have challenged this understanding. However, the idea that Jacksonian elections were fundamentally different than their predecessors stood. Yet the historians, visiting scholars, and invited speakers with whom I had contact described hotly contested elections, partisanship, stump speeches, and high elector turnout. This sounded more Jacksonian than Jeffersonian to me.

I quickly learned three things about this "new" historical narrative. First, it is not that new. It dates to the 1960s, as do I and some of my colleagues who embrace it. Second, it is not universally, or even largely, accepted. There is an active debate over the nature of early United States elections. Third, and most important for present purposes, political science and its theoretical and empirical approaches has much to offer this conversation. While contemporary political science is not absent from the debate, there is room for increased contribution from my home discipline. As a political scientist who specializes in electoral institutions and processes, I was deeply interested when my historian colleagues described an expansive collection of early republic vote returns that were unknown to me. Principal investigator Phillip Lampi nearly single-handedly collected these returns over the course of decades. These are now housed as the A New Nation Votes (NNV) project under the auspices of the American Antiquarian Society. It is not hyperbole to say that Lampi is in no small measure responsible for much of what we are likely to learn in the future about early US elections. I used a handful of these returns in my previous book, *Electing the House,* which focuses on the adoption of the single-member district system for electing federal representatives. Here I explore the returns more comprehensively for what they tell us about the development of early US elections.

The book's purpose is to explore what House of Representatives constituency-level election returns contribute to our understanding of early American electoral development. I evaluate these returns from a perspective informed by both political science and historical scholarship. Political scientists and historians ask different questions and use different approaches to address these questions. In these distinct ways both disciplines illuminate our understanding of early American elections. I seek to make this clear in the opening chapters. These demonstrate how deeply I rely on the relevant historical scholarship. For its part, political science brings well-developed theories of party and party system emergence, and empirical approaches to assess these processes. This scholarship invites one to focus on the most salient aspect of early congressional elections and what these returns reveal about elections in the early republic.

This book and the scholarship upon which it builds seeks to elucidate one of the most important questions in US political development; namely, when did the United States become a recognizably modern republic? That is, when did House elections cease to be primarily the province of elites and instead become the domain of men of typical means? When did House elections move from ad hoc and localized, to structured and nationalized? Political scientists have long studied democratic emergence and consolidation. However, this scholarship largely centers on the development and consolidation of new democracies, especially those of the twentieth century. Recalling that the United States was once an emergent democracy, these same theories and methods can tell us much about the development of early US electoral institutions, processes, their trajectories, and, ultimately, our political selves. These are exceedingly complex questions. In the United States the states organize and administer elections. Each state has its own political culture, history, institutions, and processes. We do not have a United States election; we have many state elections. This is true today and was even more so in the early republic.

This book is written for an informed but general scholarly audience. Political science theory resides in the background, not in the foreground. Likewise, the empirical analysis never extends beyond tables and graphs. My historian colleagues are fond of saying political science "flattens" history. I have tried to maintain the contours of history while pointing to several connected empirical patterns and how these might be interpreted considering political science knowledge. My political science colleagues question if the historical narrative is necessary and whether it distracts from the larger questions. It *is* necessary, and it does not distract. I balance these considerations at the risk of annoying both audiences. However, I strive to make clear that these approaches to understanding early elections are complementary, not competitive.

Here I thank those who moved this book forward. My University of Missouri KICD and Truman School of Government and Public Affairs colleagues helped in many ways. These included listening to me think out loud about ideas embedded, or not, in the manuscript. I also thank the University of Missouri Provost Office and the KICD, both of which provided a course release so I could work on the book. I also very much appreciate the research assistance I received from three of Mizzou's terrific undergraduates: Dylan Evins brought his knowledge of geography and mapping to the project and helped produce the maps in this book. History major Mason Andrews spent hours reading period newspapers for tidbits on elections and brought a sharp eye for identifying relevant commentary. Constitutional Democracy major Maggie Funston picked up where Mason left off and brough her penchant for detail work to help me find and correct missing and improperly cited references. I thank Rosemarie Zagarri and her colleagues at George Mason University's Roy Rosenzweig Center for History and New Media for hosting me to discuss their mappings of these election returns and how I might do so for this book. Finally, I thank the late Walter Dean Burnham. Many years ago, Burnham led one of my University of Texas graduate seminars. At the time I did not appreciate how deeply he influenced how I think about American elections. This is because my career and research were well off in another direction. Later when I started to think about elections and political development, I found myself, at least mentally, back in his seminar. Without these great mentors and colleagues, the book's completion would be greatly delayed.

Of course, my greatest depth of gratitude goes to my family, especially my wife, Debbie. In a global sense, Debbie gave me the gift of pursuing a scholarly career. Or, as I like to believe Crash Davis might have put it, she gave me the gift of going to the ballpark every day. To be sure, every day she gave me reasons to not think or talk about early American elections and all the other things that are best left at the office. I thank our daughters, Rachelle and Laurel, for providing similar support and distractions. Whether this book is well received or not, they will give me favorable reviews. For that I am grateful.

1 | The Development of Congressional Elections

The signature contribution of the US Constitution is that it created what James Madison called a "strictly republican" government; a representative democracy that "derives all its powers directly or indirectly from the great body of the people, and is administered by persons holding their offices during pleasure for a limited period."[1] This republican mandate is reiterated for the states in the Constitution's fourth article and in so doing establishes elections as the primary vehicle for citizen input into the government and for their control over it.

The United States has practiced electoral democracy for nearly 240 years, and much is known about the history and development of elections. The earliest elections, however, remain opaque. Although political historians have written on the early republic's electoral culture, the bases for political conflict, and political party development, we know less about the constituency-level contests for votes and office and how these furthered the development of the American republic. The founding generation struggled to reconcile its high-minded republican ideals with their intention to advance deeply disputed visions of the future United States. The electoral constituency where votes were solicited and counted was the primary battlefield in this war of ideals, and it is here we must look to understand the creation of Madison's strictly republican government.

This book illuminates the development of congressional elections in the early republic. By "development" I mean the establishment of elections as the primary means by which ordinary citizens convey their political goals, aspirations, and preferences to governing elites and hold these officials accountable for their actions in office. The defining feature of late eighteenth and early nineteenth-century American politics, a period we commonly call the first party era, was the transition from "deferential-participant" politics in which local elites exercised great influence over elections in their communities, to an electoral politics in which the enfranchised increasingly became self-determining, organized along party alliances and responsive to political issues and events. This transition occurred sometime around the "democratic revolution" of 1800, but we are confident in only its broad contours or its path in specific locations at specific times.

This book specifically studies the county, district, and state votes in US House of Representatives elections in the original thirteen states, 1796–1825. House elections are central to the development of United States electoral democracy. The representative assembly is the foundational institution in republican government. The lower chamber possesses the greatest concentration of government powers, most importantly the power to tax. Further, House elections most directly brought citizens in contact with national politics and their government. This is because these elections were typically contested in smaller, geographically defined constituencies. House elections provide a more fine-grained picture of electoral development than the selection of presidential electors, which were not even popularly elected in some states.

It is difficult to peer behind the historical veil of the late eighteenth and early nineteenth centuries to map the development of elections and the pace of this transition with confidence. This is primarily because the vote returns documenting many of these contests were thought lost to history. Some returns exist, but most were thought to be fragmentary or missing. Detailed knowledge of early elections was limited to the times and places that presented usable returns supported by documentary records.

Fortunately, this situation has been greatly remedied by newly available early republic election returns. These are the product of a long-term collection effort by the A New Nation Votes project (NNV) under the auspices of the American Antiquarian Society.[2] The collection is not complete—there remain gaps. Nonetheless, these data are ample for comprehensive, rigorous analysis of elections in the nation's first years. When combined with contemporary accounts and extant histories, the returns illuminate the development and institutionalization of mass electoral politics in the young nation in a manner not previously possible. The available returns are sufficiently numerous, and the period is sufficiently long, to reveal patterns in electoral development. The votes also capture regional differences in electoral development by encompassing New England (Massachusetts, New Hampshire, Connecticut, and Rhode Island), the Middle Atlantic (Pennsylvania, New

Jersey, and New York), border states (Maryland and Delaware) and the South (Virginia, North Carolina, South Carolina, and Georgia).[3] This enables one to address questions about early US elections that were previously informed by limited empirical evidence or simply thought unapproachable.

The primary reason some scholars describe the latter part of this period as the Era of Good Feelings is the presumed near complete demise of the Federalist Party. By the Fifteenth Congress (1817–1819) there were only 39 Federalists in the House of Representatives—and 141 Democratic-Republicans. Things only got worse for the Federalists in subsequent congresses. However, scholars have primarily observed the election outcomes, not the votes that produced these outcomes. The win-loss column is a lousy measure of party support. It potentially masks nontrivial support that is still insufficient to win elections. Sometimes this is because party support is geographically concentrated. Vote aggregation methods such as at-large elections and multimember districts diminish the importance of localized support in determining outcomes. For example, in most years New Jersey elected its representatives at-large. In 1814 New Jersey Federalists won 48 percent of the statewide vote and no representation. The Democratic-Republicans won all six House seats. That same year the Federalists controlled nearly half of the state assembly. The Federalists won assembly seats because New Jersey elected multiple assemblymen from each county.[4] The Federalist-leaning counties sent affiliated assemblymen to Trenton. This is not an isolated example; several states used at-large elections and multimember districts that precluded the Federalists from translating often robust, geographically concentrated support into representation. Further, single-member district elections, whether the districts are gerrymandered or not, provide the leading party with a "bonus" in translating votes into legislative seats. As will be seen, the Federalists enjoyed more electoral support than the size of their congressional delegations indicate.

The book is organized around three themes. The first is geography. Electoral politics differed across US regions and across geographic areas within the states. American politics—especially in the founding era—is territorial politics. Any accounting of the emergence of American republican governance must highlight the similarities and differences in electoral development across states and regions.

The second organizing principle is time. The first party era, from 1789 to 1824, spans three decades. I begin in 1796 with the elections to the Fifth Congress. This cycle marks the introduction of truly contested elections following the Federalist and Anti-Federalist period and the Washington administration.[5] When George Washington left office he opened the door for the first competitive presidential election between Federalist John Adams and Democratic-Republican Thomas Jefferson. The election revealed the presence of two distinct visions of the United States. These visions were also present in the House of Representatives, where two opposing voting coalitions emerged. The era can be subdivided into three distinct periods: the founding to the "democratic revolution" of 1800, the period from 1800 through the War of 1812, and the postwar era through the James Monroe administration. Each period captures an important stage in the development of American electoral politics. The book concludes with elections to the Nineteenth Congress (1825–1827). This election cycle marks the opening of the Jacksonian period and the second American party system.

The third organizing theme is the electoral system. The states used a variety of methods to elect their representatives. These included single-member districts, multimember districts, and statewide at-large elections. Some states required a vote plurality for election. Other states required a majority, raising the possibility of multi-round elections. Further, statehouse-controlling parties sometimes changed their election methods between elections, often for partisan advantage. The electoral calendar also shaped the emergence of developed elections. The early United States didn't have a standardized election calendar. Instead, states held their elections on often widely separated dates. For example, Maryland elected its representatives to the Eleventh Congress in October 1808. Virginia held its elections in April 1809, well after the start of the session. States sometimes elected their national and state offices on different dates as well. This often-overlooked feature of the electoral system meant that preceding elections illuminated party prospects in subsequent elections. This is especially true for regional neighbors. Combined, these system features shaped elite and mass political engagement and the formation of cross-constituency and cross-office alliances—that is, the development of political parties, party systems, and the emergence of competitive, mass participatory elections.

The book's overarching question centers on the ability of political elites to organize themselves and mass supporters to form nascent parties and elect preferred candidates. Legislative elections present a detailed picture of the parties and their strength in various regions of the states and the nation. I also explore what these elections tell us about democratic norms and practices in the early republic. Finally, I use the returns to assess how national political events (Jay's Treaty, the Sedition Act, the Embargo Act, the Hartford Convention, the Compensation Act of 1816, etc.) influenced electoral politics in the new nation. All of this is the stuff of the development of US electoral democracy.

The balance of this chapter is organized as follows: The next section discusses how one can assess whether elections have transitioned from the "deferential participant" politics of the founding to more recognizably modern and party-centered elections. I then review the extant knowledge of political party emergence and development and how this theoretical foundation elucidates early elections. Following this I consider how one can assess whether parties comprise a regional or national party system. Finally, I briefly review how the NNV election returns inform electoral development. To do so I use an 1800 Pennsylvania single-member district election, the 1816 New Hampshire general-ticket election, and Maryland county-level returns as illustrative examples. The final section overviews the balance of the book. I devote a chapter to each of the four early US geographic regions. The NNV returns hold key information that illuminates the progression of party development and the institutionalization of modern elections in the new nation.

The Development of Modern Elections

How do we know if electoral politics has transitioned from a proto-democratic "deferential-participant" period to developed elections in the sense discussed here? This is a complex question. A milestone in American political development is the transition from viewing the "spirit of party" as antithetical to republicanism to thinking parties, or at least one's party, as embodying republican values. This happened early in American history and is reflected in those standing for office and their supporters embracing partisan affiliation. With this came changes in electoral language, especially in newspapers and broadsheets where political commentary evolved from individualistic and particularistic to universal and issue-based.[6]

There is no single indicator that conclusively establishes whether recognizably modern electoral politics took root in any given place at any given time. However, there are several markers that when viewed in their totality provide insight into the development and institutionalization of elections. These are described and justified below, but all speak to the ability of parties to supplant the activities of local elites and for voters to exercise effective personal discretion in voting. The vote returns provide an invaluable resource for exploring six markers of electoral development that most directly illuminate early elections. These are the number of competitive party candidates in each election, election turnout, aggregate party support, evidence of partisanship, the number of elections in which candidates stand for office, and the electoral fortunes of incumbents. The returns also indicate whether the parties used election rules for political advantage. The use of election processes such as vote aggregation methods and districting points to electoral development because their effective use requires that partisanship reside in the electorate.

The number of candidates indicates whether parties can control candidate entry and the efficacy of nomination procedures, or at least whether norms exist for candidates to step aside to permit a more viable co-partisan to stand for election. If there are no barriers to entry then like-minded candidates may overcrowd the field and split the vote. Barriers to entry provide considerable advantage to the more disciplined party. Election turnout points to democratization, party development, electoral competitiveness, and how elections are contested. Political historians have long noticed that the early United States enjoyed high levels of elector participation.[7] However, much of this evidence comes from a limited number of elections at particular times and places. The House of Representatives returns reveal systematic patterns in participation and help explain changes in participation rates. The aggregate party vote, whether at the county, district, or state level, provides a more nuanced view of party support than whether an election was won or lost. The returns show that while the Federalists lost many elections they often did so with rather respectable levels of support. Partisanship in the electorate is a foundation of party and party system development. Partisanship, inter alia, provides the predictable bases of political support necessary for governing coalitions to function effectively, allows for the purposeful use of electoral rules for advantage, and facilitates meaningful citizen electoral engagement. Inferring partisanship from aggregate vote returns presents methodological challenges that I address later. For now, it is simply useful to note that the returns present several ways to assess party in the electorate. Multimember districts and at-large elections were used in the early United States. These returns, particularly their within party vote spreads, provide considerable information on partisanship. The geography of support reveals where parties were most and least competitive and, by extension, the differences in party constituencies. Finally, the stability of the district and county votes reveals much about whether the parties enjoyed reliable bases of support.

The methods used to elect representatives inform much about the development and viability of early US parties. It is difficult to delve deeply into the question of whether the state parties adopted election methods for electoral advantage. However, the decision to use at-large elections, multimember district elections, or single-member districts is never politically neutral. Parties are either advantaged or disadvantaged by election methods, a point not lost on the founding generation. A prerequisite for the advantageous use of vote aggregation methods is partisanship in the electorate. One must know the locations of one's supporters and opponents and have confidence their votes are reliable. Otherwise, these practices can misfire badly. Importantly, party decisions to contest an election may be an endogenous response to the rules; a party denied seats because the playing field is tilted irrevocably against it may simply concede the game even if it enjoys considerable support. A key argument of this book is that the election methods in force are an important and neglected factor in understanding the decline of the Federalist Party.

Finally, patterns in candidates standing for office indicates the extent to which incumbents are successfully reelected, and whether these electoral fortunes are plausibly related to changes in electorate partisanship, political issues and events, or other, less easily identified considerations. In these years there was no congressional career. Most representatives served a couple of terms, if that.[8] Even so, the returns indicate whether there are episodes that encouraged candidates to stand or concede election, and whether these effects disproportionately visited one party's candidates.

These indicators are "soft" in that they are attributes that one would consider in assessing the development of elections in the early republic. There is no bright line test for determining if electoral politics has moved to established, party-centered elections. This judgment can only be made by considering the returns in combination with the documentary record to produce an informed assessment of the overall state of electoral politics. This requires scholarly judgment buttressed by tangible evidence provided by analysis of votes and the allocation of legislative seats.

Political Parties and Electoral Development

The political development of elections requires the creation of political parties. Parties are the key institution that structures the programmatic differences that divide governing elites, mobilize the electorate, and enable citizens to hold governing officials accountable for their performance in office. Simply, rising party means declining deference.

Political parties are created by elites to solve institutional problems such as forming stable governing coalitions.[9] Consequently, the genesis of parties is in the legislative caucus. However, in a republic parties must have an electoral foundation. There can be no stable governing or opposing caucuses unless affiliated representatives have predictable bases of popular support. Nor can citizens convey their political preferences and subsequently hold legislators accountable for their actions without this link between representatives and the represented. The existence of a meaningful alternative to an incumbent government requires that an alternative can be identified. This is not possible in an ad hoc, unstructured political setting. Electoral parties provide that structure. Party in government, at least in republican government, requires party in the constituency.

Recent scholarship presents increasing evidence of the rise of electoral parties and consequential elections earlier in American history than previously thought. The early republic saw the erosion of the old deferential style of politics coupled with the creation of electoral parties that successfully contested elections in their jurisdictions and commanded loyalty in the electorate. Further, these competitive contests continued throughout the first party era, long after the presumed demise of the Federalists ushered in the so-called Era of Good Feelings.

What Is a Political Party?

Scholarly debate over the formation of American political parties is, as John F. Hoadley aptly put it, "a game of definitions."[10] Restrictive party definitions place their emergence in the 1830s. More flexible interpretations admit the development of national parties as early as 1796. William Nisbet Chambers, Walter Dean Burnham, and Frank J. Sorauf provide the canonical definition of a political party as "a relatively durable social formation which seeks offices or power in government, exhibits a structure or organization which links leaders at the center of government to a significant popular following in the political arena and its local enclaves . . . and generates . . . symbols of identification and loyalty."[11]

This definition has much to recommend it. It clearly distinguishes political parties from other social organizations. It emphasizes that their raison d'être is to win office. Parties seek to control the governing apparatus. The definition makes clear that party-in-government alone is not a true party. A party must have an organizational structure. In addition, party must exist in the electorate; that is, there must exist partisan identification. This points to the social role of parties. Through the creation of partisan identification, people come to think of themselves as politically like some citizens and different from others. This connects citizens with fellow political travelers and helps create political communities that advance shared interests and values. The definition further highlights parties' electoral role by emphasizing that parties link the governed and the governors. Party labels enable voters to infer much about what politicians stand for and hold them accountable for their performance in office. By creating a connection between citizens and representatives, parties produce more informed votes and greater electoral accountability. The definition requires that true parties have durability, thereby distinguishing parties from transient social movements. Finally, by pointing to party residing in local enclaves it makes clear that political parties have geographic reach.

Despite its virtues this definition is incomplete for understanding the early US parties. Two of its features have led scholars to misunderstand the development of the early parties. First, it encourages scholars to overemphasize the role of "leaders at the center of government" in the creation and maintenance of parties. Nobody doubts that political leadership played an important role in party emergence and development, but party development in the United States was more organic and decentralized than often recognized. Many of the most important party builders never held public office. Second, by emphasizing the importance of party organizations it has encouraged scholars to equate party organization with the well-defined and structured Democratic and

Whig organizations that emerged in the mid-nineteenth century. The Republican and Federalist Party organizational structure, as explained later, centered on the press. While no less an organization, this differed considerably from its later counterparts.

To prove useful the received definition must be leavened with other conceptions of party. Among these, Marty Cohen et al.'s description of parties as "the creatures of interest groups, ideological activists, and others whom we call intense policy demanders" is especially valuable.[12] In this view parties are created by "intense policy demanders" and are defined by the groups that comprise it. These policy demanders may be trade and guild leaders, planters, merchants, small-scale farmers, speculators of various stripes, and others with deep interest in government policy. These groups are motivated by policy goals that require them to elect officials that will enact these ends. Elected officials are the agents of decentralized political actors who "organize parties to get the government policies they want."[13]

This understanding of party supplements rather than replaces standard definitions. It does so by deemphasizing the role of elected officials and highly visible political elites in forming parties. If parties are defined by the groups that comprise them, this diminishes the importance of a hierarchical, top-down organizational structure. Other political actors, including groups of citizens who share common policy objectives, are instrumental in forming parties. This doesn't mean leadership isn't important, but it recommends a more decentralized and ground-level understanding of leadership. This understanding also affirms the electoral role of parties but cautions that the "most important party business is the nomination and election of office seekers who will serve the interests of the party's intense policy demanders."[14] This places boundaries on how important winning office is relative to other goals. Here "parties . . . do not care about winning for the sake of winning office." Instead, parties "care about the policy gains. . . . They make [these gains] by the election of someone committed to the maximum feasible achievement of group goals."[15] A party is not a vote-maximizing entity; it primarily pursues a vision of good governance.

Building on these ideas, I argue that five key attributes must be satisfied to say parties are present. First, parties should exhibit a structure or organization, and this structure should distinguish party leaders from party supporters. However, the organizational form of parties need not be overly hierarchical or centralized. Chapter 2 presents an extended discussion of party organization in the young republic. To foreshadow, historians recognize a well-defined party structure—something largely overlooked by political scientists because it differs from that which emerged in the Jacksonian period. Second, a party should be associated with clearly identifiable visions of good governance that distinguishes it from other parties. This vision should not be compromised for short-term gains such as winning the next election. Third, parties should perform functions that facilitate the election of affiliated candidates. These include, inter alia, nominating candidates and mobilizing supporters. Fourth, parties ought to structure the electorate and be supported by an identifiable and stable core group of supporters. Finally, and perhaps most important, parties should enjoy normative legitimacy as a means of political organization.

The rhetoric of the founding generation did not evoke this sense of normative legitimacy. George Washington's memorable farewell address cautioned against "the baneful effects of the spirit of party." Reflecting this, Richard Hofstadter argues that parties did not achieve wide-spread normative acceptance until the emergence of the "second generation" of American political leaders, such as Martin Van Buren.[16] This is a far too cautious assessment. Washington delivered his 1796 farewell message sensing party development was gaining momentum. His concerns were well justified; politicians would soon thereafter identify themselves as "party men," and voters would embrace partisanship as a means of political organization.

The founding generation reconciled parties with American political ideals. Parties were "understood as necessary to overcome the disequilibrium in Congress due to competing sectional interests and beliefs in the extent of the new national government power."[17] Parties were seen as a "temporary necessity" to ensure the viability of the American experiment in the face of efforts by others, either monied elites or Jacobins depending on one's perspective, to undermine it. The result was that parties were consciously and quickly "worked into American constitutionalism to ensure that a majority party could make a legitimate claim to represent the country's opinions, interests, and constitutional interpretations."[18]

So why and how did electorally oriented political parties emerge in the nation's early history? The development of mass parties in the United Kingdom provides some insight. Here the creation of large, often densely populated constituencies in the mid-nineteenth century induced political leaders to change their vote solicitation strategies from reliance on political favors and personal connections to broad-based policy appeals. Personal favors and patronage, of which there was little in the early United States, does not require floor action and the formation of majority coalitions. Policy does. The increased scale of British electoral politics meant that party organization and policy became the most effective means to obtain electoral support and form a government. This furthered the ability of legislators to pursue policy and reinforced the need for electoral parties. Parties emerged because office seekers no longer operated in the intimate world of personal connections and pursued ends larger than their own personal interests.[19]

This explanation resonates in the early American republic. Colonial politics was small scale; the franchise was limited, and personal connections mattered greatly. However, at the founding the franchise quickly expanded, and the original congressional apportionment was a considerable one representative for every thirty thousand persons. This often made for large constituencies. Compounding this, some constituencies were geographically immense. No representative could know more than a fraction of his potential electorate, most of whom voted. The politics of personal reputation and connections was unsustainable. This created incentives to develop means of political organization that could solicit votes on a large scale.

If political scale motivates party development, the relative ease or difficulty party organizers face in doing so depends on whether like-minded political elites can focus similarly like-minded voters on preferred candidates.[20] The key problem faced by parties is that if a party has enough supporters to elect a given number of candidates, it still must ensure that its supporters concentrate their votes on precisely this number of candidates. If party supporters spread their votes thinly across more candidates than positions available to elect, then the other party is likely to win, even with less aggregate support. To avoid spreading votes too thinly requires the establishment of barriers to candidate entry.[21] Nascent parties must figure out how to limit options by controlling candidate access to the ballot. The party can then focus voters on preferred candidates. If either part of this coordination problem fails, then party organizers risk spreading supporters' votes so thin that no affiliated candidate is elected. This must take place in the constituency. This means that electoral party development is first and foremost a constituency-level activity. It is only after constituency parties are built that these can be aggregated to the state and national levels.

Three main considerations affect the relative ease or difficulty of party development. The first is the electoral system itself. An electoral system consists of the "set of laws and party rules that regulate electoral competition between and within parties."[22] These include how constituencies are defined, the threshold for election, how citizens cast votes, nomination processes, and similar considerations. Party building is simplified or complicated by the election rules in force. Single-member district, plurality rule elections are simple. They provide like-minded political elites incentives to limit entry to a single candidate and focus voters on that candidate. Multimember constituencies, whether a legislative district or statewide, introduce a more complicated coordination problem, but also greater rewards for overcoming it. This is because a majority party that is well-organized and focuses voters on its slate is likely to win all seats. Consequently, these elections provide the greatest incentives to organize, but also present the greatest challenges in doing so. Majority rule complicates all of this by providing incentives for spoilers to enter and force multiple rounds. Consequently, entry control is even more important in majority rule elections and in multi-seat elections.

Another factor influencing coordination is political preferences, specifically the extent of unity or division in like-minded groups.[23] Divided groups are harder to coordinate than are unified groups. The state-level cohesiveness of the Hamiltonian Federalists and the Jeffersonian Republicans greatly influenced the ability of the nascent parties to effectively compete for elective office. In some states the Federalists and Republicans were relatively cohesive. At other times they were not. For example, around 1818 in New York the Republicans fractured over how best to fund and oversee construction of the Erie Canal. This produced the Martin Van Buren–led "Bucktail" faction of the New York Democratic-Republicans, who aligned against the main opposition led by New York governor DeWitt Clinton.

The final consideration that affects party development is the expectations of voters, especially expectations about the viability or reliability of office seekers. Expectations are central to facilitating coordination because "common expectations about who is and is not viable are self-fulfilling."[24] If like-minded voters differ in their expectations about the political viability or reliability of a candidate, then coordination between electors and party elites is difficult.[25] This means there must be available and shared information about the identity of candidates and their viability.

This highlights the importance of nominations and endorsements. A prerequisite for electoral parties is that like-minded political elites must encourage preferred candidates to stand for office and discourage others from crowding the field. These organizers must also focus supporters on favored candidates to win elections. This directs attention to the constituency. Despite the historical narrative of the parties of Alexander Hamilton and Thomas Jefferson being created from the "top down," party building is a constituency-level project. While centralized efforts to build American parties were the catalyst for their emergence, the path from an electoral politics dominated by local elites to party-organized politics goes through the constituencies. Nominations and endorsements were a state and local affair.

Some historians intuitively share this view, but historiography of early republic elections is seldom presented in terms of theories of party emergence and development. However, there is evidence that this approach to electoral party development, when viewed in light of the historical evidence and empirical analysis of legislative elections, has purchase in explaining the emergence of political parties in the nation's first years.

Historian David W. Houpt provides tantalizing hints of this in his study of post-founding party development in Pennsylvania. He points to the importance of electoral rules in shaping the development of the Pennsylvania parties.[26] Pennsylvania switched between at-large and district elections for US House of Representatives elections between 1788 and 1794, first using the at-large general-ticket system, then single-member districts, then returning to the general ticket for elections to the Third Congress.[27] These rule changes were strategic; they were designed to first advantage the Federalists, then the Anti-Federalists, and then again the Federalists.

This forced the nascent parties to organize to compete effectively under the rules in force. In Pennsylvania the "process of switching back and forth between at-large and district elections forced politicians to develop communication networks throughout the state, hone methods of nomination, and derive new ways of campaigning."[28] The Pennsylvania general ticket initially advantaged the Federalists because of their numerical superiority, forcing the Republicans to organize in the western part of the state.[29] The result was that by the Fourth Congress, Pennsylvania used single-member district elections, with both parties competing effectively in many jurisdictions. Importantly, both parties figured out how to limit candidate entry and focus voters on preferred candidates. At least from initial indications, the Pennsylvania Federalists and Republicans were developing effective organizations.

All of this points to the existence of a constellation of rules, processes, and political culture that either encourages or hinders electoral party development. States with unified political elites that competed under electoral rules that either strongly motivate coordination or make coordination relatively easy often enjoyed success. Elites heading heterogeneous or divided electoral coalitions in states with election rules that complicated coordination found it more difficult to form effective electoral parties. States with widespread information on the political expectations of the electorate were more likely to form effective electoral parties. In addition, the election calendar, whether there were elected governors and other statewide offices, the strength of these offices, and whether Electoral College electors were elected all affected the incentives and ability of political elites to build electoral parties.

Finally, there is evidence that partisanship took root in the electorate. This is reflected in the language surrounding elections. Electoral language changed from being individualist and focused on candidate personal attributes to being universal and issue based. The change in political language "created new loyalties; allegiances to parties as institutions" rather than groups that exemplified virtue and the true meaning of republicanism.[30] Assessing partisanship from vote returns requires care. The well-known "ecological inference" problem means that even stable aggregate party support may mask underlying volatility in the electorate. If electors are not deeply tied to parties, shifts in individual-level voting patterns may still produce the appearance of stable and predictable party support. There is no solution to this inference problem contained wholly within election returns. We must look outside these data to decide if aggregate election statistics provide useful information about individual-level behavior.

Here historical literature becomes invaluable. Historians who have looked carefully at elections in specific jurisdictions argue that partisan ties took root early and these guided voters' electoral choices across offices and temporally. This is captured in one of the rare instances where we have individually identifiable votes from the early republic. Maryland poll books recorded these votes in presidential elector and House of Representatives elections between 1796 and 1816. Here voting patterns demonstrate considerable stability in party voting over successive elections and across office levels.[31] In Maryland there was "a strong tendency of voters to maintain their partisan allegiance . . . regardless of the factors involved in any given contest."[32] Stable party voting belies the claim that the parties were shifting alliances, unable to command deep loyalty in the electorate. There is little reason to believe the Old Line State is unusual in this regard. Instead, the evidence suggests that "long before Andrew Jackson rose to prominence the electorate displayed strong grassroots partisan affiliations."[33]

With that in mind, the district-level and county-level vote receipts provide considerable information on partisan behavior in the electorate. One must interpret these data with care and pay particular attention to the finest possible gradations of the voting patterns. As will become evident, ballots from multicandidate elections and geography present signs of partisan loyalty and stability in voting. This provides good reason to believe these series reflect stability in individual votes that aggregate to the observed patterns.

The creation of electoral parties that supplanted these elites was an uneven process: they emerged earlier in some places and later in other places. Consequently, local elites lost influence quickly in many jurisdictions. In other areas they remained influential longer. Nonetheless, electoral parties developed earlier in our political history than commonly recognized, and they effectively contested elections using an organizational infrastructure that differed considerably from their mid-nineteenth-century counterparts. The parties rapidly supplanted the local gentry who dominated the "deferential-participant" political world as these men were, after all, only local.

Regional and National Party Systems

How do we know if the Democratic-Republicans and Federalists comprised a true party system in the early national era? It is one thing to argue that the Democratic-Republicans and Federalists were political parties. This is the prerequisite for a party system. This does not mean these components combined to comprise a regional or national party system.[34]

The creation of a party system requires that locally and regionally created parties link in pursuit of common goals. The question is why such parties would arrange themselves under a common label. There are several reasons. At the state level these linkages advantage the politically like-minded in capturing statewide offices such as the governorship and control of the legislature.[35] Gubernatorial elections motivate party system development because to be elected one needs support from many constituencies. This proves important in explaining differences in regional electoral development because not all states, in particular southern states, elected their governors. Similarly, these linkages advantage cross-state cooperation in winning the presidency; either in states where voters directly selected presidential electors or in states where the legislature selected electors. The likelihood of achieving state, regional, and national policy objectives is increased when like-minded elites and followers face incentives to unite under common labels.[36] The common label provides voters with information about the political and policy objectives of political elites and supplies a powerful symbol around which to rally political engagement. These labels, if meaningful, oblige office seekers to increasingly campaign on national issues and answer for national policy in the constituency.

Political scientists have accepted approaches for assessing whether parties comprise a national system.[37] While measurement strategies differ, all capture two fundamental premises. The first is that in a national system, parties should not be highly fragmented and should be competitive across regions. Fragmentation—the presence of many small parties that have not yet coalesced around overarching principles—indicates that well-developed parties have not emerged. Highly territorialized party politics also signals the absence of a party system. The second component of nationalization is the relative uniformity in response to political events across geographic units. A national political issue or event should be reflected in party vote shares across regions. This is true even if the base level of support for the parties differs across these regions. If candidates are immune to changes in national politics, this indicates politics is localized and candidates win or lose based on constituency-specific considerations and their own personal attributes. Overall, the absence of a large number of uncontested or safe seats for a party in a particular region, similar party vote shares across regions, or modest differences in state or district-level party performance compared with its national performance all point to a national system. The opposite is true as well.

One must apply these standards to historical elections with care. As with the definition of political parties, scholars sometimes impose an overly high bar for the party system in the young republic. US party politics has always had a regional flavor. Through much of the twentieth century the Republican Party failed to compete effectively in the South. For example, from the Fifty-Seventh Congress (1901–1903) until the Sixty-Sixth Congress (1919–1921) no Republican was elected to the House of Representatives from any of the core ex-Confederacy states. Thereafter, Republicans enjoyed only episodic victories in these states. In contrast, Republican candidates dominated elections in the intermountain West and Northwest. American politics certainly had a territorial component, but the occasional party victories outside of their regional homes, combined with each party capturing the presidency and the prevalence of high-profile national issues such as health and safety reforms, entry into World War I, and others, demonstrate there was a national two-party system. In addition, in the early republic and today, legislative candidates and districts differ in the extent to which their elections are vulnerable to national political events. Some candidates enjoy a significant "personal vote" owing to their standing with constituents. Parties draw districts to produce "safe seats" that are insulated from national events. Today the parties have geographic bases of party support, and there exist differences in the extent to which legislative elections respond to national political events. Still, one would certainly agree that the United States has two national parties. In the early republic there was geographically concentrated party support, and candidates benefited from a "personal vote." Determining whether this was a feature or *the* feature of the first party era is an empirical question to which this book speaks.

Another consideration is that nationalization is not a static concept. It is not a one-directional characteristic such that once a party system becomes nationalized it remains so. The United States has witnessed several periods when the extent of nationalization has waxed and waned. An example of this is the transition from the very nationally competitive post–Civil War party system to the early twentieth century when, following the election of 1896, the Republican Party dominated national politics for three decades and the Democratic Party retreated to its base in the South. The same pattern may well exist in other periods of American political history.

I assess whether regional or national party systems emerged in the first party era using an empirical strategy that has seen application in the study of party system development. It is quite simple. Beginning with the state and regional legislative vote returns, I determine the number of competitive parties, their relative performance in state and regional elections, and their responsiveness to national political events. This assesses whether both parties seriously contested significant numbers of elections across states and regions. If both parties contest many elections across regions, this indicates that a national party system exists. In contrast, if one or the other party concedes a region, then this indicates no such system exists. Likewise, the extent to which party vote shares move in tandem across regions, especially in response to political events, indicates whether a party system exists. Overall, the best measure of party system development remains the "intraocular" test; do the vote receipts across jurisdictions provide evidence for the development of regional or national party systems?

The development of a party system is important for the emergence and consolidation of electoral democracy. This is because such a system is the foundation for the promotion of national-level policies and governance. Nationalized party systems encourage the provision of public goods such as defense and trans-state road systems rather than policies that advantage concentrated interests at the expense of dispersed interests.[38] In its absence government is parochial, with each party seeking to distribute particularistic benefits to its geographically concentrated supporters. Laws are crafted to benefit territorially based clients rather than to meet common national needs. A national party system also links spatially separated citizens who share common political identities and preferences. This has immense benefits for governance because representatives see the connections between their own actions and a broader political community.

Political scientists and historians are skeptical that a national party system emerged in the first party era. The received view is that "the political coalitions that formed in the early national period . . . had a pronounced sectional basis."[39] Though the Federalists acquired supporters in the South and some strength in the Middle Atlantic states, their presumed base was New England. The Jeffersonian Republicans drew much of their strength from the Middle Atlantic states and eventually made substantial inroads in New England. But their home was the South, especially Virginia. Regional patterns in the Electoral College vote, for example, indicate deeply geographically polarized party support.

One reason many scholars doubt the emergence of a national party system is because the mechanisms that might be expected to bind cross-regional alliances—patronage and policy—were arguably insufficient to motivate the creation of a national party system. Scholars generally agree that "patronage parties" did not exist before the Jacksonian-era spoils system.[40] Since officeholders had few patronage positions to distribute, there was little incentive to develop a national party system to capture government and control the allocation of these positions. Even more restrictive is the view that the United States did not become a true national, two-party system until the twentieth century because national fiscal responsibilities were insufficient to motivate national electoral coordination.[41]

These arguments raise several questions and cautions. While patronage and federal expenditures were probably insufficient to motivate cross-state electoral coordination, there were certainly major policy issues capable of motivating party system development. The most important of these was the "great principle" over the reach of the national government relative to the states.[42] This question encapsulated the founding-era differences between the Democratic-Republicans and Federalists over the relative stations of the national and state governments. The "great principle" was contested electorally and in the courts, as reflected in the *McCulloch v. Maryland* (1819) resolution of the meaning of the Article I "necessary and proper" clause and the Article VI "national supremacy" clause. This was captured in a host of subsidiary issues including Hamilton's plans for assumption of Revolutionary War debt, a national bank, and the policy prescriptions in his Report on Manufactures. Other issues such as the Alien and Sedition Acts, foreign affairs as reflected in the Jay Treaty, the Embargo Act of 1807, and other matters of policy presented national implications. These considerations alone were more than sufficient to motivate broad, nationally oriented political parties; that is, a party system. A party system develops in response to the nationalization of policy, but the nationalization of policy furthers the creation of a national system.

Finally, one should not make too much of the nominal number of parties that found local support in the early republic. The variety of "party" labels in play through the first party era do not reflect true parties. Instead, these are typically factions within the Federalist and Republican Parties, such as the aforementioned New York "Bucktails," which were a faction of the dominant Democratic-Republicans that wrestled with DeWitt Clinton over control of the Erie Canal Commission. These labels were often created to "rebrand" the Federalist or Republican Party in certain locations. An important example is the "Quids." Candidates identified as Quids or other labels denoting the same were a third group typically composed of Republicans. This group only enjoyed organizational life in Pennsylvania and New York, although the term makes occasional appearances in other regions. Men rarely self-designated as "Quids"; rather, it was a derogatory term applied by others. Typically, Quids self-identified as "Constitutional Republicans" or other names and are best understood as a faction within the Democratic-Republican Party. The term's derogatory connotation itself points to party development because "quid" generally meant neither this nor that, or, as might be interpreted, one who stands for nothing. This is not a flattering designation.[43]

Examples of NNV Election Returns: Pennsylvania, New Hampshire, and Maryland

This section illustrates how the NNV returns contribute to our understanding of early American electoral development. I use the Pennsylvania 1800 Third District single-member district election, the New Hampshire 1816 at-large election, and several Maryland county-level returns to show how the NNV votes illuminate candidate entry, turnout, party support, evidence of partisanship, the geography of support, and other markers of electoral development. I apply the approaches here to the election returns in subsequent chapters.[44]

A few remarks on the returns are necessary before proceeding. First, there are statewide returns, district returns, and county returns. Not all of these are necessarily present for the same election. For example, a state general ticket return may be complete when some of its constituent county returns are missing. Likewise, a district return may be complete when some of its county returns are missing. Conversely, a district return may be missing when some of its constituent county returns are present. Each of the regional chapters details the present and missing returns. An important consideration is whether there are systematic patterns in the present and missing returns. For example, perhaps for some reason returns from Democratic-Republican jurisdictions are more likely to survive than those from Federalist jurisdictions. This would present clear problems for analysis. Fortunately, there are no obvious patterns to present and missing returns.

Second, for some purposes, such as determining aggregate party support, I use all votes cast in the election. For other purposes, such as counting the number of party candidates in an election, I only count candidates who received at least 5 percent of the vote. This eliminates candidates who received a trivial number of votes, which was common in an era of handwritten ballots.[45] Third is the question of candidate partisanship. I use the party affiliations assigned to candidates in these data. The NNV returns code candidate party affiliation as reported in the period newspapers. If there is no recorded affiliation, or the candidate has minor party affiliation, I code party affiliation as "other." Scholars consider some candidates to have different affiliation than that in the returns. However, it is affiliation as reported at the time of election that matters. Ex-post attribution of party affiliation to a candidate risks assigning that candidate a label that might not have been obvious to electors at the time.[46]

Finally, counties present challenges for early republic analysis. This is because the states created counties, subdivided counties, and otherwise changed their boundaries throughout the era. For example, in 1801 New York changed the boundaries of at least ten counties. In 1808 it created three new counties. I address these challenges by using census-assigned codes to identify counties. These codes allow one to precisely match the vote returns and population to counties at the census year.[47] For some analysis I focus on counties with boundaries established and stable throughout the era. The county-level maps use their historic boundaries.[48] In the era, congressional districts were often formed from one or more counties, with the district boundaries determined by the county boundaries. This has important implications for analysis. While there was no constitutional requirement that legislative districts have equal population, there were good faith efforts to avoid gross distortions in district populations. This could be achieved by combining multiple less populated counties into a single district, or by apportioning multiple representatives to a densely populated county. This balancing was rarely perfect, but it reflected that the early republic recognized that people were to be represented and that the era's population was mobile and dispersed.[49]

To illustrate the use of these returns, first consider the 1800 single-member district election in Pennsylvania's Third District. In 1800 the

Third District consisted of Chester and Delaware Counties just west of Philadelphia. This is the simplest of all elections. Here Federalist John Hemphill defeated Democratic-Republican Joseph Shallcross 2,732 to 2,389 votes. No other candidates stood. I discuss nominations in the following chapter, but these developed in Pennsylvania by the late 1790s and are especially important in competitive districts.[50] This district was competitive. That Hemphill and Shallcross were the only candidates points to effective nominations, or at least to a norm of standing aside so that like-minded candidates do not overcrowd the field.

The number of electors in a single-member district is simply the sum of votes. Here this equals 5,121. This shows election scale. The election was not an intimate affair; it engaged thousands of men. I argue in the next chapter that the number of electors, rather than the turnout rate, is the more important figure for understanding electoral development.[51] Calculating the turnout rate requires an estimate of each state's potential electorate. Pennsylvania suffrage was nearly universal for adult white men. In addition, free African American men voted. I use two approaches, the first at the state and district levels, and the second at the county level. The first is to use the proportion of the state's population identified by Walter Dean Burnham as eligible to vote.[52] Pennsylvania's population in 1800 was 602,545. Burnham calculates its potential electorate as 123,900. This means 20.6 percent of Pennsylvanians could vote. The population of Chester County was 32,093 while Delaware County's was 12,809. If 20.6 percent of these counties populations could vote, this returns a voting-eligible population of approximately 9,000 and a turnout rate of 57 percent.

The second approach I apply when focusing on counties is to use the census to calculate turnout as the proportion of adult white males who voted.[53] In Chester and Delaware Counties the census returns an adult white male population of 9,222 and a turnout rate of 56 percent. In some instances, I use county returns to estimate state-level turnout. I do so when there are insufficient complete district returns to obtain reliable estimates of state turnout, but there are enough county returns to do so. Beyond the number of county returns, the counties should have geographic range sufficient to capture the state's political regions. Estimating state-level turnout from county-level returns presents one challenge: rarely—very rarely—the calculated turnout rate exceeds 100 percent. This may be due to several factors, including changing county boundaries, misrecording of votes, men voting at a proximate location outside their home county, ballot stuffing, and other reasons that are impossible to discern from the returns alone. This concern primarily arises in southern elections and, to emphasize, even here this is a very rare occurrence. Still, for this reason, I typically calculate state turnout rates estimated from county returns using county medians, not means. This reduces the influence of outliers and arguably provides a more accurate estimate of "typical" turnout. In practice, both methods of calculating state-level turnout rates provide similar interpretations. The important point in the present example of Chester and Delaware Counties is that the number of electors and the turnout rate show that men of typical means exercised their suffrage liberally.

Partisanship in the electorate is more difficult to assess. One single-member district election reveals little about party ties. It may be that the men who voted Democratic-Republican in 1800 voted Federalist in 1802, and vice versa. Multiple elections help. So does geography. Recalling V. O. Key Jr.'s well-known comparison of voting in the towns of Somerville and Ashfield, Massachusetts, that illuminated the partisan origins of the New Deal realignment, one can compare early republic votes in congressional districts and counties over time.[54] The aggregate vote in different communities, especially when observed over several elections, indicates whether the parties enjoyed distinct bases of support associated with location. In 1800 both Chester and Delaware Counties leaned Federalist. However, some towns and villages displayed partisan differences. In Delaware County, for example, Concord township voted Federalist while a strong majority of Darby township electors voted Republican. These townships bookend the county on its western and eastern boundaries, suggesting a geographic party divide. One should not overinterpret these differences, but sequential elections combined with location clarifies the popular foundations of each party.

The 1816 New Hampshire election is more complex. New Hampshire used the general-ticket to elect its six representatives. The general ticket is an at-large system whereby voters submit the names of candidates—usually handwritten—to be elected. Electors receive as many noncumulative votes as positions elected and may submit an incomplete ballot. Accordingly, in 1816 a New Hampshire elector could submit up to six names, and the six candidates with the most votes were elected. This voting method was also used in multimember district elections. One can simply think of New Hampshire as a six-member district.

In the nation's first years the Federalists won most New Hampshire

House of Representatives elections. However, in 1816 the Republicans swept the election. The region's elections spanned nearly the entire year. New Hampshire elected its governor and other executive and judicial offices in March. New England neighbors Massachusetts, Connecticut, and Vermont held their state legislative and congressional elections in the late summer and early fall. New Hampshire elected its representatives and presidential electors on Monday, November 4, by which time great excitement had built in anticipation of the election.

The Republicans and Federalists both met in Concord in early summer to nominate their House of Representatives candidates.[55] Throughout the fall local newspapers reported these party endorsements, exhortations to vote, and excoriations of the opposition. As shown in the figure 1.1 electioneering notice, the Republican *New Hampshire Patriot* described the Federalist list as comprised of closet royalists who shall "abridge the liberty of speech and of the press," submit to "foreign insults," and continue to accumulate national debt. It also charged the Federalists of supporting Connecticut's elite Standing Order that controlled that state's politics. The condemnation that the Federalists were "2500 Dollar Men" refers to the deeply unpopular Compensation Act, enacted the previous spring. The act increased congressional salaries to $1,500 per year. Presumably the Federalists, if elected, would increase salaries even further. Not surprisingly, the nominated Republicans shared none of these vices, instead supporting "no shackles to freedom," "no arbitrary restraints on the rights of conscious," and "manful resistance to all foreign encroachments."[56]

Importantly, *The People's Advocate*, a Republican newspaper, informed its readers that some at the party caucus voted to "highly disapprove" of the nomination of Arthur Livermore, whom it described as a "dishonest politician" who possessed "unprincipled ambition."[57] This was perhaps understandable because in 1800 Livermore was a Federalist presidential elector who cast his ballot for John Adams. Nonetheless, by election day Livermore's support at the nomination caucus erased any misgivings Republicans voters had had about him.

Table 1.1 presents the final vote. Those elected are in italics.

Multimember district returns reveal much about nominations and partisan attachments. First, the party caucuses nominated all the leading candidates. Electors knew these candidates, and these were the only ones who received nontrivial numbers of votes. There were other candidates, including Republicans George Prescott and Daniel Young, but

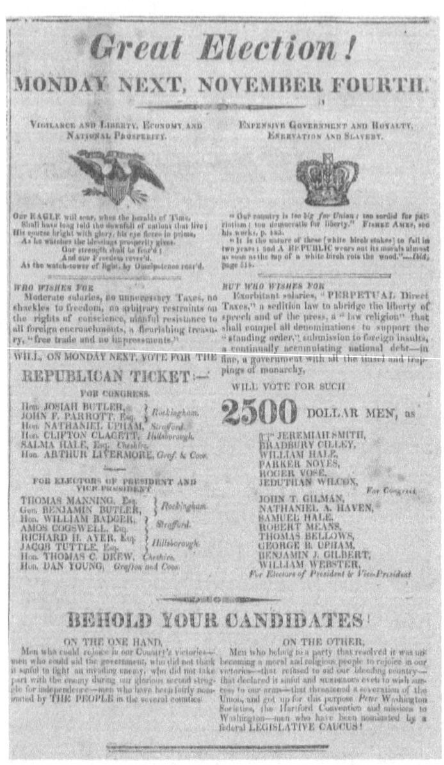

Great Election!

MONDAY NEXT, NOVEMBER FOURTH.

VIGILANCE AND LIBERTY, ECONOMY AND NATIONAL PROSPERITY.

EXPENSIVE GOVERNMENT AND ROYALTY, ENERVATION AND SLAVERY.

Our EAGLE will soar, when the heralds of Time,
Shall have long told the downfall of nations that live;
His course bright with glory, his eye fierce in prime,
As he watches the blessings prosperity gives.
Our strength shall be fear'd;
And our Freedom rever'd,
As the watch-tower of light, by Omnipotence rear'd.

"Our country is too big *for Union*; too sordid for patriotism; too democratic for liberty." FISHER AMES, see his works, p. 485.

"It is the nature of these [white birch stakes] to fall in two years; and A REPUBLIC wears out its morals almost as soon as the top of a white birch rots the wood."—*Ibid*, page 514.

WHO WISHES FOR
Moderate salaries, no unnecessary Taxes, no shackles to freedom, no arbitrary restraints on the rights of conscience, manful resistance to all foreign encroachments, a flourishing treasury, "free trade and no impressments,"

WILL, ON MONDAY NEXT, VOTE FOR THE

REPUBLICAN TICKET:—

FOR CONGRESS.

Hon. JOSIAH BUTLER, } *Rockingham.*
JOHN F. PARROTT, Esq. }
Hon. NATHANIEL UPHAM, *Strafford.*
Hon. CLIFTON CLAGETT, *Hillsborough.*
SALMA HALE, Esq. *Cheshire.*
Hon. ARTHUR LIVERMORE, *Graf. & Coos.*

FOR ELECTORS OF PRESIDENT AND VICE PRESIDENT.

THOMAS MANNING, Esq. } *Rockingham.*
Gen. BENJAMIN BUTLER, }
Hon. WILLIAM BADGER, } *Strafford.*
AMOS COGSWELL, Esq. }
RICHARD H. AYER, Esq. } *Hillsborough.*
JACOB TUTTLE, Esq. }
Hon. THOMAS C. DREW, *Cheshire.*
Hon. DAN YOUNG, *Grafton and Coos.*

BUT WHO WISHES FOR
Exorbitant salaries, "PERPETUAL Direct Taxes," a sedition law to abridge the liberty of speech and of the press, a "law religion" that shall compel all denominations to support the "standing order," submission to foreign insults, a continually accumulating national debt—in fine, a government with all the tinsel and trappings of monarchy,

WILL VOTE FOR SUCH

2500 DOLLAR MEN, as

JEREMIAH SMITH,
BRADBURY CILLEY,
WILLIAM HALE,
PARKER NOYES,
ROGER VOSE,
JEDUTHAN WILCOX,
For Congress.

JOHN T. GILMAN,
NATHANIEL A. HAVEN,
SAMUEL HALE,
ROBERT MEANS,
THOMAS BELLOWS,
GEORGE B. UPHAM,
BENJAMIN J. GILBERT,
WILLIAM WEBSTER,
For Electors of President & Vice-President.

BEHOLD YOUR CANDIDATES!

ON THE ONE HAND,
Men who could rejoice in our Country's victories—men who could aid the government, who did not think it sinful to fight an invading enemy, who did not take part with the enemy during our glorious second struggle for independence—men who have been fairly nominated by THE PEOPLE in the several counties.

ON THE OTHER,
Men who belong to a party that resolved it was unbecoming a moral and religious people to rejoice in our victories—that refused to aid our bleeding country—that declared it sinful and [illegible] even to wish success to our arms—that threatened a severation of the Union, and got up for this purpose *Peter Washington* Societies, the Hartford Convention and missions to Washington—men who have been nominated by a federal LEGISLATIVE CAUCUS!

Figure 1.1. New Hampshire: *Patriot and State Gazette*, October 29, 1816

these candidates received few votes. In general ticket and multimember district elections I calculate the number of electors as the sum of votes cast for the leading party candidates. This top-of-the-ticket approach defines turnout as the act of showing up at the poll to record a ballot even if one does not cast all allocated votes. This approach yields 29,169 electors. This is a "lowball" figure, as some electors may have solely voted for less competitive candidates. Extrapolating from the 1810 and 1820 censuses, there were 230,000 New Hampshire residents in 1816. This translates to a potential electorate of about 49,200. Turnout was a robust 59 percent. The number of voters and the turnout rate clearly show large-scale, party organized elections.

With respect to partisanship, it appears that about 53 percent of electors were Republicans and 47 percent were Federalists. The question is, how do we know that some of Butler's or Upham's voters, for example, didn't vote for Federalist candidates, or vice versa? We don't—at least not with certainty. However, this isn't very plausible. To see this,

Table 1.1.New Hampshire US House of Representatives Election, 1816 (winners in italics)

Within Party Finish Order	*Republican*	*Votes*	*Federalist*	*Votes*
1	*Josia Butler*	15,569	William Hale	13,600
2	*Nathanal Upham*	15,562	Jeremiah Smith	13,582
3	*Clifton Claggert*	15,551	Jeduthun Wilcox	13,578
4	*Salma Hale*	15,416	Roger Vose	13,536
5	*John F. Parrott*	15,231	Bradbury Cilley	13,493
6	*Arthur Livermore*	15,231	Parker Noyes	13,477
7	George Prescott	308		
8	Daniel Young	249		

consider the within party finish order and the votes separating these candidates. The leading Republican, Josia Butler, received 15,569 votes while the sixth-place Republican candidate, Arthur Livermore, received only 338 fewer votes. Likewise, the first-place Federalist, William Hale, and the last-place Federalist, Parker Noyes, received nearly equivalent votes. Such tight spreads argue against within party candidates having different supporters. Each party ran a slate, and voters cast straight tickets for their preferred list. The vote difference between the top of the ticket and the bottom of the ticket is certainly ballot roll off, meaning some electors did not cast all their allocated votes. The leading party—in this case, the Republicans—swept the election, as is typically the case in highly majoritarian general-ticket elections characterized by party cohesion among political elites and their supporters in the electorate.

County-level returns are especially useful for interpreting at-large elections. This is because aggregate returns obscure local concentrations of party support. In 1816 New Hampshire's six counties displayed noticeable differences in the vote. The Federalist stronghold was in the southwest along the Connecticut River. Here the Federalists won both Cheshire and Grafton Counties with a 56 percent vote share. While impressive, this was too little to compensate for losses in the other counties, including the drubbing they took in neighboring Hillsborough County. The county vote reflects the differences in the social and economic features of these areas that manifest in party support.

Ballot structure and substate returns, especially when strengthened by temporal analysis, demonstrate how vote aggregation rules affect party fortunes. The returns show that the presumed Federalist demise after 1812–1814 is exaggerated, at least in New Hampshire. In 1816 the Republicans swept the election, but by only a narrow margin. The Federalists would have won two seats if the state had districted along county lines, as was common in the period. Localized areas of Federalist support remained even in counties won by the Democratic-Republicans. This is demonstrated by Federalist performance in statehouse elections, where seats were apportioned to towns and cities. In these elections the Federalists won approximately 45 percent of the seats.[58] While their subsequent support declined, as late as 1819 Federalist House of Representatives candidates won in nearly fifty communities, including the sizeable towns of Hanover, Sanbornton, and Newport, sometimes by large margins. Importantly, after 1816 New Hampshire congressional election turnout declined. This is likely because the Federalists and their supporters recognized they could no longer win at-large elections. New Hampshire shows the vitality of early nineteenth-century House elections, at least until the combination of diminished support and unfavorable election methods rendered Federalist efforts futile.

Table 1.2 shows how a sample of Maryland county-level returns illuminate whether partisanship resided in the electorate. These are from Anne Arundel, Fredrick, and Prince Georges Counties. The table presents each party's median vote, the mean absolute deviation from it, and the number of elections upon which these figures are based. The median absolute deviation (MAD) measures vote stability. The smaller the deviation from the median, the more stable the county-level party vote. I only calculate these figures when there are seven or more contested elections with complete returns. This reduces the influence of outliers and abnormalities, and is the minimum number of elections for these figures to convey useful information. I focus on contested elections because a conceded election reveals little information about the deferring party's support. A party may enjoy support even though affiliated candidates decline to seek office. In addition, all three counties' boundaries were established before 1796, and remained stable throughout the era. The county returns speak to partisanship in several ways. First, these are among the most fine-grained votes available. Second, to the extent that county returns are available, these foster analysis across multiple elec-

Table 1.2. Maryland County-Level Party Vote and Deviation, 1796–1824

County	*Median Republican Vote*	*Republican MAD*	*Median Federalist Vote*	*Federalist MAD*	*Elections*
Ann Arundel	57	8	43	8	10
Fredrick	45	11	55	11	14
Prince Georges	46	5	54	4	10

tion cycles. The county returns also illuminate district elections. The returns show where the Republicans and Federalists enjoy their most, and least, support, including within districts.

To illustrate, consider Anne Arundel County. Here there are returns for ten elections. The Anne Arundel County Federalists conceded elections to the Eighth, Ninth, and Seventeenth Congresses, but this leaves ten contested elections. The median Anne Arundel Republican and Federalist vote is 55 and 44 percent, respectively. The median absolute vote deviation for both parties is about 8 percent. This shows how concentrated each party's vote is around its median. A concentrated vote indicates stable partisanship, whereas a dispersed vote indicates the opposite. There is no formal demarcation between "large" and "small." I leave it to the reader to decide such matters. To place this in context, the smallest Republican percentage was 36 percent (1798) and the greatest percentage was 70 percent (1800). The Jeffersonian Republican wave of 1800 was an abnormality. Of the remaining elections, four Democratic-Republican vote shares hover in the 50 to 60 percent range. If one excludes the 1798 and 1800 elections, the parties' median absolute vote deviations are reduced by nearly half.

One should not overinterpret vote variation in geographic areas, whether these are counties or districts. The creation of new districts and new counites may increase the homogeneity of these geographic units. On the one hand, homogeneous districts help identify the bases for partisanship by pointing to why some districts or counties support one party rather than another. This is especially true if areas previously supportive of one party are repositioned in another district or newly formed county. I emphasize those figures calculated using several returns from counties with long-standing boundaries. Ann Arundel, Fredrick, and Prince Georges Counties meet this standard, each having boundaries established before the founding. Even so, as with all aggregate-level indicators of partisanship, vote deviation is most useful when interpreted considering other information. Small cross-party and cross-county differences signify little.

The table shows that the Federalists were strongest in Prince Georges County. Even though their typical vote share was about the same as in Fredrick County, the vote dispersion is much smaller. This indicates a partisan electorate. Fredrick County was competitive, with both parties averaging close to 50 percent of the vote across the ten elections. The Federalists won nine of the eleven contested elections. Even with tight margins, the stability in the Fredrick party vote ensured Federalist wins. Overall, the table shows differences in party strength across counties and suggests some counties are characterized by stable partisan attachments while other counties are less so.

The Plan of the Book

The book is divided into three sections. This first section, consisting of this and the following chapter, presents the primary questions of interest, the theoretical and empirical foundations, and a review of the political and social context for elections in the early republic. Specifically, chapter 2 reviews the early republic electoral setting. Here I discuss early republic election practices. This centers on franchise, electioneering, nominations, and balloting. This chapter also presents a more detailed discussion of early US political parties and how these should be considered for proper understanding of national electoral development. The chapter's purpose is to enable the reader to better understand the historical context of early republic elections and interpret the empirical analysis.

The four chapters of the next section present the empirical analysis. I devote one chapter each to the Middle Atlantic, border states, New England, and South. Here I detail whether the parties successfully limit entrants and focus their supporters on these candidates. This requires that one count the number of candidates who compete for office. If parties and voters properly coordinate, there should not be more candidates seeking office than the election method supports. I also assess voter participation. The number of men who vote speaks to whether elections are the domain of elites or men of more typical means. It also indicates the organizational requirements needed to effectively contest elections.

Turnout indicates whether parties are capable of mobilizing supporters. Elector participation should be low when parties are unformed or noncompetitive and increase when party competition is vibrant. The chapters also explore the party vote and partisanship, geographic patterns in party support, and patterns in candidates standing for election and reelection. This tells us how much support each party enjoyed given the election methods in use and where this support resided. The votes allow one to isolate pockets of party support that are lost in aggregation. I also discuss the effect of election rules and processes on party competitiveness. As suggested previously, election rules are not neutral. The chapters display instances where the Federalists were so disadvantaged by the election processes as to diminish their incentive to contest House seats.

Each chapter presents, as much as possible, a census of elections emphasizing those contests that illuminate the development of elections. No election will display all markers of maturation previously discussed, but it is likely that as elections become more institutionalized, more of these markers will be present than not. This raises the problem of getting lost in the weeds, making it difficult to obtain an overall sense of the development of US electoral democracy. I avoid this as much as possible by focusing on the broad patterns that speak to the book's argument. Many of these elections confirm this argument, while others are less supportive. That's okay. Early republic legislative elections present an immensely complicated tapestry. We are interested in the major patterns; the individual components of this tapestry are primarily of interest to the extent that they illustrate broader themes and other similarly situated elections.

The final chapter synthesizes the empirical analyses into a coherent statement about the development of elections in the early United States. The evidence points to regional transitions from deferential-participant politics in the late eighteenth century to a more recognizably modern electoral world in the first years of the nineteenth century. This transition was not uniform. It first emerged in the Middle Atlantic and border states, propagated out to New England a bit later, and never fully took root in the deep South. That said, the Federalist Party persevered, and there was much more robust two-party competition than generally understood. The establishment of recognizably modern elections took root in several states. All of this transpired earlier, and maintained itself longer, than previously thought. Taken in total, the election returns indicate that in the proper intellectual and political climate, elections became the primary vehicle for citizen input into government earlier and more robustly than previously understood.

Conclusion

The received story of the development of US elections is that the electoral world was ad hoc, dominated by local elites and, after 1800, the Jeffersonian Republicans. This system failed to solidify into an institutionalized and modern process until the rise of the Jacksonian Democrats and Whigs in the 1830s. By now it is clear that I think evidence from early House elections makes this understanding a simplification to the point of being terribly misleading. House elections became more systematic, competitive, and recognizably modern earlier in our history than commonly recognized. Better understanding this process is important not only for its own sake but also because it says much about the development of political parties in a new nation. The United States is rarely discussed by social scientists interested in party development and democratization because our interest lies in the new democracies of the twentieth and twenty-first centuries. Of course, the United States was once an emergent republic, and deeper knowledge of this transition informs more general questions about democratization and party development.

To the extent that the empirical analysis is convincing, it motivates a new interpretation of the Jacksonian-Whig era. This period is thought to present a significant break from the previous era. The evidence presented here challenges this interpretation. Rather than being a departure from the first party era, the Jacksonian period was an acceleration and expansion of it. The late eighteenth century and early nineteenth century were a school in the art of electoral organization and politics, and its students learned their lessons early and well. These were not forgotten. This helps explain the remarkable expansion of elections as the primary entry point into politics for most of the enfranchised in the first third of the nineteenth century, including the legions of new immigrants to the United States. In this sense, understanding the development of elections in the early republic not only tells us much about the establishment of democratic institutions; it also tells us much about our political selves.

2 | Elections in the New Republic

The winter of 1789–1790 witnessed one of the most important House of Representatives elections in US history. James Madison and James Monroe sought election to the First Congress from the Virginia Piedmont Fifth District. The seat was vigorously contested. Patrick Henry threw his considerable political influence behind Monroe by placing Madison's Orange County home in a district weighted with counties that leaned Anti-Federalist.[1] Protesting to Thomas Jefferson, Madison complained that Henry grouped "the counties into districts to . . . associate with Orange such as are most devoted to his politics, and most likely to be swayed by the prejudices excited against me."[2] The election was decided on a bitterly cold February day with a foot of snow on the ground.[3] Despite the weather and Patrick Henry's best efforts, Madison won with 1,308 of the 2,280 cast votes.[4]

Madison earned his victory the hard way. That winter he traveled throughout the district to speak with voters. Madison devoted particular attention to Culpeper County and Monroe's own Spotsylvania County. These counties, he thought, "will determine the election."[5] Madison reassured voters that he would vigorously pursue a Bill of Rights and reminded ecclesiastical dissenters of his commitment to religious freedom.[6] For his part, Monroe brought impeccable credentials to the election. He was a war hero who participated in the celebrated Christmas night crossing of the Delaware River with George Washington and was severely wounded in the ensuing Battle of Trenton. Monroe played a leading role in the Virginia ratifying convention, reluctantly supporting the Constitution contingent on the adoption of a Bill of Rights. He deeply objected to the federal government's ability to directly tax citizens, and his commitment to fundamental rights required no reassurances. Next to the diminutive Madison, the six-foot-tall Monroe looked every bit the citizen-soldier.

Madison and Monroe campaigned through personal appearances and in print. Personal friends and political opponents, they often traveled the campaign circuit together. In doing so they presented themselves to voters and publicly debated their respective understandings of constitutionalism. One such debate was held on the portico of a Culpeper County Lutheran church on a day so cold that Madison suffered permanent frostbite scars. He later described these marks as his "battle scars."[7] The election saw high-profile endorsements, wealthy benefactors, and the candidates' supporters perform diligent fieldwork. Turnout was respectable, especially considering the weather: at 44 percent of the eligible electorate, it was comparable to many twenty-first-century legislative elections.

The Madison and Monroe contest is the only House election featuring two future US presidents. While fascinating, that's not why it is important. The election is important for its apparent modernity. Patrick Henry sought to gerrymander the district although the term "gerrymander" wouldn't exist for another twenty-five years.[8] Madison responded by focusing his campaign on the "swing" Culpepper and Spotsylvania Counties. Importantly, the election was about politics, not men. Madison and Monroe, to be sure, were both gentlemen of great stature, but on this dimension they were indistinguishable. For two men drawn from the same social and economic caste, they embraced markedly different political agendas. Madison advocated for a strong national government. Monroe demanded a greater sphere for the states. Political values and issues, not social stature, distinguished these candidates.

The campaign was anything but staid, as would be expected given the divisive Virginia politics surrounding the Constitution's ratification. Voters paid little heed to the names and social standing of the men who sought their votes. George Washington once surmised that the natural aristocracy, a class to which Madison and Monroe belonged, were "no more than a drop in the ocean."[9] If so, then some two thousand men who comprised the great sea determined the outcome. These men voted in accordance with their views on the new Constitution, their religious affiliations, their personal and community ties, and other considerations intrinsic to any election. The candidates had to earn each vote. It's unclear how typical the Madison and Monroe contest was for the period. If the election was atypical, it was also a harbinger of things to come.

This chapter provides a foundation for understanding elections in the early republic. The next section discusses political culture; in particular, the "deferential-participant" culture that characterized early United States politics and reasons why this culture rapidly dissipated.

Following this, I discuss party organization and nomination methods. The early Democratic-Republican and Federalist Parties were organized through the partisan press. The press provided a structure well suited to the period's political and social environment. The parties also adopted systematic nomination processes that effectively winnowed the field and focused electoral supporters on these candidates. I then discuss the right to vote. While there certainly existed very real and troubling exclusions to the suffrage, most adult white men could vote. The de jure and de facto franchise expanded rapidly. The turnout figures presented in later chapters demonstrate that the enfranchised exercised this prerogative liberally.

The chapter's penultimate section focuses on period campaigns and elections. Here I discuss electioneering including the casting of votes, ballot structure, and the extent of electoral secrecy. While some believe that voting viva voce was ubiquitous in the early republic, voting by handwritten and preprinted ballots was far more common. Literacy posed few problems for completing a ballot, as almost all white Americans could read and write. Further, procedures existed to maintain privacy in voting. Campaigns were typically organized around festivals, celebrations, and party-sponsored events. These forums also provided a venue for persons excluded from the suffrage to influence electoral politics. The relationship between electioneering and party development is reciprocal; electioneering motivated the organization of political parties, and the political parties furthered electioneering.

Early republic elections and the political culture that surrounded them differ in important ways from modern elections. Yet the common reference of the Enlightenment, liberal and republican values, and the revolutionary inheritance moved the Americans steadily in a direction that made elections the foundation for political and governing legitimacy. Votes had to be solicited and contested. This process developed and solidified in these first elections. Parties emerged and maintained themselves as a national force. They recruited and nominated candidates for office, stood for distinct visions of the future United States, and commanded loyalty in core supporters. If not fully modern, the first elections established the fundamental importance of competitive elections for choosing political leaders, providing them with political legitimacy, and establishing a trajectory that anticipated the mass party-based elections in the Jacksonian Era.

Political Culture in the Early Republic

The received interpretation of early republic electoral politics centers on the existence of a "deferential-participant" political culture. Political historians describe the first party era as transitioning from "traditional, notable-oriented and deferential politics to . . . party, electorate-oriented and egalitarian" politics.[10] The former political universe dates from the colonial era. Early to middle colonial-era elections, to be frank, were often dull affairs. Men stood for office, sometimes without their knowledge or consent, there was no electioneering to speak of, and turnout was sometimes so low that in some elections only a few voters cast ballots. Those who voted did so on the "basis of men rather than measures."

In an influential study Ronald P. Formisano defines this "deferential-participant" political culture as

> the acceptance of the view by the whole society that, whether by chance or simply by habit, people would naturally delegate power to a select minority. The belief that this minority would govern in the interest of the entire population was the unifying spirit that bound the society together. In such a society moral cohesion was supplied by the sense of deference and dignity, [and] it was possible for the broad mass of the people to consent to a scheme of government in which their own share would be limited.[11]

In this political world the small electorate was largely disengaged. There were few political issues, even fewer that engaged public discussion, and office seekers seldom debated or even addressed public policy.[12] Richard Hofstadter puts it succinctly when he states that "men were elected not because of the group they were associated with or what they proposed to do about this or that issue but because of what they were."[13] People deferred to their social and economic superiors in matters of governance. This meant that ordinary citizens looked to elites to be their governors and for guidance in exercising their franchise.

Orthodox scholarship argues that the deferential-participant culture did not give way early or easily. Indeed, it lasted until the Age of Jackson and the emergence of modern political parties.[14] The natural aristocracy—not the natural democracy—drove the politics of the new republic. A restricted franchise and modest national governing responsibilities presented political elites few incentives to develop electoral parties. In this view, early republic elections shared more in common with their colonial predecessors than those contested in the mid-nineteenth century.[15]

This argument is increasingly difficult to sustain because it is grounded in two untenable assumptions. The first is that postrevolutionary Americans still subscribed to central tenants of British "virtual" representation. The most important of these is that it is that typical citizens justifiably have limited electoral roles because "those elected by the few are presumed to represent all."[16] This is defensible so long as "there is a communion of interests and a sympathy in feelings and desires between those who act in the name of any description of people and the people in whose name they act, though the trustees are not actually chosen by them."[17] The Americans, as reflected in the Revolutionary War slogan "no taxation without representation," rejected virtual representation and demanded actual representation. Implicit in actual representation is the idea that the individual is the best judge of his own well-being and that of his community. The power of these ideas is reflected in evidence that by the late colonial period—in some places, even earlier—"middle-class democracy" had begun to emerge.[18] The electorate was broader and more active than commonly assumed, and while they may have elected elites to the legislative chambers, they did so without significant duress or coercion. The second assumption is that the deferential-participant political culture maintained itself in the post-founding era because of the absence of organized political parties. The rise of parties meant "the influence of family and local notables could be expected to decline. . . . Party elites . . . would become more important relative to other elite groups."[19] Simply, "rising party" means "declining deference."

Perhaps the strongest argument against the revisionist account of American electoral development—namely, that the United States developed into a recognizable "middle-class democracy"—is that the revisionists "have not really documented their case."[20] However, scholars increasingly present a significantly more nuanced and democratic picture of the early republic. Recent scholarship describes a founding-era political culture that was noticeably more party-oriented, participatory, and engaged than earlier scholarship allowed. This political culture was vibrant, nondeferential, and possessed sufficient organizational capacity to mobilize voters to turn out in impressive numbers.[21] Previously unrecognized forms of electioneering emerged "under the radar" of previous scholarship, and early deferential norms and practices quickly "combined with, and paved the way for, democratic politics."[22] The timing and extent of this transition remains an open question to which this book speaks. What is clear is that sometime between the late eighteenth century and the Jacksonian era the status of the old elite diminished, and with it, their political authority.[23] The evidence presented here shows that this transition emerged earlier, maintained itself longer, and was stronger and more vibrant than established scholarship often recognizes.

Historians have started to leverage the NNV returns to question whether the early nineteenth century was as lacking in party competition as is often assumed. These scholars have documented a competitive partisan landscape in the early nineteenth century and an "extraordinary surge" in voter turnout between 1800 and 1816.[24] The initial analyses of these returns provide evidence that the Federalists remained a "powerful and vibrant political opposition" well into the nineteenth century and "were able to capitalize on the existence of localized support and find ways to win elections long after they had peaked as a national political force."[25] Likewise, political scientists have uncovered an emergent "electoral connection" between representatives and their constituents.[26] Voters responded to, and held representatives accountable for, their legislative actions. In turn, representatives anticipated constituents' responses to their actions and accounted for these reactions in their decisions to seek reelection or election to subsequent office.[27] Historical campaign documents such as pamphlets and newspaper commentary provide considerable evidence that representatives' voting records were important to early elections.[28] Nationally, about 70 percent of incumbents stood for reelection in the first party era. Of these, about 80 percent were reelected.[29] However, there was little in the way of a congressional career. Representatives served an average of about two terms.[30] The early republic political career, such as it was, followed a trajectory from local office to the state legislature, to the US Congress, and then back to the statehouse. Representatives who voted at variance with their constituents' interests, even if they survived initial electoral challenges, were less likely to culminate their careers in the statehouse.[31]

The existence of a vibrant, participatory, political culture and an "electoral connection" is not easily reconciled with standard accounts of period politics and party development. This presents a puzzle for election scholars who argue that modern democracy requires political parties with deep organizational structure. Historian Andrew W. Robertson distills the puzzle when he questions "how Americans could be so caught up in politics, policy, and partisanship without the elaborated political organizations that were typical of American and British mass-based parties later in the nineteenth century."[32] An electorate "caught up in politics, policy, and partisanship" describes a party-structured democracy where citizens have well-defined preferences over government policy, identify with like-minded citizens from whom they are often geographically and even temporally separated, and vote in large numbers. As is sometimes said of ducks, if it walks like one and talks like one, it's probably one. If the new nation didn't have party organized elections, then one must explain why the Americans "spoke and acted" as if it did.[33]

Political Parties in a New Nation

Most political historians take a conservative view of party development. They generally agree that true national parties did not emerge in the United States until the 1830s. In this view, the election of 1800 did not establish a lasting system of national political parties, and to whatever extent parties emerged they rapidly devolved in the Era of Good Feelings and certainly did not coalesce into a national party system. The early proto-parties lacked formal and institutionalized nomination methods and did not present programmatic policy options; their organizational structure, if it could be called that, was ad hoc and based on networks of political elites that were linked by family ties, Revolutionary War service, efforts to advance or preclude the Constitution's ratification, and other connections.[34] These scholars concede that political elites attempted to create organized parties in the late 1790s. However, the presumed post-1800 decline of the Federalists removed incentives for further party development.[35] Without significant opposition, so the argument goes, the Republicans had little need to create deep organizational structures. Instead, they "relied heavily on the congressional caucus and communication through congressional networks."[36] Accordingly, "the early parties . . . were more like factions or stable coalitions of limited duration than the highly articulated organizations of the Democrats and Whigs" of the 1830s.[37] The Federalists and Republican parties "acquired neither legitimacy nor an institutional life as entities apart from particular crises."[38]

There are good reasons to be skeptical of the late development thesis. Recent scholarship, especially when buttressed by vote returns, supports much earlier and lasting party development. David Hackett Fischer in *The Revolution of American Conservatism* was among the first to challenge the late development consensus. Fischer places the establishment of fully functioning parties firmly in the early 1800s. In doing so, he emphasizes the continuing electoral relevance of the Federalists. In his words, "A younger generation of Federalists . . . responded to the Jeffersonian movement with energy, flexibility and effect. . . . They deliberatively tried to create popularly oriented vote-seeking political organizations which might defeat Jefferson with his own weapons."[39] These Federalists sponsored newspapers and engaged in Jeffersonian-style electioneering and campaign rhetoric for their own electoral advantage. They successfully did so in at least ten states, remaining very much alive.[40] Further, much to the chagrin of the first generation of Federalists, these younger Federalists admirably performed that most party-specific function—opposition.

Current scholarship increasingly concurs and places the rise of parties in the early nineteenth century. Around 1800, "parties moved from factionalism through polarization into the expansion stage. . . . The development of a permanent party system had begun to take place."[41] Political scientists largely agree that by "about the third or fourth congress . . . political parties had come into existence. Shifting factions had become settled. . . . They had a partisan press and rudimentary campaign organizations."[42] The Republican and Federalist Parties organized themselves through a national network of presses, local activists, and supporters. Further, political issues including foreign affairs and questions about the scope and powers of the national government began to permanently separate the young parties.[43] By the early 1800s candidates were no longer hesitant to describe themselves as "party men," and the "spirit of party" no longer carried a negative connotation.[44]

Still, many scholars maintain a conservative understanding of the early parties that also acknowledges limited party development. In this view parties did not become established in the new states that entered the Union after 1796, fractionalized in other states, and largely evaporated in the South. This perspective recognizes that the first party system "possessed some vitality" in Maine, Massachusetts, New Jersey, Delaware, and Maryland, and there also were "numerous isolated instances elsewhere of Federalists still offering challenges to their republican adversaries."[45] For example, the late historian Richard P. McCormick conceded that even after 1815 there remained "vestiges of the old party organization" in some areas, and partisan affiliation "lingered on," but apparently this had little effect on elections and how they were contested. Still, these passages reveal misgivings, acknowledging that the Federalists did not abruptly perish but instead remained "amazingly vigorous" well into the mid-1820s. Unfortunately, McCormick relegated this point to a footnote, where it resides to this day in our understanding of early US party politics.[46] The first party system defies easy classification.

This assessment raises several important points. First, does it comport with the empirical evidence provided by House of Representatives election returns? For example, the Democratic-Republican and Federalist Parties were well-established in early Ohio.[47] Second, it emphasizes that party competition and Federalist viability was localized. This presents the challenge of identifying those areas that supported robust party competition. It also introduces the question of why some areas developed party-organized elections while others did not. Third, if Federalist organization remained vibrant in some areas well into the 1820s, this means the first parties achieved legitimacy and structed elections until the Age of Jackson.

The state parties never fully standardized. This is expected and remains true today. Political parties are primarily electoral organizations, and states control the administration of elections. This was especially true in the early republic when there was no national election calendar and states elected offices using a variety of rules and processes. For example, most House of Representatives elections to the Seventh Congress (1801–1803) were held between April 1800 and January 1801, with three states electing representatives *after* the start of the March 1801 session. Some states elected their representatives from single-member districts; some elected representatives at-large, and Pennsylvania, New York, and Maryland used single-member districts augmented with multimember districts.

Scholars point to the dearth of Federalist officeholders after 1812 as evidence that the party's support evaporated. For example, the Fifteenth Congress, convened in 1817, counted 39 Federalist representatives compared to 146 Democratic-Republicans. At the risk of repetition, the win-loss column is a lousy measure of party strength. Federalist candidates mounted respectable campaigns in many contests, only to lose the seat. Some of these losses occurred in states that used at-large elections that in the presence of party-line voting awarded the leading party all seats. Party-line voting for nominated slates is itself an indicator of partisanship and party organizational capacity. As Elbridge Gerry's namesake practice demonstrated, the parties also districted for advantage. Districting for advantage points to party development because it requires the cooperation of like-minded state legislators and the ability to identify the geographic locations of sympathetic and stable voting blocs. Purposeful districting only works if voters are anchored by partisan attachment. Districting for advantage also included creating multimember constituencies to overwhelm geographic concentrations of the other party's supporters. This method is especially advantageous because it creates a district-scale general ticket election. The same evidence that argues for diminished party—few Federalist wins—may instead point to the opposite; namely, that the Democratic-Republicans pulled out all the stops including advantageous electoral rules, effective nominations, mobilization, and other tools in the kit to impede a credible Federalist threat. None of these practices work in the absence of party electoral organization and party in the electorate.

Finally, even in the absence of nefarious districting, the single-member district system offers the majority party with disproportionate legislative seats. A party that can command 30 to 40 percent of the aggregate vote will be fortunate to elect 20 percent of the chamber, if that much. Yet, a party that receives a 30 to 40 percent vote share is surely a serious party. This is especially true if this support is geographically concentrated. Just as today, well-chosen rules and well-chosen geography can shape legislative representation and mask underlying party support.

Party Organization and the Partisan Press

Party organization depends on the electoral environment. An organizational structure that is well-suited for one setting may not perform well in another setting. In the United States the incentives that foster and shape party development principally reside at the state level.[48] Consequently, political parties are primarily state-level organizations built from the constituency up. Elections in the first party era differed across states and from those in later years. They were contested under a variety of vote aggregation rules, franchise requirements, calendars, and other considerations that shape party organization.[49] Decentralization meant that "as parties made their appearance, their forms did not always match twentieth-century expectations of how parties should look."[50] Although the early state-level organizations differed in important respects from their later counterparts, they fulfilled the functions of political parties and eventually comprised something approaching a national system.[51] Party organizations of the type developed in the Age of Jackson didn't exist in the first party era in large part because these would have been ineffective.

In the early republic, the Republicans and Federalists were organized through the partisan press. Newspapers *were* the national party organization; they "embodied the parties in a quite literal sense."[52] Newspaper editors, both national and local, were the principal party organizers.[53] The genesis of this organizational structure dates to the constitutional ratification period when several newspapers including the Philadelphia *Gazetteer* and the Boston *Centinel* aligned with the Federalists and Anti-Federalists, respectively. The Adams and Jefferson administrations created the partisan press. They did so by providing favored papers subsidies to print and disseminate information on government activities. These subsidies and subscription support from an increasingly partisan electorate transformed newspapers into party organs.[54] The number of newspapers grew at a prodigious rate. By the early 1800s there was a national network of Federalist and Republican newspapers that reached virtually all Americans. High literacy rates ensured that newspapers were widely read.[55]

The foundation of this party organization was provided by two newspapers: the Republican *National Gazette* and the *Federalist Gazette of the United States*.[56] These papers disseminated political content that was further distributed through a battery of local outlets. Local presses supplemented this content in a manner relevant to their states and communities. The press linked political elites in the center of government to followings in the electorate to pursue shared political goals. This made the press "the political system's central institution, not simply a forum or atmosphere in which politics took place."[57] Newspapers faithfully transmitted the views of national and local leaders for partisan purposes. In doing so, they "created and reinforced a new sense of "virtual" partisanship that existed in the minds of the newspaper audience."[58] Historian Jeffrey L. Pasley captures the near equivalence between early republic newspapers and parties. The early newspapers "filled many of the gaps left by the party system's uneven development." They maintained party presence between elections and "connected voters and activists to the larger party, and linked the different political levels and geographic regions of the country."[59] The press created a sense of belonging, partisan identity, and "common cause" that connected electors and activists across time and place.[60] Party organization and activity was not episodic because the party press was not episodic. In the first party era, newspapers and their editors did what party organizations and their leaders did in later years.

Newspaper language changed in these years. No longer focusing on candidate character and imagined conspiracies, the parties instead engaged in "substantive discussion of public concerns."[61] Local editors framed national themes and debates in a manner appropriate for their audiences. This included embracing sloganeering and debating policy.[62] These changes in language did not happen suddenly or uniformly, and the old nomenclature sometimes maintained even after the electoral world had clearly shifted. For example, in 1818 New York's dual-member Fifteenth District saw a contest between the Clintonians, led by Robert Monell, and the Bucktails, led by Samuel Campbell. A local Republican newspaper wrote of the candidacies:

> It is highly gratifying to the friends of Mr. Monell, to find that wherever his domestic virtues and intrinsic worth is known, he receives the unanimous suffrages of the people. He will undoubtedly be elected. Mr. Campbell has deservedly many friends in this county. In some towns, his lenity and humanity, in executing the office of Sheriff, has rendered him extremely popular. He has many domestic virtues also. He must not, however, endeavor to rule this county, or grasp the highest offices in the gift of the people.[63]

The language of friends, virtue, and humanity echo that of earlier decades. What the text masks is the deeply divisive politics of the election. Samuel Campbell, while a decent man, was apparently ambitious. Robert Monell's "virtues and intrinsic worth" must not have been widely known because he received nowhere near the "unanimous suffrages of the people." Of the over 5,500 men who cast ballots that day, he received 52 percent of their suffrages, which would be expected given New York politics and the competing tickets. Editors also sought to reach specific groups. In Delaware, for example, the Federalist papers appealed to Quakers; likewise, New Hampshire Republican papers reached out to Baptists.[64] All these features of the Jacksonian political culture appeared before the War of 1812 and maintained itself throughout the first party era.[65] Early in the era newspapers displayed many of the elements of the "Jacksonian" campaign.

Nominations

Candidate nomination is a key function performed by political parties. The presence of formal and accepted nomination methods is a principal indicator of party establishment and strength. Parties act as ballot gatekeepers to avoid spreading electoral support too thin to win office. To do so, the groups that control nominations must be recognized as legitimate and receive sufficient deference from jilted office seekers and their supporters to stave off intramural challenges.

The importance of nominations for party formation is the subject of considerable theoretical research. The primary purpose of nominations is to reduce the number of candidates, thereby precluding intraparty competition in the general election. Nominations ensure that no more affiliated candidates stand than there are seats available to win. Formal nominations also provide voters with information on the identity, viability, and reliability of candidates. Candidates that have the imprimatur of fellow political travelers are presumably well-vetted and will behave accordingly in office. A core element of party development is figuring out how to limit political options by controlling candidate access to the ballot and focusing voters on selected candidates.

Most scholars agree that structured congressional nominations developed in several states by 1800. Party balance—the extent to which the Democratic-Republicans and Federalists competed on relatively equal footing—was a primary consideration motivating formal nominations.[66] In the nation's first years the state legislative caucuses fulfilled this responsibility. However, delegate conventions soon became common in the Middle Atlantic states and New England.[67] This presents two questions. First, did these processes institutionalize, or did they atrophy after the presumed Federalist demise? Second, were nomination meetings "genuine decision-making bodies," or "cosmetic devices" designed to give a color of popular authority to the leaders' decisions?[68] Simply, did formal nominations exist to give the appearance of public input in decisions reached in the parlors of political elites?

Some scholarship supports the latter conclusions arguing that control over nominations "was exercised in a semi-secret fashion through some form of legislative caucus or state convention." Further, these conventions were "short-lived appearing only at election times."[69] William Nisbet Chambers concludes that "early conventions . . . were . . . very irregular in their operation. . . . Called *ad hoc* by caucuses, town meetings, or coteries of leaders, they had no continuing life from election to election."[70] Nobel E. Cunningham Jr. in his landmark *The Jeffersonian Republicans* cautions that "popular participation in [nominating conventions] should not be confused with popular initiative in the introduction of party machinery. In the 1790's one rarely finds effective party organization spring from the so-called 'grass roots.' Instead, the organization of the Republican party and the introduction of smoothly function party machinery were due largely to the leadership of a few dedicated and influential political leaders."[71] Men of typical means could participate in these processes, but the levers of power were held by others.

Recent scholarship offers a more generous assessment. As early as the mid-1790s "nomination processes in a number of states already included a number of modern elements."[72] Conventions emerged in New England, and while these were originally called and controlled by a "junto," they were eventually attended by "sizeable groups of popularly elected delegates." [73] This was also true in Delaware, Pennsylvania, New Jersey, and other states. New York saw the development of increasingly "grass roots" nomination methods. Perhaps surprisingly, it was the Federalists that effected this change. Leading New York Federalists denounced legislative caucuses as "a subversion of republican principles and an 'assumption of power highly derogatory to freemen.'"[74] They pointed to their district-nominating conventions as proof of commitment to the popular nomination of candidates. One supporter spoke for many when he opined that these were beneficial "both to the candidates . . . and to the citizens generally, that the people should have an opportunity of expressing their opinion generally and fairly" on the nomination of candidates.[75]

Primary sources, especially newspapers, reveal more structured and lasting nomination methods than generally recognized. These included district and state conventions, mechanisms for transmitting votes from satellite meetings to a central nomination body, procedures for determining the credentials of meeting participants, rules of procedure, and other markers of a formalized process for nominating candidates. Nomination methods were not generally the same for the two parties. The Democratic-Republicans often adopted a tiered system of committees while Federalists preferred more general meetings.[76]

The 1804 Pennsylvania Fourth District consisting of Cumberland, Dauphin, Huntingdon, and Mifflin Counties illustrates an early Democratic-Republican nomination and the occasional failures of these processes. The nominations proceeded from township meetings to the county and, ultimately, the district. The district meeting required "certificates" to prove delegates elected from the townships were qualified to attend the county meeting. Here some of the attendees challenged some Dauphin County delegates' qualifications. As a result, no nominations were made.[77] The result was four Democratic-Republican candidates ultimately stood in the two-seat district. This had no practical effect, as the Fourth District was solidly Democratic-Republican and the Federalists offered no serious opposition. Still, one suspects the Democratic-Republicans would have resolved their differences had the district been competitive as they courted disaster had the Federalists mounted a strong challenge.

This example of failed nominations notwithstanding, both parties developed formalized nomination processes in many locations that anticipated their Jacksonian era counterparts. These ensured that "the parties usually agreed on the appropriate candidates and gave adequate publicity to these slates."[78] By the first years of the nineteenth century, nominations had largely been wrestled from local political elites and placed in the hands of party organizers and rank-and-file voters. These took seriously the role of supporters—and took on an institutional life of their own. Political elites, to be sure, remained important. However, they did so primarily in their role in organizing meetings and conventions and making sure they were well attended. This is a first, but a very important, step in electoral development.

Who Could Vote?

One of the most remarkable features of the early republic was how many Americans voted. The United States had an exceptionally liberal franchise. This flies in the face of conventional wisdom. Certainly by twenty-first-century standards, the founding-era franchise was deeply restricted. Women, African Americans, the indigent, tradesmen, lessees and tenant farmers, and a host of others were often excluded from the vote. White men, and not all these men, possessed the right to vote. In this view, electoral democratization began in the Jacksonian Era with the mass enfranchisement of white men that came with national party development.

The conventional wisdom contains its grain of truth. States in the early republic often imposed property and tax-paying requirements to vote. Most women and free African Americans could not vote and would have to wait until the twentieth century to fully exercise this basic prerogative of citizenship. However, as is often the case, conventional wisdom's grain of truth masks a larger reality. Here it greatly understates how widespread the franchise was among white men and how ineffectual franchise restrictions often were in practice. The received figure is that about 75 to 80 percent of white men possessed franchise at the founding and that these numbers increased in subsequent years.[79] By way of comparison, in the British Isles the suffrage was asymptotically small, and universal manhood suffrage was not obtained until the twentieth century.[80] Historian Chilton Williamson in *American Suffrage* argues that the "predominant mood of the period, regardless of how reactionary it may have been in other particulars, was not reactionary by and large in regard to the suffrage."[81]

In the nation's early years New Hampshire, Pennsylvania, and Georgia had the least restrictive franchise laws, with something approaching universal white manhood suffrage. The most restrictive suffrages were in Virginia, Rhode Island, and, to a lesser extent, New York. In these states about 60 percent of white men enjoyed suffrage in statehouse and US House elections. Other states fell between these bookends, with most approaching the higher end of the spectrum.[82] Overall, in the 1790s the large majority of adult white men could vote, and those who could not vote would soon find paths to suffrage.[83] Importantly, there is no obvious regional pattern that explains the differences in state franchise.

This invites one to step back and consider how the founding generation thought about suffrage and why there were any qualifications to vote at all. Period franchise debates centered on whether voting is a privilege or a right. The privilege interpretation was dominant in England and in the colonies prior to the revolution. The words "franchise" and "suffrage" themselves convey the idea that voting is a privilege. "Franchise" in period English captured the notion of being invested with a privilege. "Suffrage" invokes prayer, especially prayer on another's behalf.[84] This language implies that voting is a privilege that the state could grant or withhold, not an inherent right.

In the United States, however, the national discussion over the right to vote was steeped in the language of natural rights. Blackstone's *Commentaries* influenced the founding generation when he wrote that all people have a natural right to vote and that the only acceptable restriction on voting was one's lack of political independence. [85] A property requirement to vote is permissible only "to exclude such parson as are in so mean a situation as to be esteemed to have no will of their own."[86] Those with "no will of their own" included, inter alia, slaves, tenant farmers, indentured servants, women, and the urban working classes. As a matter of principle, the natural right to vote belongs to all members of the community, but in practice some may be excluded from the franchise to prevent those upon whom they are dependent from exercising undue political influence. This justification for restricting the suffrage was that failure to do so would "increase the power of wealth in election and reduce the effectiveness and honesty of government officials."[87] In an era before the universal adoption of secret ballots, the dependent would presumably vote as those who controlled their economic livelihoods instructed.

This concern was justified. In the 1792 New York gubernatorial election, for example, Federalist William Cooper, father of author James Finimore Cooper, threatened "tenants and debtors with ruin if they did not vote as they were told."[88] He also threatened to have anyone arrested if they "challenged the legality" of these votes.[89] Likewise, Cumberland County, New Jersey, witnessed "men of large estates or who have many debtors . . . influence a great many voters in an undue manner counter to the spirit of the constitution."[90] Scenes such as these played out in other jurisdictions in the nation's first years. Many believed with justification that a property requirement diminished the political influence of men such as William Cooper.

The second pillar of the right to vote was having a long-term interest in one's community.[91] If the property qualification ensured that voters enjoyed political independence, it also spoke to one's "stake in society." Those with "real property" (land) were thought to be more "committed members of the community" and possessed a "personal interest in the policies of the state, especially taxation."[92] Tenants, indentured servants, and laborers might move to better opportunities wherever and whenever these might arise. Property owners, in contrast, had a vested, long term interest in the maintenance and prosperity of their community. The property requirement was thought beneficial in so far as it ensured that voters were civically responsible and remained subject to the laws promulgated by those whom they elected.

Ownership of real property was the most important economic barrier to voting. Virginia imposed one of the more restrictive property qualification by requiring fifty acres of land or twenty-five acres and a house. Connecticut required a freehold worth $7 per year or a $134 personal estate. However, property-holding requirements were far from universal. Some states had no freehold requirements at all. Other states imposed property requirements, but these were often modest and effectively disappeared by the early nineteenth century. For example, Delaware required a freehold of fifty acres of property from 1734 to 1792, after which it eliminated this requirement. Maryland abolished its property requirement in 1801. To vote in lower chamber elections Massachusetts required a freehold that generated only £3 pounds of income annually. These and similar requirements were not especially high bars to voting.

Paying taxes as a prerequisite for voting was a more liberal alternative to a property requirement. This is because this standard could more often be met by artisans, mechanics, and others who generated income by their skills and labor, but who did not own real property. In the nation's first years several states adopted a tax-paying requirement as an alternative to owning property.[93] Of the ten states that adopted a tax requirement, four—Connecticut, New Jersey, South Carolina, and New York—after 1820 used it as an alternative, rather than a supplement, to the property requirement. Other states, such as Pennsylvania, had no property requirement and required only that one pay a modest state or county tax to vote. In contrast, Virginia and Rhode Island maintained a property requirement, but no tax alternative, thereby imposing a higher barrier to voting than states that relied solely on a tax requirement or a tax as an alternative to property.

As restrictive as these qualifications seem today, the language of natural rights promised that voting barriers would be challenged early and strenuously. The first attempts to broaden the franchise centered on substituting tax payment for property ownership and providing blanket enfranchisement for men who served in the army or militia. Besides being a less restrictive mechanism to demonstrate independence and commitment to community, tax paying resonated with the core justification for the revolution, which rallied around the call for "no taxation without representation."[94] The political justification for franchise predicated on tax payment is different than that for property ownership. Whereas property speaks to independence and one's stake in a community, taxes speak to one's acceptance or rejection of the government policies to which one financially contributes. If taxes underwrite military adventures or roads, one who pays for military adventures or roads is entitled to a voice in these decisions.[95] Further, when taxes were levied, most adult men paid them. Consequently, with "taxation of adult males universal, a taxpaying suffrage was almost universal suffrage."[96]

Economic changes further reduced barriers to the polls. Property requirements defined in nominal currency diminished in real value over time. For example, New York's 1777 constitution required that voters for the state assembly possess a freehold worth £20. By 1790, inflation had rendered the £20 equivalent a modest barrier to the vote.[97] Similarly, states that maintained property requirements in terms of acreage found that population migration to less populated areas of the state created new voters wholesale.[98] In South Carolina, for example, men who migrated to the western parts of the state obtained the suffrage by virtue of settlement.[99] Land, or the lack of it, had the opposite effect in New England. Primogeniture was abandoned in the United States by the revolutionary period, meaning that inheritance often reduced parcels below freehold requirement. This put additional pressure on these states to abandon land ownership as a qualification for franchise.[100]

These voting requirements presuppose that they were enforced. The enforcement of legal restrictions to vote for white men was often lax or nonexistent. The value of one's property was sometimes overlooked. In other cases long-term tenancies were treated as freeholds.[101] In many locations the property and taxpaying requirements were simply ignored.[102] When elites were recalcitrant, citizens sometimes had recourse to extraordinary measures to codify broader franchise. In Delaware restrictive franchise laws, especially for upper-chamber and gubernatorial elections, were challenged with the threat of calling a state constitutional convention to fully democratize franchise for all branches unless the lower-chamber restrictions were eased. The state's political elites blinked, and the 1791 Delaware state constitutional convention reduced lower-chamber voting qualifications to a tax-paying requirement.[103] Finally, Roman Catholics and Jews were enfranchised, although New York required Quakers to take loyalty oaths.[104] The important point is that the focus on de jure suffrage ignores the de facto reality on the ground. By 1800 there is convincing evidence that the monetary qualifications "were divorced from freeholds and from tax assessments."[105] Some states simply required potential voters to take a "freeman's oath" testifying that they were eligible to vote and could meet property or tax requirements. The "freeman's oath" eventually took the form of something of a registration requirement rather than a substantive restriction on franchise.[106] Property and related requirements remained on the books until the age of Jackson, but these were often deadwood.

None of this means that the desperately poor, vagabonds, women, and African Americans were admitted to the franchise in significant numbers. Women, even those who met property or tax requirements, were disenfranchised in all states except New Jersey. New Jersey enfranchised unmarried property-holding women until this suffrage was revoked in 1807.[107] The early nineteenth-century disenfranchisement of New Jersey women was itself a sign of party development. The rise of party politics made electoral politics notably more verbally and even physically contentious. By the norms of the early nineteenth century, women were expected to be a calming influence and exemplify nonpartisan virtues such as "Republican Motherhood." The home was to be a refuge from partisan warfare. Political venues increasingly became a space for men.

Free African Americans were prohibited from voting in most southern states, but were enfranchised in other states subject to property or tax requirements. Historian Van Gosse's meticulously researched documentary evidence reveals that free African American men voted in often substantial numbers in the Middle Atlantic and New England in the early antebellum period. For example, in 1820 Black men voted in their hundreds in several south-central and western Pennsylvania counties. At about the same time New York's African American men constituted about 5 percent of the potential electorate.[108] The Black electorate generally supported the Federalists, and in some jurisdictions their numbers were sufficient to tip the political scales to one party or the other.[109] This was the case in New Jersey, which revoked the African American suffrage concurrently with women.

Any discussion of early US suffrage must account for an empirical reality that one will encounter repeatedly in the follow chapters. Namely, the number of electors in early House elections is often immense. This is true at the county, district, and state levels. One can easily determine these numbers from votes, and one can use the censuses to determine what proportion of men voted. This allows one to assess the de facto franchise and whether the electorate was primarily comprised of elites or men of typical means. As will become clear, the de facto franchise was expansive, and the electorate included a large cross-section of American men.

Electioneering in the Early Republic

The development of American political parties and electioneering are deeply intertwined and inseparable. Electioneering practices depended on the extent of party development, but electioneering itself furthered party development. Unlike in the colonial period, election campaigns in the new nation were often long, structured, and vigorously contested.[110] Electioneering initially resembled that in earlier years. However, unlike in colonial elections, political deference combined with egalitarian rhetoric, popular participation, and the increased importance of political issues to pave the way for well-organized partisan campaigns.[111]

In the nation's first decade, candidates stood for election on their personal attributes and seldom directly solicited votes. Elections were often lightly contested, and polling was typically conducted by voice vote, leaving voters vulnerable to pressure. Elections were intended to produce a local consensus and confer the endorsement of the community on a favored candidate. Since republican theory and rhetoric rejected campaigning, electioneering practices sought to ensure that office holders appeared to emerge through "spontaneous" and uncoordinated community consensus.[112]

Candidates pretended to be above politics while working diligently toward their own election. They did so by "making interest"; that is, discreetly "constructing a hierarchical network of influence" that would translate into electoral success.[113] The foundation of an interest was the candidate's "friends." These friends undertook the task of obtaining support for his election. In doing so they implied their connection to the office seeker was personal, not political. They helped the candidate by expounding on why he was worthy of election. These solicitations emphasized the candidate's independence, integrity, fidelity, and similar qualities. Sometimes supporters resorted to more nefarious tactics, such as spreading false rumors that other potential candidates did not seek the office or had withdrawn from consideration.[114] Since "making interest" was considered antirepublican, contending interests accused each other of doing so. Interests, not parties, were the foundation of the first American elections.

The politics of interest and deference were predicated on the belief that voters were capable of judging office seekers' characters, but not public policies. Consequently, those standing for office seldom discussed ideology or issues.[115] Rather, election rhetoric centered on candidate character, family status, and community standing. When speaking to electors, candidates sought "to please everyone and promise little in the way of specifics."[116] They did so by making "decorous speeches designed to impress the lower orders with their knowledge."[117] This "sprouting" sought to placate voters while avoiding any discussion of policy.[118] Such politicking was a local affair. Those standing for office did not typically link their candidacies with like-minded candidates in other districts or those seeking other offices. This was necessary to preserve the appearance of republican ideals that rejected coordinated electioneering. Suitability for office depended on personal attributes, and these are not easily linked to other political aspirants. Even for the highest offices, electioneering did not extend beyond state boundaries.[119]

Electioneering consisted of political theater in which candidates appeared to subjugate themselves to ordinary citizens to win their votes. The more important the office, the more the candidate flattered the freeholders.[120] These men addressed voters as "gentlemen" in obsequious language while "humbly begging" them for their support. Such flattery was delivered with "a certain affability carefully modulated between reserve and familiarity."[121] The candidate would express his wish that he would "merit the approbation" of voters and that he was "pleased to have the honor" of being his constituents' "obedient servant." On election day the candidate's friends often conducted an "electioneering tour" to gather voters at their homes and take them to the polls. These tours reinforced the egalitarian appearance of electoral politics by "permitting common men to be flattered and treated as cherished friends by men of higher status—gentlemen who otherwise tended to socialize only with one another."[122] The candidates often "treated" potential voters with refreshments to encourage their support. Such treating sometimes turned into extravagant and expensive affairs featuring roast ox, beer, rum punch, and other fare.[123] Interest politics demonstrates that despite our nostalgia for a purer form of electoral democracy, the "pure unmediated election was a fantasy of republican theory."[124]

The political culture of the 1780s and 1790s proved evanescent while providing a foundation for a new style of electioneering. Large-scale participation combined with "sprouting" and "courting" made freeholders feel that they were a valued part of the community and the political equal of any other man. Sometime around 1800 this rhetoric transformed into reality. By the last years of the eighteenth century it was clear that the purely local and gentlemanly approach to elections was in decline and would never reemerge.[125] Campaigns organized around community festivals and national celebrations. These events provided a forum for politicking and party organizing and often featured large and passionate crowds. Celebrations also provided a space for the disenfranchised to participate in electoral politics. Here candidates faced unpropertied white men, women, free Blacks, and even children. These men and women influenced elections by their presence and peripheral involvement. Men, enfranchised or not, sometimes engaged in "rough play" to intimidate political opponents.

Women also played an important role in early elections. So-called female politicians expressed their own political views and politicked for favored candidates and parties, even delivering speeches that were reprinted in newspapers.[126] For example, at a June 1800 rally protesting the Federalist-promulgated Alien and Sedition Acts, the "Republican Females of Chester County," Pennsylvania, presented the militia with a flag in appreciation for "their exertions in the cause of liberty, when it appeared declining, never to revive."[127] That same year the "Ladies of Cheshire," Massachusetts, engineered a nationally visible political event by making a "mammoth cheese." Supporters transported the 1,200-pound cheese by sled, boat, and wagon to Jefferson's Monticello as an election gift. The cheese's journey to Virginia captured national interest for weeks, and with it a great deal of commentary from enthused Republicans and dismissive Federalists.[128] The "Ladies of Cheshire" produced what was quite possibly the first national-level electoral spectacle. What is beyond doubt is that the Chester and Cheshire women not only made their political voices heard but in doing so challenged period ideas of proper gender roles.[129] These and similar undertakings capture the important, yet circumscribed, role women played in early elections.

The 1799 Virginia US House of Representatives election between Federalist John Marshall and Republican John Clopton illustrates this transition to a more modern style of elections. Although the complete vote returns are lost to history, Marshall won the election by 114 votes out of what certainly been more than a thousand cast.[130] Here an observer named Mumford describes two local ministers, a Mr. Blair and a Mr. Buchanan, casting their votes in the heretofore tied election.[131]

> There were shoutings and hurrahs perfectly deafening. Men were shaking fists at each other, rolling up their sleeves, cursing and swearing with angry and furious denunciations. Some became wild with agitation. . . . Parson

> Blair came forward. A swaggering fellow, just above him said, "Here come two preachers, dead shot for Marshall." Both candidates knew them intimately and rose from their seats, and the shout was terrific.
>
> "Mr. Blair," said the sheriff, "who do you vote for?" "John Marshall" said he. Mr. Marshall replied, "your vote is appreciated, Mr. Blair. . . . [And then] Parson Buchanan was at the sheriff's elbow.
>
> The whole Federal party, and the Democrats too, thought this vote was certain, beyond the possibility of a doubt, for Marshall. "Who do you vote for, Mr. Buchanan?" "For John Clopton," said the good man. Mr. Clopton said, "Mr. Buchanan, I shall treasure that vote in my memory. It will be regarded as a feather in my cap forever." The Astonishment expressed in Mr. Marshall's face, in Parson Blair's countenance, by the friends of Mr. Buchanan generally, can only be imagined. . . .
>
> When our friends entered the carriage on their return home, Parson Buchanan said, "Brother Blair, we might as well staid [*sic*] at home. When I was forced against my will to go, I simply determined to balance your vote, and now we shall hear no complaints of the clergy interfering in elections."[132]

Here many components of deferential-participant politics are found. First, the parsons felt little urgency to vote; both had to be encouraged to turnout. Second, voting was public. Parsons Buchanan and Blair declared their votes before the crowd, and the election was known to be tied when the latter voted. Third, Parsons Blair and Buchanan, while certainly men of standing in their communities, had none of the social stature of the candidates. Nonetheless, the candidates addressed them in the formal manner appropriate for gentlemen. This would have been true for all men who voted that day.

The election also displays attributes of a more modern style of electioneering. There was a large, boisterous, and partisan crowd at the polling place. The election was not solely or even primarily the province of elites. Enfranchised men, and certainly many others, were there in numbers. Further, the electorate knew the partisan affiliation and the issue stands of the candidates. Marshall, for one, declared that "every citizen has a right to know the political sentiments of the man who is proposed as his representative; and mine have never been of a nature to shun examination."[133] It's hard to imagine a sentiment more at variance with the deferential-participant political culture.

Importantly, the Virginia Thirteenth District tended Republican, so Marshall had to win the votes of moderates.[134] The candidates' partisan associations and issue positions mattered to the electorate. Marshall clarified and even moderated his own for the sake of election. To do so, he expressed opposition to the Alien and Sedition Acts. He also expressed reservations about closer ties with Great Britain, instead advocating neutrality in foreign affairs.[135] The crowd also suspected the partisan leanings of the clergymen; they were expected to vote Federalist even though Parson Buchanan's vote was ultimately driven by a desire to absolve the ministry of influencing the election. Parsons Blair and Buchanan were reluctant to vote and had to be cajoled to the poll. Somebody had to do the cajoling, and given their anticipated votes that person was certainly a Federalist. Finally, the campaign was contested in the press and broadsides. The Federalist Richmond-based *Virginia Gazette* and the Republican *Aurora* published several essays supporting their preferred candidate and attacking his opponent.[136]

The transitional period saw the contrast between parties and their newspapers become sharper and more than sufficient for men to vote on the basis of issues and ideology. The parties were increasingly associated with specific principles and polices, and these "gradually became values for their own sake."[137] For their part, newspapers enlarged their election coverage and printed more partisan content. Editors moved beyond calls to elect "good men" and instead pointed to the political differences that separated candidates.[138] The Democratic-Republican *Philadelphia Aurora* and the Boston *Independent Chronicle*, for example, admonished their readers to vote for "PRINCIPLES, AND NOT MEN."[139] The *Aurora* demanded that candidates provide clear policy alternatives because we "can distinguish between black and white—but do not believe that a grey part can exist long."[140] Newspapers also devoted premium space to campaign material under the heading "Electioneering," something uncommon in the deferential period.[141]

The politics of deference ended sometime around the election of 1800. The approach to electioneering that supplanted it did not immediately take root. These changes came faster in some places than others, but they inexorably progressed. The emergence of party-centered electioneering built on existing practices and developed new ones that were appropriate for this evolving stage of US political history. These created an increasingly partisan electorate and different expectations for how candidates engaged constituents. The result was "more structured and party centered electioneering."[142] That is, the emergence of mass, partisan elections. Parties achieved normative legitimacy by reconciling nationalism with partisanship. They did so by each claiming to be the "true expression of the revolution and American republican ideals."[143] Consequently, one could be a partisan and a nationalist.[144] To be sure, some still referred to the "despotism of party," but this no longer equated parties with interested factions. Instead, it referred to parties seeking conformity on a broad range of issues rather than just a few salient ones.[145] Republicans defended the need for cohesion by equating party politics with a "natural force, upon which depends on all order in the universe."[146] When a party embodies the revolution and republican values, united political action is a virtue, not a vice.

Party legitimation also legitimized their leaders. Previously viewed as demagogues, party organizers including local office holders and newspaper editors proudly displayed their partisanship. These men increasingly shaped campaign strategies. They did so by formalizing nominations, transmitting party messages and exaltations, and, most importantly, by mobilizing the electorate. Pennsylvania Republican leaders, for example, devised election strategy at "centrally organized meetings." Party leaders also sent representatives to other counties, "providing money, printed matter, or political expertise" to help affiliated candidates.[147] Slowly at first and then more rapidly, these leaders began to craft coherent political programs, gatekeep candidate access to the ballot, mobilize voters, and coordinate with state and national political allies. By fostering structure, coherence, and participation, these leaders contributed greatly to the "democratization of American politics through electoral means."[148]

Increased party legitimacy and importance changed the way candidates campaigned and the way voters interacted with them.[149] These changes anticipated many presumed Jacksonian-era innovations. Candidates reached out to voters, mingled with them in taverns, marched with them in parades, and delivered stump speeches that directly solicited votes.[150] Parties and candidates also began targeting their messages toward ethnic and religious groups. For example, Pennsylvania organizers encouraged German immigrants to vote as a bloc to preserve their political standing. Appeals to social class were increasingly common in urban areas.[151] Some, most often Federalists, complained this new electioneering style dishonored republican foundations and traditions.[152] However, within a few years Federalists were delivering as many Fourth of July orations and publishing as many pamphlets as the Jeffersonians.[153] These new-style candidates and party leaders came to see themselves not as "corrupters of the purity of polls or as demagogues who despoiled patriotic holidays," but rather as those who harnessed these events to further republican ideals and save community festivals from "irrelevance or subversion."[154]

Community celebrations remained the central event in electoral politics. However, there was an important shift in the purpose of these festivals. In the deferential period freemen used festivals to further their own participation in the political process; in the post-deferential period they used these events to determine who would make policy.[155] The most important celebrations were Independence Day and George Washington's birthday, but traditional local celebrations remained important political events. Festivities included church services, militia drills, parades, cannon fire and fireworks, and dinners followed by patriotic and partisan toasts.[156] Newspapers reveal considerable overlap in celebration committees and election committees.[157] These events "brought party workers together, identified the candidates, and informed voters about the issues."[158] Party organizers caucused at celebrations and distributed printed ballots.[159] Not surprisingly, the best-organized committees also produced the most and the best-attended celebrations.[160] Importantly, patriotic celebrations created a "sense of national unity" and helped nationalize party politics by "extending the 'community of allegiance' beyond state and regional boundaries."[161]

Conclusion

By the early nineteenth century, there is evidence that US elections were contested by well-organized parties and affiliated candidates before a relatively expansive and active electorate. Candidates secured their nominations through increasingly formalized processes that were dominated by politically engaged, but not necessarily elite, organizers. They competed on political issues and deeper differences over proper republican government. In doing so, each party's candidates could count on a relatively stable core group of voters. Further, the Federalist Party maintained a viable electoral presence in many areas. In these respects, the first party era is more similar than distinct from the Jacksonian period.[162]

This new electoral politics eventually established itself nationally, but there remain important questions about the timing, extent, and regional differences in the development of early US elections. The Middle Atlantic and border states show clear, sustained electoral development. Maryland politicians, for example, solicited votes through rallies and speeches. They also sought to attract wide-scale attention by holding elaborate parades.[163] Similar politicking existed in Pennsylvania, New Jersey, and New York. New England retained a more distinctive style of politics, but candidates spoke directly with voters, and party organizers dutifully mobilized supporters on election day. In the South electioneering was more limited but could still be found in commercial towns such as Wilmington, North Carolina.[164]

By the early nineteenth century, party leaders developed something approaching regional party systems. It is less clear if these comprised a national system, about which I will say more in the book's concluding chapter. System development, whether regional or national, was furthered by the national press, and by the decentralized election calendar. Most states held their fall elections on dates that followed local tradition. The election season was truly seasonal. This sometimes extended to offices within a state so that gubernatorial, statehouse, and other offices might be decided on different days. The staggering of elections created a sense of anticipation and excitement. Elections in one state were often seen as foreshadowing elections in another state. The outcomes of preceding elections motivated party supporters and organizers to maintain the momentum or turn the tide, depending on the case.[165]

The increasing role of party did have negative consequences, the most significant of which was diminishing the electoral role of women. Celebrations became more about party, and party was increasingly circumscribed by franchise. As the ruckus spirit of party clashes intensified in the early nineteenth century, women were increasingly expected to abandon their partisan identities and instead act as "pacemakers and mediators."[166] The home was to be a refuge from party warfare, and women were expected to rise above politics and embody the virtues that united rather than divided Americans.[167] As such, women entered a political fallow period that extended into the Jacksonian era and only reemerged with the Seneca Falls Convention and the rise of abolitionist politics.

In a fitting epitaph for the old style of electioneering, in November 1816 the Federalist *Alexandria Gazette* published a letter by Henry Lee Jr., then seeking election to the US House of Representatives. In it Lee harkened back to the virtues of the deferential period, lamenting that party spirit was "the source of all of our woes." Writing in a tone and tenor long out of fashion in in most places, Lee encouraged voters to select "the most worthy" candidate based on character and standing, meaning, of course, himself. Lee was hopelessly out of step with his Virginia electorate, and he lost badly.[168] The movement toward party-structured elections and campaigning was irreversible. By the early nineteenth century, political parties were the primary organizers of American elections. Parties and candidates appealed directly to voters, and men voted without regard to the preferences of their social superiors. The electoral world was changing.

3 | The Middle Atlantic States

Electoral democracy as we know it first emerged in the Middle Atlantic states. Party-structured elections were a staple of the middle seaboard by the first years of the nineteenth century. As will be seen, robust voter turnout, partisan loyalty, and other markers of electoral development were present by the late eighteenth century and maintained throughout the era. The region was politically contentious. This is reflected in hard-fought campaigns, aggressive districting, and other elements of a competitive and structured electoral setting. This makes Pennsylvania, New Jersey, and New York central for understanding the development of early American elections. While each state had its own political history, traditions, and culture, there are common threads that link these regional neighbors.

The Middle Atlantic quickly saw public opinion separate into two groups that eventually solidified into Democratic-Republican and Federalist leaders and supporters. These differences centered on national concerns including foreign policy. Newspaper editor John Binn, for example, wrote in his Philadelphia *Democratic Press* that "the correct demarcation of parties in the state, ought to be dated from 1795, at the period when Mr. Jay's treaty was submitted to the Senate. . . . The adoption of the British treaty accurately decided the fate of parties."[1] In addition, the French and Haitian revolutions, the Barbary Wars, the War of 1812, and the Hartford Convention, along with domestic issues such as the reach of the national government relative to the states, Hamilton's plan for the Bank of the United States, the Alien and Sedition Acts, and a host of other considerations affected Middle Atlantic electoral politics. Philadelphia's standing as the nation's first capital magnified the local importance of national politics.[2]

Regional party development was present by the final years of the eighteenth century. For example, by the end of the Adams administration the New Jersey Federalists had to "contend with a state-wide opposition party."[3] The Democratic-Republicans, as they came to be known, developed first in the northern part of the state, especially in Essex,

Morris, and Sussex Counties. Their reach eventually extended to south Jersey.[4] At first it was uncommon for party labels to be attached to candidates, but by the late 1790s "the terms 'Federal' and 'Republican' began to acquire distinctive meanings."[5] This forced politicians to choose the banner under which to align and established expectations for how representatives would act in Congress. As one elector insisted, if a man "were elected as a Republican . . . he was expected to vote as a Republican in the Legislature."[6] The New Jersey Republicans built a political machine originating at the township level. These men organized county conventions and a biennial state convention. At these, "Congressional tickets were agreed upon in accordance with regular rules."[7] The Federalists lagged in this regard but by 1800 were standing slates as well. Finally, many of the staples of modern elections, including rallies, door-to-door canvasing, endorsements, and parades, were a staple of regional politics.

The Middle Atlantic states were politically combative. Pennsylvania's relatively egalitarian state constitution, combined with its heterogeneous social composition and regional divisions, primed the pump for party organized elections. New York's political divisions were even more complex. These existed not only between Democratic-Republicans and Federalists, but also across institutions, with the legislature and governor battling for influence. This was further complicated by conflict and shifting alliances among the state's most prominent families. The Clintons, Livingstons, Van Rensselaers, and several lesser families dominated New York politics throughout much of the era. The Democratic-Republicans sometimes split into competing factions under various leaders including Aaron Burr, George and DeWitt Clinton, and Peter Livingston. Alexander Hamilton led the Federalists until his death at the hands of Burr; thereafter it was piloted by a group of like-minded men including Elisha Williams, Jacob R. Van Rensselaer, and William W. Van Ness.[8] These alliances were often comprised of identifiable groups including "Quids," "Martling Men," "Tammanys," "Clintonians," "Bucktails," and "Old Federalists."[9] A contemporary observer aptly described New York politics as a "labyrinth of wheels within wheels."[10]

Residents didn't have to look hard for state-specific issues to divide them. In Pennsylvania "Citizen" Genet attempted to export the French Revolution to the streets of Philadelphia. Taxes—including the hated "Window Tax" of 1798 that sparked "Fries's Rebellion"—along with the perennial issues of economics, roads, religion, and the myriad of other considerations intrinsic to a large, heterogeneous state provided plenty of fuel for political organization. In New York the Erie Canal was the most important early nineteenth-century political issue. Federalists initially championed the canal. This precipitated a statewide debate over whether and how to fund the canal—estimated to cost a staggering $7 million in a state that had only $21 million in private capital.[11] When it became clear that no federal funds would underwrite the project, Democratic-Republican DeWitt Clinton broke with his party by securing legislative support for the canal. He subsequently won the governorship in 1817 on a pro-canal platform. Further complicating New York politics, candidates ceased to stand under the Federalist label beginning in 1818. This is largely because the Federalists never fully recovered from their response to the War of 1812 and the internecine party warfare endemic to the state. Thereafter, many of these men stood as "Clintonites," which included many formerly labeled Federalists as well as disaffected Democratic-Republicans.[12] Regardless of label, "it became the fixed purpose of the Republicans to defeat" these men, and vice versa.[13]

Each state had areas of Democratic-Republican strength and areas where the Federalists were stronger. In Pennsylvania the south-central counties including the German-dominated areas tended Federalist. The northern and central areas included Democratic-Republican strongholds, but here too there were Federalist-leaning counties. Philadelphia city was competitive. New York's Hudson Valley, including Albany, Rensselaer, and Columbia Counties, was reliably Federalist. Democratic-Republican areas in the south and west included Long Island's Suffolk County, as well as Rockland, Orange, and Delaware Counties. New York City (Manhattan) leaned Democratic-Republican, but both parties were competitive in the city and in some of its immediately adjacent districts. New Jersey Democratic-Republicans dominated largely Presbyterian East Jersey, which was mostly northern and coastal, and shared political affinity with New York City. West (southern) Jersey leaned Federalist and tended Quaker, with Philadelphia serving as its political and social anchor.[14] This "east-west" division, which still shapes New Jersey politics, was not as sharp as commonly believed. New Jersey, to use the contemporary chromatic characterization, was a purple state. Both parties drew support from several areas.

House Elections and Markers of Electoral Development

The Middle Atlantic states conducted hundreds of House elections between 1796 and 1825. Three pieces of information are necessary to place the state and regional elections in context. These are the state populations, the sizes of their potential electorates, and their apportionments. Table 3.1 presents these figures. The columns are labeled by Congress, corresponding to the years 1796–1800, 1802–1810, 1812–1820, and 1822–1824.[15] The populations and estimated potential electorates are from the first year of the decennial census. For analysis, I update these figures throughout the apportionment cycle. With respect to their potential electorates, Pennsylvania and New Jersey had remarkably egalitarian constitutions with near-universal white male franchise. New York maintained a more restrictive franchise, but even here most white men were eligible to vote in House of Representatives elections. Franchise was at least partially extended to African American men in in all three states.[16] Single (unmarried) New Jersey women and African American men possessed the suffrage until 1807.[17] In 1800 the region was home to over a quarter of the nation's population and an even larger share of its voting population. By 1820 New York and Pennsylvania alone accounted for a third of the nation's electorate.[18]

Table 3.1. Middle Atlantic Population, Potential Electorate, and Apportionment, 1796–1824

	Congress			
State	*5th–7th*	*8th–12th*	*13th–17th*	*18th–19th*
Pennsylvania				
Population	434,373	602,545	810,091	1,049,458
Electorate	110,800	123,900	163,400	212,900
Apportionment	13	18	23	26
New York				
Population	340,120	589,051	959,049	1,372,812
Electorate	98,600	118,200	191,800	286,300
Apportionment	10	17	27	34
New Jersey				
Population	184,139	211,149	245,555	277,575
Electorate	39,500	40,700	48,000	55,300
Apportionment	5	6	6	6

Turning to election returns, Pennsylvania presents 195 complete district returns. The returns lack only three districts in 1796, two in 1804, and one each in 1806 and 1818. The returns include 131 single-member districts, 40 dual-member districts, 19 three-member districts, and 5 four-member district elections. Likewise, New York is only missing a handful of returns. Here there are 272 complete districts. New Yorkers elected most of their representatives from single-member districts, although there were some multimember constituencies. These include 233 single-member districts, 37 dual-member districts, and 2 three-member district elections. New Jersey used the general ticket to elect its representatives.[19] The sole exceptions are in 1798 and 1813, when New Jersey used single-member districts and dual-member districts, respectively. The New Jersey general ticket and district returns are complete. The Middle Atlantic states also present hundreds of county-level returns. There are 536 Pennsylvania useable county returns, 597 New York county returns, and 175 New Jersey county returns. The New Jersey county votes are especially important because the general ticket reveals little about ground-level party support. The counties present the most fine-grained picture of party support available and provide a useful check on district-level and state-level analyses. Overall, the Middle Atlantic election returns at the state, district, and county levels are remarkably complete.[20]

I use the returns to evaluate the measures of electoral development discussed in chapter 1. These include the number of party candidates in each election, elector turnout, aggregate party support, evidence of partisanship, and candidate terms and reelection patterns. I also discuss the use of districting and seat allocation rules for political advantage. No single measure provides conclusive evidence of electoral development. Viewed collectively, they inform whether the empirical patterns are supportive of significant electoral development. These measures also highlight similarities and differences across regional neighbors and the distinctive features of Middle Atlantic House elections.

Evidence of Effective Nominations

The number of party-affiliated candidates in a district or at-large election is the first indicator of developing elections. Only parties can control candidate entry or foster norms that discourage excessive candidate entry. The number of viable candidates captures whether political elites respect both the formal and informal rules of the game. Having few overcrowded fields indicates the presence of effective nominations methods. Even if formal nominations are underdeveloped, it speaks to whether aspirants to office are willing to stand aside for more viable candidates. Understaffed elections provide different information. Parties, even well-developed ones, may forgo elections if they cannot compete effectively. This is especially true in multimember districts and at-large elections. In the presence of party voting, the majority party will likely win all seats. Minority parties find these difficult to staff because one must convince multiple candidates to stand and inevitably lose.

To illustrate, in 1812 in Pennsylvania there were nine single-member district elections. Candidates from both parties ran in all districts. The Federalists stood a single candidate in each district. A single Democratic-Republican stood in seven districts, and more than one stood in two districts. The correct number of Federalists stood in all districts while the Democratic-Republicans overcrowded the field twice. Jointly the parties fielded the optimal number of candidates in seven elections. Overall, in Pennsylvania there were ninety-two contested single-member district elections. One Democratic-Republican stood in eighty-five elections, and one Federalist stood in eighty-seven elections. These correspond to "success" rates of 92 percent and 95 percent, respectively. Perhaps most importantly, of Pennsylvania's contested single-member district elections, the Democratic-Republicans and Federalists jointly fielded a single candidate in eighty elections.[21] Simply, the large majority of these elections were contested by one Democratic-Republican and one Federalist.

Pennsylvania hosted thirty-two dual-member district elections, seventeen three-member district elections, and five four-member district elections for which there are complete returns. The party and joint success rate is impressive. The Federalists and the Democratic-Republicans did nearly as well in multimember districts. The success rates drop only slightly in multimember districts. This modest decline is not surprising. These nomination and entry decisions are more complex. Most of this drop-off is because the district's minor party fails to field a full slate. For example, in 1810 the Democratic-Republicans swept the three-member second district. Only one Federalist candidate completed, and he received nearly the same vote as two Quids.[22] This underscores the difficulty of recruiting high-quality candidates to stand for election when defeat is likely.

New York hosted 137 contested single-member district elections.[23] Both parties stood one candidate in 121 of these elections. The Federalists did slightly better than the Republicans by properly staffing 131 elections to the Democratic-Republicans' 127. The percentages are nearly equivalent for the dual-member district elections. Overall, both parties fielded two competitive candidates in twenty-three elections. The districts electing more than two candidates were typically uncompetitive.

New Jersey elected five candidates at-large in 1797 and 1800 and six candidates from 1803 to 1824. The exceptions to at-large elections were in 1798, when New Jersey used single-member districts, and in 1813, when New Jersey used dual-member districts. The Federalists and Democratic-Republicans stood the proper number of candidates in the district elections. Even though the Federalists initially championed the general ticket, they were terribly disadvantaged by it and only contested five of these elections. When both parties contested the election, they nearly always stood the proper number of candidates, with the Federalists understaffing just one election, and that by a single candidate.

Regionally, the number of competitive party candidates says much about nominations and entry norms. First, if the election is contested, then both parties almost always stand the proper number of candidates. Parties seldom overstaff these elections. Spoilers are rare. Second, the party success rate decreases only slightly as the number of district seats increases. Multimember districts and at-large elections present more challenging entry problems, but the parties manage these challenges by running tickets. Third, parties are more likely to understaff multimember district elections. The likely reason for understaffing is that these elections are often uncompetitive, thus presenting the minority party with obstacles to candidate recruitment. Finally, there are few differences between Federalist and Democratic-Republican ability to field the correct number of candidates. Sometimes the Federalists do a bit better and sometimes the Democratic-Republicans do a bit better.

The Number of Electors and Turnout

Turnout speaks to citizen engagement in politics. The raw number of electors is especially important for understanding early republic elections. The number of voters captures the scale of elections. Party organization and mass communication are necessary in large-scale elections.

The numbers also confirm who is voting. If these numbers are large, then by definition typical men dominate mass politics. This does not mean turnout rates are unimportant, but the action is in the numerator. Scholars may dispute the potential electorate and turnout rates, but it's the number of electors that speak most directly to how elections are contested.

To place turnout in context recall the table 3.1 state populations and potential electorates. Taking 1800 as a reference, Pennsylvania's population of just over 602,000 was second only to Virginia's 807,000. However, Pennsylvania's electorate of nearly 124,000 ranked well ahead of Virginia's because of the latter state's large enslaved population and relatively restrictive suffrage. Nearly 587,000 people lived in New York, which housed the nation's second-largest potential electorate of 118,200. New Jersey's smaller population of 211,000 returned a correspondingly smaller potential electorate of 40,700.

Overall, approximately 283,000 Middle Atlantic residents could vote in 1800. These numbers grew rapidly over the next two decades, largely because of population growth. The US population grew from just over five million in 1800 to approximately nine and one-half million in 1820, an increase of over 80 percent. This growth was not uniform across states. Between 1800 and 1820 Pennsylvania's population increased by well over 3 percent annually and New York's by an astounding 6 percent annually. In contrast, New Jersey, like many smaller states, grew at an anemic 1.5 percent annually. By 1820 New York's potential electorate of 286,300 was the nation's largest, and the region's electorate numbered approximately 624,000. While fueled by population growth, the electorate also grew because of the elimination of many de jure suffrage restrictions and the increased willingness of local election officials to overlook those that remained on the books.[24]

Pennsylvania elections capture the era's high voter turnout. The top panel of figure 3.1 shows the raw number of voters; the bottom panel is the turnout rate.[25] Keeping in mind these are "lowball" estimates in those years missing district returns, the number of men that voted was impressive. From 1800 forward, the fewest number of voters in House elections was nearly 55,000 (in 1800), and the maximum was approximately 131,000 (in 1820). After 1810, Pennsylvania saw approximately 90,000 men cast ballots in a typical election cycle *excluding* the 1820 spike. The 1800 turnout rate was 45 percent. Between 1810 and 1824 it stabilized at about this level. The 1808 increase, which brought over

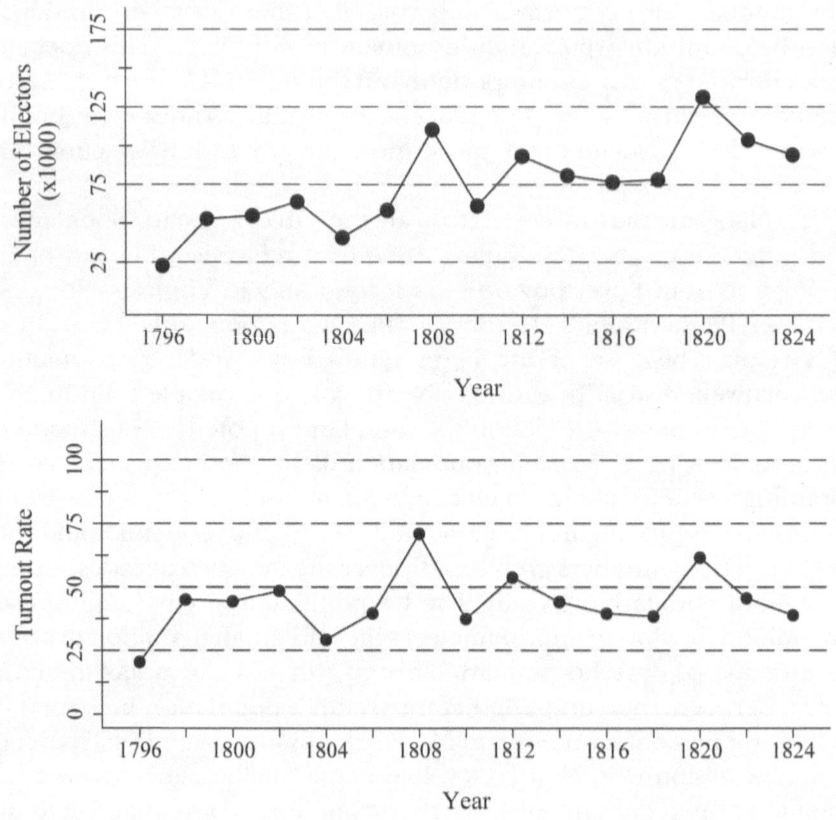

Figure 3.1. Pennsylvania: Number of Electors and Turnout Rate

110,000 men to the polls, was likely driven by internal divisions in the Democratic-Republican Party. Conservative governor Thomas McKean split the party ranks. After an unsuccessful attempt to impeach McKean, the liberal wing of the party nominated Simon Snyder as its preferred candidate. Snyder, who was opposed by Federalist James Ross, won the election with a 61 percent majority. The 1820 surge was also driven by gubernatorial politics. In this case, Democratic-Republican governor William Findlay's alleged financial impieties contributed to his defeat by Federalist Joseph Hiester.[26] Gubernatorial politics spilled over to congressional elections with positive effect on turnout.[27] This provides evidence of linkages across elections to different offices.

Figure 3.2 displays the number of New York and New Jersey voters.[28]

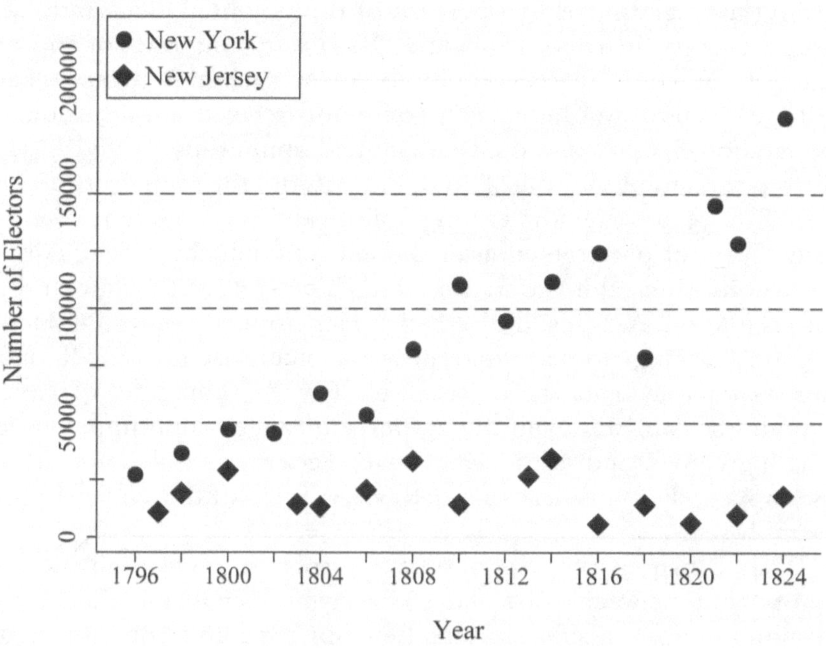

Figure 3.2. New York and New Jersey: Number of Electors

After 1810, New York typically saw well over 100,000 men cast ballots in a typical election cycle. In high-turnout years more than 175,000 men voted. Early New York turnout hovered in the 35 to 40 percent range. It then increased to over 50 percent until a sharp decline in 1818. The reasons for the decline center on gubernatorial politics and congressional party competition. With respect to gubernatorial politics, in 1817 DeWitt Clinton won a special election to the governorship as a Republican in a race that the Federalists declined to contest. He subsequently won in 1820 under the Federalist banner. With fewer "Federalists" competing as such and now subsumed under the "Clintonian" label, elections became less structured. The lack of a competitive, top-of-the-ticket race the previous year, combined with few candidates embracing the Federalist label, depressed turnout. However, turnout rebounded in 1820. Much of New York's increase in electors simply owes to population growth. This points to the capacity of political parties. Organizing an electorate of 150,000 requires, well, organization.

New Jersey turnout is clearly different. Between 1798 and 1814 turnout averaged nearly 50 percent of the potential electorate, with three elections (in 1800, 1808, and 1814) returning rates of approximately 70 percent.[29] Party competition drove such high turnout. Each of these elections was immensely competitive. For example, 1800 saw over 29,000 electors, and the Democratic-Republicans elected all seats with 51 percent of the vote. The Democrats did the same in 1808, this time with 33,400 electors casting ballots and a 56 percent vote majority. Turnout plummeted after the exceptionally hard-fought 1814 election in which the Federalists won 48 percent of the vote and no representation. As a result, the Federalists stopped contesting House elections. Facing no serious opposition, many Democratic-Republicans stayed away from the polls as well. For the remainder of the era turnout was consistently in the 25 percent range—and dipped as low as 11 percent. Importantly, New Jersey Federalists did not suddenly lose support. For reasons explained below, they continued to win state assembly seats.

District turnout provides another perspective on participation. In Pennsylvania between 1802 and 1810 a typical single-member district election saw about 4,000 electors. Between 1812 and 1820 this figure hovered closer to 3,500, but this apparent decline is an artifact of increased apportionment—there were more districts. In New York the median number of single-member district electors between the Fifth and Twelfth Congresses was approximately 4,150. This figure increased to nearly 6,400 for the rest of the era. Districts, of course, differed in population, making comparing the number of electors difficult. To provide a sense of scale, consider the number of electors relative to state apportionment. Between 1802 and 1810 there were nearly 4,100 Pennsylvania electors for every apportioned seat. Between 1812 and 1820 this figure increased slightly, to just over 4,200. These figures match well with the number of electors in Pennsylvania's single-member, dual-member, and larger district elections, which averaged approximately 3,900, 9,060, and nearly 12,000, respectively. In New York approximately 5,000 men voted for every apportioned seat, with high-turnout elections seeing as many as 8,000 electors per seat. New Jersey's contested elections present similar figures. In 1800, 5,800 men voted per seat. This level was again reached in 1808, 1813, and 1814, when there was an average of 5,250 electors for each apportioned House seat. Whether measured statewide, at the district level, or in terms of apportionment, Pennsylvania and New York saw impressive House election participation throughout the first party era. New Jersey did too, but only when the Federalists contested the general ticket.

The votes show that mid-Atlantic elector turnout was robust. This finding is not new; historians provide scattered evidence of vigorous turnout in Middle Atlantic elections in the first years of the nineteenth century.[30] These more comprehensive figures show that previous indications of an active electorate are not anomalous. Turnout shows that typical men thought voting was worth their time. Men of ordinary and even modest means voted in large numbers. New Jersey shows that turnout levels depend critically on the extent of party competition, which depends to some extent on the electoral rules in force. Voter engagement demonstrates that by 1800, Middle Atlantic elections were no longer structured by personal connections and informal electioneering. The numbers were simply too large. One cannot effectively complete for office in a constituency with thousands of voters without party organization. Elites can no longer influence men by personal qualities and connections, much less intimidate and control them.

Party Support

Political historians are especially interested in party support, including its level, stability, and geographic dispersion. The Middle Atlantic states present different patterns of support, making it useful to consider them separately. Aggregate party support then presents the question of whether there is stable partisanship in the electorate. Evidence for this comes from multicandidate ballots, which were present in all Middle Atlantic states and from the geography of party support.

AGGREGATE PARTY SUPPORT. Figure 3.3 presents Pennsylvania statewide party votes by year. The graph shows several notable features. First, it shows the early collapse of the nonaffiliated vote. By 1800, candidates had to identify with a party to compete effectively. There are spikes in nonaffiliated and other party support in 1806, 1810, and 1816, but these never exceed a fifth of the vote. Second, there is a significant increase in Democratic-Republican support in 1800 through 1804, but thereafter it levels off. From 1806 forward the Democratic-Republicans are the majority party, but they are hardly crushing the Federalists. The election of 1808 marks an upsurge for the Federalists, as it did na-

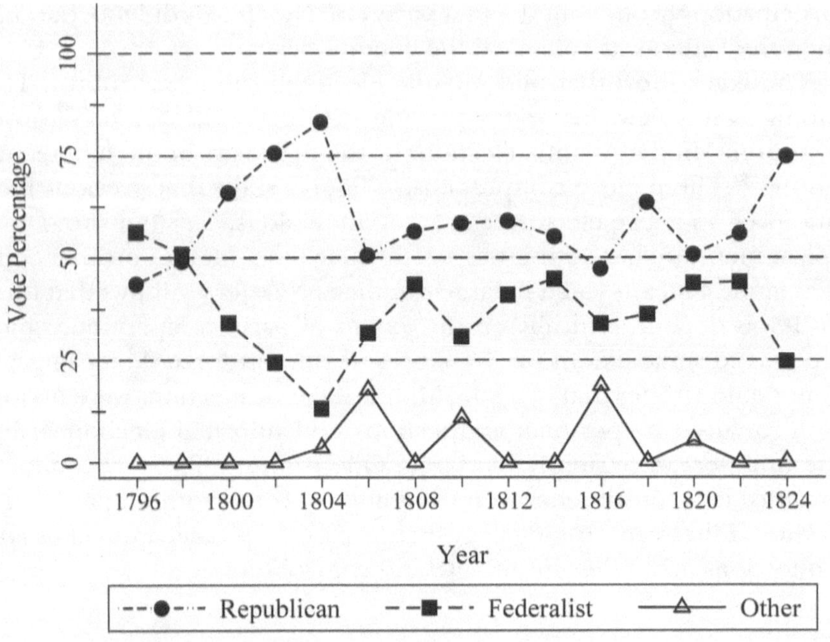

Figure 3.3. Pennsylvania: Party Vote Shares

tionally. This signified no improvement for Pennsylvania Federalists in their quest for congressional seats. Only two Federalists were included in Pennsylvania's delegation to the Eleventh Congress. Thereafter, the Federalists routinely won about 35 to 45 percent of the statewide vote. For each party some years are better than others, but the Democratic-Republicans and Federalists enjoy fairly stable support. This stability, while only suggestive, is consistent with each party enjoying a core group of supporters.

New York and New Jersey are more complicated. Figure 3.4 displays New York party vote shares. As in Pennsylvania, there is an early collapse of the unaffiliated vote. The Federalists were the stronger party until 1800. The Democratic-Republicans dominated until about 1806, after which the two parties competed on roughly equal footing for a decade. As in Pennsylvania, there is an upsurge in the Federalist vote in 1808. Unlike Pennsylvania, this produced dividends. New York's Federalist representation in the Eleventh Congress increased from two to eight members. However, almost half of these seats were lost in the following election cycle. Beginning in 1818, candidates largely stopped run-

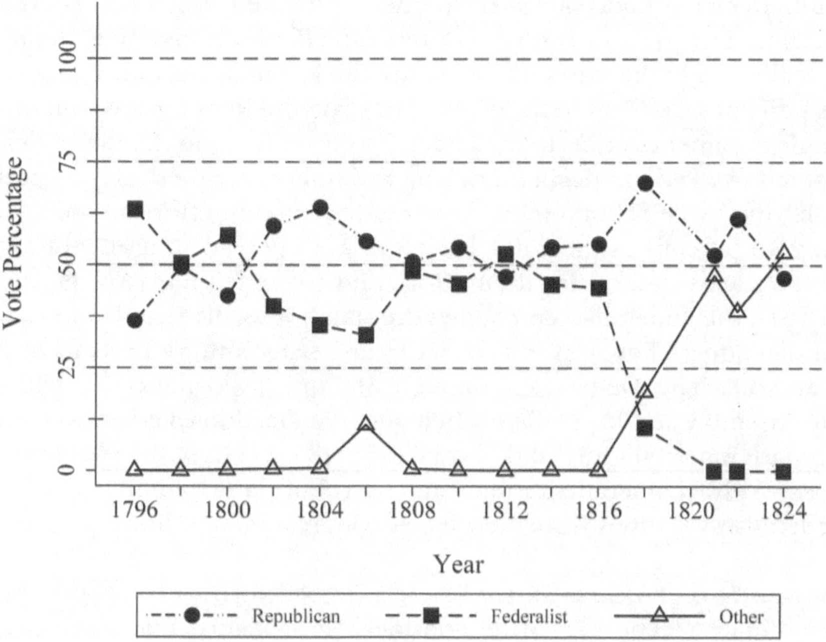

Figure 3.4. New York: Party Vote Shares

ning under the Federalist umbrella. This does not mean that New York Federalists stopped seeking election. Both Federalists and Democratic-Republicans ran under other labels and sometimes won election. From 1818 to 1824, 102 candidates ran under a party label other than Democratic-Republican or Federalist.[31] Some were Federalists subsumed under the Clintonian label. These men included Henry Storrs and John D. Dickenson, both of whom won two post-1816 House elections, as well as Peter Jay, son of founder John Jay, and Joshua Sands, who served as collector of the Port of New York until Thomas Jefferson removed him from this post in 1801. Sands was subsequently elected to Congress as a Federalist. These men possessed too much political stature to hide their backgrounds. In 1818 three of the four winning candidates who stood under a label other than Democratic-Republican or Federalist had previously won office as a Federalist. The New York "other vote" chorus sang with a strong Federalist accent.

New Jersey was a political snake pit, and this is reflected in the volatility in its vote. The volatility owes little to changes in the political orientation of electors and primarily to whether the Federalists contested the election. In 1798 and 1800 the Democratic-Republicans and Federalists virtually tied in the statewide vote, with the Republicans winning 52 and 51 percent majorities in these years. In 1798 the Republicans won three single-member districts to the Federalists' two. In 1800 the Republicans won all five general-ticket seats. The Federalists declined to contest the following two election cycles. They made a modest effort in 1806, winning 26 percent of the vote. They won a 44 percent plurality in 1808 with no seats to show for their effort, and conceded the 1810 election. In 1813 the Federalists controlled the statehouse, districted, and called for elections. They won four of six House seats with 53 percent of the state vote. The Democratic-Republicans quickly regained control of the Assembly and immediately held at-large elections. Federalist voting strength waned slightly, and despite their 48 percent of the vote won no seats. With Democratic-Republican control of the Assembly secure, the Federalists withdrew from New Jersey congressional politics.

EVIDENCE OF PARTISANSHIP FROM BALLOTS AND GEOGRAPHY. Multicandidate elections provide considerable evidence that stable party attachments resided in the electorate. To see this, consider table 3.2, which presents the 1808 New Jersey general-ticket results. By 1800 the New Jersey press describes the parties as presenting tickets. The table confirms this by showing that each party ran a slate. The leading Democratic-Republican candidate, Henry Southhard, received 18,705 votes, and the last elected Democratic-Republican candidate, Jacob Huffy, received 18,586 votes. The first losing Federalist candidate, John Beatty, received 14,702 votes. The sixth-place Federalist, Samuel W. Harrison, received 14,496 votes. There were no other viable candidates.

Recalling that New Jersey required handwritten ballots, the votes give every appearance that electors knew their party slate and wrote straight tickets for their preferred party.[32] Only 119 votes separate the leading and trailing Democratic-Republican candidates, and 206 separate the corresponding Federalist candidates. The top-to-bottom differences are certainly ballot roll-off. One could argue that this provides less evidence of partisanship than pressure at the polls. This explanation is at variance with what we know about early voting practices. Over 33,000 men voted in the election. It would be absurd to think any but a tiny fraction of these men could be coerced at the polls. Then, as today, it would be difficult if not downright dangerous to attempt to pressure, much less

Table 3.2. New Jersey General Ticket Results, 1808 (winners in italics)

Finish Order Within Party	*Republican*	*Votes*	*Federalist*	*Votes*
1	*Henry Southhard*	18,705	John Beatty	14,702
2	*Adam Boyd*	18,691	William Campfield	14,677
3	*William Helms*	18,684	William Coxe	14,677
4	*Thomas Newbold*	18,657	John Neilson	14,673
5	*James Cox*	18,649	Aaron Ogden	14,609
6	*Jacob Huffy*	18,586	Samuel W. Harrison	14,496

Note: No other candidates received votes beyond single digits.

intimidate, large numbers of New Jersey men. In addition, electors had to write the name of each candidate.[33] The party association mattered much more than the names of the candidates. Occam's Razor says electors voted straight tickets for their preferred party, especially since this pattern is repeated in all elections that both parties contested.

This approach is equally applicable to multimember constituencies in which each party stood at least as many candidates as available seats. Thirty-two of Pennsylvania's two-member district-elections met these criteria. The median within party vote difference between the first- and second-place candidates was about 3 percent, or 120 votes. The voters were equally party-centric in Pennsylvania's twelve three-member district elections. Here the median vote difference between each party's first-place and third-place candidates was about 175 votes, or, again, 3 percent. There are only minor differences in the cohesiveness of Republican and Federalist electors. Party voting in New York's dual-member districts was even more unified. Here the median difference between a party's first and second candidate was about 1 percent.

Naturally, there were elections where the within-party-voter difference between leading and trailing candidates was larger, but these were anomalous. This typically happened when the parties fail to control entry, and more party-affiliated candidates stood than available seats. For example, in 1822 one of Pennsylvania's three-member districts featured a viable fourth Federalist who drew votes from the party's other candidates.[34] This resulted in the election of the leading Federalist and two Democratic-Republicans. However, elections where this happened were rare.

The aggregate vote obscures geographic concentrations of party support and how this speaks to partisanship in the electorate. This is revealed by district-level and county-level votes. Pennsylvania Democratic-Republicans and Federalists maintained core support in several competitive districts that maintained itself across election cycles. For example, between 1812 and 1820 the Federalists swept the balanced four member Philadelphia First District in 1814, 1818, and 1820. The Republicans did so in 1812, while 1816 produced a split delegation. Similar patterns exist in the southeast Second and Seventh Districts, and the western Fourteenth District.[35] Party strength also resides in districts and counties where affiliated candidates did not win. For example, between 1812 and 1820 there were twelve Pennsylvania districts hosting a combined thirty-six elections where the Federalists won at least 40 percent of the vote. Federalist candidates won twelve of these elections, accounting for twenty-one House seats. Federalists also lost several close elections. In the southeast dual-member Second District, the Federalists won once and lost four elections by thin margins. In the Third District, Federalist candidates lost three of four elections despite a median party vote share of 48 percent. Federalists never won the western Eleventh District, despite consistently polling about 45 percent of the vote. Of course, sometimes things cut in the Federalist favor. In the Fourteenth District, comprised of Allegheny and Butler Counties, the Federalists won four elections, with a median vote share of 58 percent. Following the 1810 census and subsequent reapportionment and districting, Federalists won four times in the Schuylkill and Berks Counties district, averaging 56 percent of the vote.

The district vote provides evidence that elections became more competitive, and the vote became more structured as the era progressed. Between 1802 and 1810 there were only three districts where the Federalist vote typically exceeded 40 percent. These included the southeast Third District, where the Federalists won twice in three contested elections, and the south-central Sixth District, where the Federalists won once in four attempts, and the western Eight District, where the Federalists gained strength at the end of the decade. In the following apportionment cycle, the number of districts where the Federalists command an average of at least 40 percent of the vote increases to seven, keeping in mind that the number of districts increased as well. Still, the Federalists were certainly holding their own. Between the first and second decades of the century, the district-level vote variability declined. Prior to 1812 the vote median absolute deviation (MAD) for both parties approached 10. From 1812 forward, the Federalist figure was about 7, and the Republican figure was slightly lower. It is possible that this is an artifact of increases in the number of districts and their homogeneity.[36] This question is better addressed at the county level. However, the increase in party competitiveness in the aggregate vote, combined with reduced variability in the vote, certainly suggests strengthening partisanship.

While districts are typically created in response to the census and apportionment, counties present a challenge because these are regularly created and boundaries changed, often at irregular intervals. In some years counties were added wholesale. For example, in 1800 Pennsylvania had thirty-four counties. By the end of the era there were fifty-one Pennsylvania counties, counting Philadelphia city and county separately. In 1800 alone Pennsylvania created eight new counties by breaking up previously massive Allegany County in the far west. Between 1810 and 1812 parts of Luzerne County were used to create new counties, including Bradford and Susquehanna. The number of New York counties also rapidly increased, in this case from twenty-nine to fifty in the same period. New Jersey, in contrast, maintained thirteen counties throughout the era.[37]

The Pennsylvania county votes confirm the district patterns and provide further details. The creation of counties and changes in their boundaries motivate placing emphasis on those counties that were established or largely unchanged throughout much of the period.[38] With that in mind, twenty-seven counties returned complete returns from at least seven contested elections. The average number of observed and contested elections in these counties is just over eleven. The median Democratic-Republican vote across these counties and years was about 55 percent while the median Federalist vote was about 43 percent. These are clearly the more competitive counties, and many were also more established counties, as evidenced by their longer election track-records. Indeed, ten of these counties presented returns for at least twelve election cycles. Throughout the era both parties maintained an average absolute vote deviation of about 6.5. The Republican margins are a bit larger after 1812, but the vote volatility is about the same.

Each party dominated in certain Pennsylvania counties. The Federalists were nearly unassailable in Adams and Delaware Counties. They also did well in Chester County, winning ten of fifteen election cycles, although the county was competitive. These counties are in the southeast and south-central regions, and their boundaries achieved stability in the earliest days of the era. With Allegheny County's permanent boundaries established by 1802, the Federalists won its vote in seven of twelve elections, including in five consecutive cycles beginning in 1814. The Federalists lost many other counties, but with competitive margins. For example, they won Montgomery County only once in twelve cycles. However, excluding three uncontested elections, their typical losing margin was about 11 percent.[39] Similar patterns exist in Bucks and Westmoreland Counties. Berks, Lancaster, and Allegheny Counties were also typically competitive. Philadelphia city was immensely competitive, with the Federalists gaining the upper hand in the latter half of the era. Philadelphia County, however, was Democratic-Republican.

The New York vote was also often competitive. Between 1802 and 1810 there were forty-one district elections in which the Federalists won at least 40 percent of the vote. These include at least four elections each in five districts centered in the southeast and the Hudson River Valley.[40] Between 1812 and 1818 there were fifty-eight contested elections in which Federalist candidates received at least 40 percent of the vote. These translated into twenty-four district wins and twenty-eight House seats. The variability in the district-level party vote also decreased between the first and second decades of the nineteenth century. In the century's first decade the MAD in both party's votes was about 7. In the second decade through 1816, it drops to about 5. There was an increase in competitive districts as the era progressed. This, however, did not keep pace with the increase in New York's apportionment.

New York's county-level party support displays identifiable geographic patterns. The Federalists did well in the northern Saint Lawrence region and the upper Hudson River Valley. The latter area was dominated by the traditional Dutch families. Keeping in mind that many candidates declined to run under the Federalist label after 1816, the Federalists regularly won in the Hudson River Valley's Albany, Columbia, and Rensselaer Counties. In terms of districts, Federalist strength resided in the Tenth District centered on Rensselaer County, and in the Sixteenth and Eighteenth Districts centered on Oneida and Saint Lawrence Counties in the northern and northeastern part of the state. For their part, Republican geographic clustering is present in the Finger Lakes region, including Cayuga, Onondaga, and Senaca Counties. Democratic-Republicans also did well in many other areas, especially the counties bordering Vermont in the northeast, including Essex, Clinton, and Saratoga Counties. They also dominated the southern border with Pennsylvania, including in Allegany, Delaware, and Tioga Counties. In and around New York City, the Republicans controlled the city, as well as nearby Rockland and Orange Counties, and Suffolk County, which forms the larger part of Long Island.

Finally, beginning in 1818, candidates running under party labels other than Democratic-Republican did well in areas that previously supported Federalist candidates. This provides evidence that Federalists who shed the party label continued to reach and receive support from the same constituents. This is indicated by the county figures. Prior to 1818 the Republicans received an average county vote share of about 55 percent, with the Federalists about ten points lower. The typical deviation in both parties' vote was about 5, providing evidence of partisanship in the electorate. This vote stability is more prevalent in some counties than others. For example, the vote deviation in the Federalist strongholds of Albany, Columbia, and Rensselaer Counties is typically quite small. The same is true in Democratic-Republican–leaning areas including Cayuga, Delaware, and Suffolk Counties. In comparison, the vote deviation was significantly larger than the state average in Montgomery, Queens, and Steuben Counties. One thing these latter counties have in common is that each party won the vote multiple times. The larger vote deviations in these counties were likely due to fluidity in partisanship, perhaps due to migration or changing demographics. Regardless, partisanship appears stable in many but not all areas.

New Jersey's county returns are especially important for understanding the state's early elections. The general ticket obscures the geographic distribution of party support. New Jersey is well suited to explore county-level variation in the vote to assess partisanship. This is because when both parties competed, it was more competitive than its grossly disproportionate election outcomes indicate. The New Jersey counties also inform much about early elections because there are relatively few of them and their boundaries are stable.[41] First, considering the 175 complete county returns, the Federalists won about a quarter of these returns. However, the Federalists won about half of the 86 county returns from the election cycles that they seriously contested. Second, focusing again on contested cycles, the New Jersey vote displays a less-pronounced regional pattern than is often expected. The Democratic-Republicans certainly did best in the north, and the Federalists won more often in the middle and south of the state. Northern Essex County was Republican, with seven victories returning an average vote share of 83 percent. The Republicans did comparably well in Morris and Sussex Counties. The Federalists were strongest in Burlington and Middlesex Counties, which span the state's middle, but also as far north as New York's Staten Island. The most-contested counties include Hunterdon, Monmouth, and Salem, which run from the northwest southward. The Federalists dominated southeastern Cape May County, but the Republicans won generally competitive southern Cumberland County five times. Even though each party had its supporting regions, both parties drew votes from all parts of the state.

There is only a modest relationship between party strength and population. The Federalists won consistently in Burlington County. The Republicans did so in Essex County. Hunterdon County was competitive. These were the state's three most populous counties. As noted, the Federalists did well in Cape May County, the state's least populated county. Finally, the county vote shows that if New Jersey were districted, as it was in 1813, it would have elected divided House delegations. In 1814 the Federalists won six counties by an average of two-thirds of the vote. Among these, Middlesex and Summerset in the north, and Burlington and Gloucester in the mid-state area, were natural candidates for combining into two single-member districts. These counties continued to send Federalists to the state assembly after 1814, indicating they would do so in House of Representatives elections as well.

Figure 3.5 illustrates these patterns by mapping the county-level returns from the 1814 election. The darker shaded counties are those in which the Federalists received a larger share of the two-party vote. As expected, the Democratic-Republicans did best in the north while Federalists were strongest in the south. The largest Republican margins were in the northern tier counties including Essex, Morris, and Sussex. The Federalists ran strongest in the middle and southern counties, including Burlington, Middlesex, Summerset, and Cape May. Other counties, including Cumberland, Hunterdon, and Monmouth, were more balanced. However, each party won votes on the other party's home turf. The figure also shows why the Democratic-Republicans were advantaged by the general-ticket system. New Jersey's most populous counties were in the north. Their advantage in these counties provided their margin to win the general ticket.

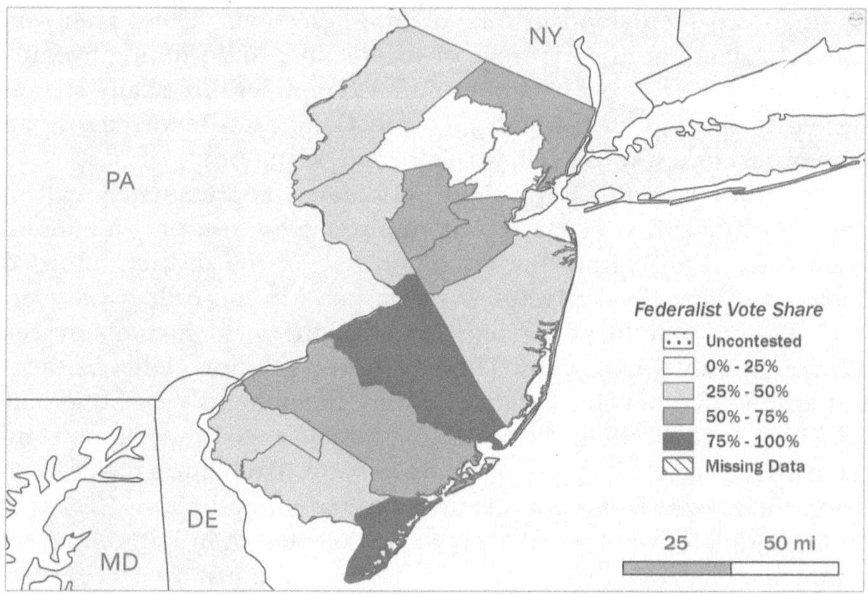

Figure 3.5. New Jersey: County-Level Returns, Fourteenth Congress

Patterns in Standing for Election and Reelection

Service terms and reelection rates also inform early elections and party competition. Early representatives typically served few congressional terms and often concluded their political careers in the statehouse. In Pennsylvania 286 distinct candidates stood in the district elections for which there are complete returns. Of these men, just over half stood only once. Of those who lost their first election, the large majority, over 70 percent, declined to stand again. Of the remainder, sixty-three stood twice, and sixty-nine stood three or more times. Among those who won their first election, 85 percent stood in three or fewer elections, and won, on average, two elections. Still, nearly three-quarters of Pennsylvania elections featured an incumbent. Incumbents typically did well when they stood for office. From 1800 forward, eighty Pennsylvania incumbents stood in a combined 142 elections. This included sixty-one Republicans and sixteen Federalists. These men won 109 times and were defeated in thirty-three elections. Republican incumbents won almost as often as they stood. Federalist incumbents won about as many elections as they lost. Of course, there were some persistent office seekers. Eighteen men stood in four or more elections. These men won regularly, standing in an average of six elections and winning five. Republican John Rea from Chambersburg exemplifies this group. He was elected to the Eighth through Eleventh Congresses before losing an intramural contest with a fellow Democratic-Republican.

New York presents 416 unique candidates, approximately half of whom lost their first election. Among those who lost, only a handful stood twice. Throughout the era about half of the districts afforded open seats. First-election winners rarely stood in more than two elections. Throughout the period only 125 elections saw an incumbent seek election, mostly Republicans. These men won election eighty-six times and lost in the other thirty-eight elections. Incumbents were noticeably safer before 1812, when the reelection rate averaged over 80 percent. From 1812 forward it was closer to 62 percent. While the smaller number of incumbent Federalists cautions against generalizations, as a rule these candidates were more likely to be defeated than Republican incumbents.[42] Overall, incumbents typically stood in just over three elections and won, on average, about 2.5 elections. As in Pennsylvania, this average is weighted by men who stood multiple times and won. These names are familiar and include Federalists Robert L. Livingston and Killian K. Van Rensselaer. However, these men are the exception to the rule.[43]

New Jersey incumbency patterns are more difficult to assess. This is because of the general ticket and the number of elections that the Federalists declined to contest. However, taking the period's full roster of fifty-four candidates, on average these men contested just over three elections and were elected in about 2.5 of these contests. The Republicans, as one would expect, drove these figures. Democratic-Republicans contested, on average, just over three elections and, not surprisingly, won almost all these contests. Federalist candidates stood in approximately two elections, and wins were nearly unknown.

Incumbent electoral fortunes suggest responsiveness to political events. Assessing this is complicated by the relatively few incumbents and because Democratic-Republicans held most seats. That said, Pennsylvania elections between 1810 and 1814 were challenging for incumbents. Of the twenty-three incumbents that stood in those years, nine were defeated. In 1810 five of twelve incumbents lost. Two losing candidates were Republicans, and one was a Federalist. However, of the two "nonaffiliated" losing incumbents, John Porter was previously elected from the First District as a Republican and William Milnor was previously elected from the Second District as a Federalist. The loss of the party label, whether voluntarily or not, most certainly damaged the reelection prospects of these men. New York saw one or two incumbents defeated each year until 1824, when six of seven lost. These Republican losses effectively signaled the end of the first party era in New York. The important point is that Pennsylvania and New York incumbents, whether early in the era or later, and whether Democratic-Republican or Federalist, were not immune to electoral accountability. Electors could and did vote them out of office.

These figures confirm that there was little in the way of a congressional career in the early republic. Pennsylvania elites were more likely to contest multiple elections, but this was less so in New York, and it appeared even less common in New Jersey. There were exceptions. At the far end of the spectrum Irish-born Pennsylvanian William Findley served a remarkable eleven terms in the House of Representatives, spanning the Second–Fifth and Eighth–Fourteenth Congresses. New Yorker Killian K. Van Rensselaer, of the New York dynasty of the same name, served five terms between 1801 and 1811. New Jersey Republican Henry Southard stood in a remarkable nine elections and won eight times.[44] Democratic-Republican John W. Taylor was elected seven times between 1812 and 1824 and became Speaker of the House of Representatives in 1820. For Findley, Van Rensselaer, and others who sought longer congressional tenure, voting these men out of office was no small matter. Then as today, incumbents enjoy electoral advantages, including name recognition and the support of party leaders and those who will work toward their reelection. However, these assets can be fickle. Ill-advised chamber votes, failure to court ongoing support, and the emergence of strong challengers produced losses for even established incumbents.

Leveraging Electoral Rules for Partisan Advantage

Voting methods affect party fortunes. The single-member district system, even if neutral in the sense of applying to all parties, still advantages the majority party. The concluding chapter discusses this in more detail, but one can see that at least some of the Middle Atlantic Federalist demise owes to how single-member district, plurality rule, elections translate votes to seats. This is true whether districting was nefarious or not. The Democratic-Republicans won many seats because of their modest, but safe, majorities in numerous districts. The 1808 election in Pennsylvania illustrates this nicely: Federalists won 43 percent of the statewide vote and no single-member districts. In 1812 the Pennsylvania Federalists polled a median district vote share of nearly 40 percent and won just one House seat. In New York's 1808 and 1810 elections there were thirteen contested single-member district seats in each cycle. The Federalists translated 49 and 45 percent of the statewide vote into five and three seats, respectively. Advantaged by the single-member district system, in 1814 the New York Democratic-Republicans translated their 54 percent of the statewide congressional vote into nineteen of the state's twenty-seven House seats.

Nefarious districting certainly existed. This includes not only the gerrymander but also the creation of multimember districts to absorb geographic concentrations of the other party's supporters. The latter approach placed the opponent's supporters in a new, larger district controlled by the districting party. In New Jersey the Democratic-Republicans relied on at-large elections to translate their majority support into electoral sweeps in nearly every congressional election. To be effective, all of these strategies require that voters display partisan loyalty. If electors are not anchored by party, these practices can easily produce wins for the other party.

Pennsylvania presents a clear example of creating a multimember district for advantage. Table 3.3 illustrates this districting, which took place between the 1800 and 1802 elections to the Seventh and Eighth Congresses. The top rows display the results of the 1800 elections in the southeast Third and Seventh single-member districts. These districts were centered respectively on Chester and Lancaster Counties. Federalist Joseph Hemphill won the Third District, and Federalist John Whitehall won the Seventh District in close contests that bucked the Jeffersonian tide. Following the 1800 reapportionment, the Democratic-Republicans redistricted for elections to the Eighth Congress. In doing so they combined the old Third and Seventh Districts into a new three-member Third District. This new district appended the north-central Democratic-Republican–leaning Berks County to Chester and Lancaster Counties. The bottom half of the table shows the outcome of this election. The addition of Berks County swamped the Chester and Lancaster Federalists in a sea of Republicans. Not surprisingly, Democratic-

Table 3.3. Districting for Partisan Advantage: Pennsylvania, 1800 and 1802 (winners in italics)

Congress District	*Candidate*	*Party*	*Vote*	
7th (1801–1803)	3rd (SMD*)	*Joseph Hemphill*	*Federalist*	2,732
		Joseph Shallcross	Republican	2,389
	7th (SMD*)	*Thomas Boude*	*Federalist*	2,274
		John Whitehill	Republican	1,927
8th (1803–1805)	3rd (3 members)	*John Whitehill*	*Republican*	9,396
		Isaac Anderson	*Republican*	9,365
		Joseph Hiester	*Republican*	9,236
		Jacob Bower	Federalist	4,932
		Joseph Hemphill	Federalist	4,853
		Thomas Boude	Federalist	4,829

* single-member district

Republicans won its three seats. Hemphill and Boude were turned out of office despite their regional support remaining virtually unchanged.

The 1802 returns are important for other reasons. First, they provide further evidence that the parties controlled candidate ballot access and that partisanship resided in the electorate. The candidates account for all cast votes. There were no "spoilers." The nearly equivalent within-party votes strongly indicates that electors cast straight tickets with minimal roll-off. Only 160 votes separate the first-place Republican finisher, John Whitehall, from the last-elected candidate, Joseph Hiester. Only 103 votes separate Jacob Bower, the first losing Federalist, from last-place Thomas Boudle. The Third District voters—which included voters from the preexisting counties and new voters from Berks County—knew their candidates and cast straight tickets for them. This, combined with the geographic concentration of party support, provides further evidence of partisanship in the electorate. The same Chester and Lancaster electors that voted for Boude and Hemphill in 1800 most certainly did so again in 1802. The addition of Jacob Bower and his nearly equivalent vote shares to the mix strongly indicates that if the Federalists stood any candidate of reasonable quality, the vote distribution would be unchanged. Second, these elections display robust elector turnout. More than 4,200 and 5,100 electors cast ballots, respectively, in the two single-member district elections, and over 14,000 voted in the newly created three-member district.

Pennsylvania Democratic-Republicans benefited from other multimember districts. Of Pennsylvania's forty-one dual-member district elections, the Democratic-Republican candidates swept nearly 90 percent of these as well as fourteen of nineteen three-member district elections. Most of the Republican victories surely owe to declining Federalist fortunes, but others likely result from the absorption of pockets of Federalist support. One of these suspect districts is the post-1810 two-member Second District, centered on Chester and Montgomery Counties. This was one of Pennsylvania's most competitive districts, with its elections often decided by razor-thin margins. The Democratic-Republicans won both seats in 1812, 1814, 1818, and 1820. The Federalists won in 1816. Both counties were competitive, but the Federalists did slightly better in Chester County while Democratic-Republican strength resided in Montgomery County. If each county had been a single-member district, the Federalists and the Democratic-Republicans would have each elected five representatives over the cycle. The combined district enabled the Democratic-Republican to elect eight of ten representatives.[45]

In 1808 New York's Democratic-Republican–controlled Assembly concocted a complex but effective districting to benefit its candidates in New York County and the surrounding areas. The Assembly removed Kings County from New York's Second District, primarily consisting of New York City. In its place it added rural Rockland County. Rockland was heavily Republican and expected give the Democratic-Republicans an edge in competitive New York City. Kings County was attached to the First District, previously consisting solely of Queens and Suffolk Counties. Separating competitive Kings County from New York County (Manhattan) would do no harm in the competitive First District and perhaps even provide an advantage there too. It worked. The New York district and its two seats, while previously leaning Republican, became safer with the Rockland votes. The First District, while very tight, also delivered its seat to the Republicans. The Federalists knew they had been harmed by the districting. The addition of the rural Rockland district to the commercial interests of Manhattan Island led to complaints that the districting was intended "to preserve power in the hands of those at present possess and abuse it."[46] The Republican response to this charge is unrecorded but presumably included something about fairness in love and war.

The New Jersey general ticket enabled the Democratic-Republicans to translate their majority support into electoral sweeps in nearly every congressional election. Beginning with elections to the Seventh Congress (1802–1803), the Democratic-Republicans elected sixty-one representatives to the Federalists' four. These four came in 1813 when the Federalist-controlled New Jersey Assembly created three dual-member districts. This was a good year for the Federalists. They won 53 percent of the state vote and the dual-member mid-state and southern districts. The districting probably drove that year's increased turnout, which likely drew in peripheral voters, especially Federalists. A net vote swing of a few percent combined with districting was enough to profoundly change the partisan landscape. The following year the Republicans reacquired control of the Assembly, restored the general ticket, and called for immediate elections. This, combined with party-line voting by electors, sunk Federalist prospects. The Federalist 48 percent state vote might as well have been 10 percent. The handwriting was on the wall, and the Federalists simply declined to contest subsequent congressional elections.

This raises the question of how the Federalists managed to briefly control the statehouse when they were shut out of congressional elections. They were able to do so because the New Jersey General Assembly was selected from counties. Counties elected multiple assemblymen, typically three members.[47] Since counties can't easily be combined or gerrymandered, the Republicans couldn't use their Assembly majorities for electoral advantage. The contrast between the House elections and the Assembly elections demonstrates the power of the election system in determining the outcome. There were no changes in the electorate; only the vote aggregation methods for each office differed. Under one, the Federalists couldn't win a seat; under the other, they held their own. By 1814 the Federalist share of Assembly seats began to decline precipitously. However, as late as 1817 they still held sixteen of forty-two seats.[48] While the Federalists were the minority party, they were not extinguished as a political force.

Conclusion

The Middle Atlantic states display party-oriented and competitive elections throughout much of the first party era. There are important state-level differences, but Pennsylvania, New York, and New Jersey share more similarities than differences. In all states the Democratic-Republicans ascended to preeminence in the early 1800s, but the Federalists remained competitive through much of the era. This was longer so in Pennsylvania than in New York and New Jersey. However, even in these states the Federalists had geographic redoubts of support.

One sees the emergence of effective nomination early in the era. This is reflected in the number of viable candidates that stood for office. Parties seldom overcrowd the field. This is true for single-member district elections, and in the more complex multimember districts and at-large elections. On the voter side, electors focused their ballots on leading candidates. Spoilers, local favorites, and those who stood without party sanction received few votes.

The returns show that Middle Atlantic parties enjoyed stable levels of popular support and provide considerable evidence that voters were anchored by party ties. The relative stability of each party's aggregate vote is consistent with the parties having a well-defined core of supporters. Multicandidate ballots provide the further evidence that electors voted the party, not the candidate. In multimember districts and at-large elections, the parties effectively ran slates, and electors appear to have voted straight tickets. This is substantiated by the geographic distribution of party support. Some areas were reliably Democratic-Republican, and some, though fewer, were Federalist. It is impossible to state with absolute confidence that voters maintained such party-line voting in the absence of identifiable ballots, but these constituency-level patterns are so strong that the burden of proof resides with those who doubt partisanship in the electorate.

Party-organized elections and partisanship also help explain Middle Atlantic turnout rates, both high turnout and lower turnout. Election turnout was typically robust in the Middle Atlantic states. Men came to the polls in large numbers. By the final years of the eighteenth century, elections were no longer contested in the intimate world of friends, family, and personal connections. Rather, elections were contested in constituencies that counted thousands of electors. Mid-Atlantic turnout was comparable or higher than that in present-day congressional elections. This maintained itself throughout the era in New York and Pennsylvania, and only collapsed in New Jersey when the Federalists ceased to contest House elections. Overall, the returns provide considerable evidence that organized parties mobilized their supporters.

The parties used electoral rules for advantage. This also points to partisanship in the electorate because of the risks incurred if voters are fickle. It is not advisable to use electoral rules and processes for advantage unless one is confident in the location and reliability of the party vote. Electoral rules advantaged the Democratic-Republicans, who were able to turn often modest advantages in popular support into electoral sweeps, either at the district level or statewide. This is especially true in New Jersey. The choices of districts and vote aggregation methods reveal that political leaders knew where their supporters and their opponents resided. The rules themselves have significant implications for political behaviors, especially turnout. With New Jersey's reintroduction of the general ticket in 1814, electors saw little reason to go to the polls. The outcome was a forgone conclusion.

Middle Atlantic electoral support, turnout, candidate entry, and reelection fortunes are not immune to political events. The vote responds to political circumstances beyond congressional and national politics. Gubernatorial politics, for example, appears to move turnout in Pennsylvania and New York. The importance of gubernatorial and other statewide and national offices requires cross-constituency mobilization efforts. As will be seen in the concluding chapter, the regional party vote is connected through most of the era. The states' votes didn't move in lockstep but responded similarly to the same political tides. This is important, because cross-state electoral linkages are necessary for party-system development.

In the Middle Atlantic states, party competition was robust, and the rumors of the Federalist death were exaggerated. The Federalists certainly saw a secular decline in their vote. However, they maintained support, albeit diminished, throughout the era. The Federalists maintained redoubts of support that remained reasonably stable. In Pennsylvania and New York this is captured in congressional districts. In New Jersey this is reflected in the county-level vote. The Federalist vote weakened, especially after 1816. The pace of this decline was accelerated in New York by the salient Erie Canal issue. In New Jersey, Federalist congressional aspirations were extinguished by the general ticket. The Federalist vote was insufficient to win seats, but it hardly collapsed. The Federalists remained a threat to the Democratic-Republicans and commanded sufficient support to justify Republicans keeping a warry eye on its candidates.

4 | The Border States

The defining characteristic of Delaware and Maryland during the first party era is that both states were electorally competitive. Delaware House elections were consistently decided by razor-thin margins, often by scores of votes out of thousands cast. The Maryland Democratic-Republicans controlled Baltimore city and county and the large number of votes that came with it. The outstate vote was more competitive. The Democratic-Republicans dominated some districts, and the Federalists won regularly in other districts. This balance was maintained at least through 1818, and the Federalists continued to win in some areas for several more years. The border states arguably had the greatest partisan balance of any region in the young nation.

Despite its diminutive size, Delaware possessed considerable social, religious, and economic heterogeneity. Its three counties north to south are New Castle, Kent, and Sussex. New Castle merged the perhaps surprising combination of a Democratic-Republican majority and an economy centered on commerce and manufacturing. The Federalists drew support from the agricultural south, which was dominated by the old families. Southern Delaware was the state's major slaveholding region. Religious divisions also shaped Delaware politics. These reflected immigration patterns. The north trended Presbyterian and Quaker and had the greatest concentration of Scots-Irish. The southern Federalists were originally Anglicans, but by the founding increasingly professed the Methodist Eucharist. The political salience of these divisions is captured in a Kent County circular that entreated neighbors to not elect a Presbyterian, especially "an Irish Presbyterian just imported."[1] The politics of deference lasted longer in southern Delaware in part because of the prominence of the established families and because the region lacked a dynamic urban area such as Wilmington.[2]

Maryland also presented considerable demographic heterogeneity. This had significant implications for its political culture. Between the first years of the eighteenth century and the founding, Maryland's political culture transformed from southern to one more akin to that of the Middle Atlantic states. The settlement of the western part of the state contributed to this change. Many of those who settled there came from Pennsylvania and were of German extraction. For example, Fredrick County in the Shenandoah Valley and Washington County in the far southwest contained significant German populations. These families had nothing to do with tobacco and the slavery-based economy that came with it. The political orientation of these areas was closer to that of their kin in Lancaster rather than that of the Tidewater elites.[3] Partially because of its demographic changes, Maryland developed a strong, long-lasting two-party system despite the absence of an elected governor. As will be seen, these features produced elections that more closely resembled those in the Middle Atlantic states than those in the South.[4]

Maryland parties developed early. The Federalists were strongest in rural areas, including the lower Chesapeake and the upper-central region centered on Fredrick County and the Cumberland Valley. The Democratic-Republicans fared best in the upper Chesapeake, in the city of Baltimore, and in Baltimore County. Maryland maintained state-level partisan balance even though individual districts often provided an overwhelming share of their vote to one of the parties. The Democratic-Republicans benefited from the 1800 Jefferson surge, but the War of 1812 gave the Federalists a political benefit that lasted through about 1818, when they began a slow but irreversible decline.[5]

Delaware and Maryland election practices were similar. Both states maintained a liberal suffrage exclusive of race and gender. Delaware divorced property from voting in 1792 and imposed only a taxpaying requirement. Maryland dropped its property requirement in 1801 and never adopted a tax requirement.[6] Delaware and Maryland also had similar voting practices. Maryland required a secret ballot. Electors recorded the name of their preferred candidate or candidates on a piece of paper that was then folded and handed to the election judge. The penalty for a judge who unfolded the ballot before formal counting was a hefty fine.[7] The Delaware Constitution of 1792 also required voting by ballots. Regional voting by written ballots excluded, or at least greatly limited, voting viva voce.

Electioneering was the norm in the border states. Candidates and their supporters canvased for votes. It was not uncommon for opposing candidates to appear together in debates, although sometimes the debate was unexpected for one of its participants.[8] Barbecues, stump speeches, parades, and similar activities were common.[9] Candidates often held lavish gatherings to garner support. For example, in 1809 Maryland's Anne Arundel County crowds were enticed by a "splendid and profuse" barbecue that featured an "animated" speech by Federalist John C. Herbert.[10] Not to be outdone, the Democratic-Republicans hosted no fewer than nine barbecues the same day. The *Alexandra Herald* captures the flavor of these events by reporting on a candidate fete that included food, debate, and general politicking.[11]

> In the district composed of Prince Georges and Anne Arundel, Com Barney opposes J. C. Herbet, the sitting member. There was a very large concourse of voters at Bladensburg on Saturday, at a barbaque [*sic*]. The Candidates were both present, and addressed the people til a late hour with considerable warmth and energy. The information we have from Washington is, that the democratic party are sanguine of the commodore's election, and bets are running in his favor.

Maryland voters were well-fed in the election season, which steadily lengthened from its beginnings in summer to a calendar that eventually started in midwinter.

Competitive elections also tempted citizens to bet on their outcomes.[12] In the case of the Barney and Herbert contest, more bets were lost than won on election day. Federalist J. C. Herbert defeated the Republican Joshua Barney by fewer than fifty votes out of the 3,163 that were cast. Such remarkably competitive elections demanded that candidates campaign, including making stump speeches at well-attended barbecues. Nothing in period reporting suggests the electioneering was unusual or inappropriate. Whatever reservations the old Federalists had about electioneering, these did not restrain politicking in Maryland. It was politics as usual, and none of it resembled the reserved practices of traditionalists.

The parties and their candidates campaigned on both state and national questions. As in Pennsylvania, Delaware's parties initially divided over the Jay Treaty.[13] As the era progressed, electoral appeals grounded in policy became routine. In 1804, for example, the New Castle County Democratic-Republican Committee reported that it would "rest the fate of the approaching general election . . . on the comparative review . . . of the measures and policy of the former and present administrations . . . believing that the public suffrages will give a decided preference to the friends of the latter."[14] The policy and governing differences between the Democratic-Republicans and Federalists mattered to electors in both states.

Delaware and, to a lesser extent, Maryland provide counterexamples to the presumed Federalist demise. Delaware's Federalists remained competitive throughout the first party era, indeed sometimes dominant. Maryland Federalist support diminished after 1818, but the party maintained areas of electoral strength. The political geography of both states is especially conducive to analysis of regional voting patterns. Delaware's counties voted along partisan lines, with New Castle's Wilmington being a Republican stronghold, while the Federalists drew their support primarily from rural Sussex and Kent Counties.[15] Much larger Maryland provides greater variation in regional politics. Maryland's well-known eastern and western shores, urban Baltimore, and a near frontier environment in its western counties provided a microcosm of the larger regional politics in the Middle Atlantic, the South, and even in the newly admitted western states.

House Elections and Markers of Electoral Development

The historical record argues that Delaware and Maryland were among the most electorally developed states in the early republic. Early Delaware and Maryland congressional elections were contested in clear, simple, and well-structured electoral settings. This is confirmed by the vote returns, which show these elections were often competitive. The Delaware returns are complete. Delaware had the nation's smallest population and only three counties. It elected one representative through 1810. Beginning in 1812 it elected two representatives at-large through 1820, after which it reverted to a single representative. The Maryland district returns are complete, and there are only a small number of missing county returns. Maryland elected almost all its representatives from single-member districts. The Old Line State created a two-member district following the 1800 census, when its apportionment increased from eight to nine. This district simply added a representative to the existing Baltimore city and county district. These total 108 single-member district elections and twelve dual-member district elections. Maryland's apportionment remained unchanged from 1800 to 1824. Consequently, so did its districts. Maryland had twenty counties including Baltimore. Maryland's county boundaries also remained fixed throughout the

Table 4.1. Border States Population, Potential Electorate, and Apportionment, 1796–1824

	Congress			
State	*5th–7th*	*8th–12th*	*13th–17th*	*18th–19th*
Delaware				
Population	59,096	64,273	72,674	72,749
Electorate	9,600	9,800	11,300	11,600
Apportionment	1	1	2	1
Maryland				
Population	319,728	341,548	380,546	407,350
Electorate	46,300	46,800	51,800	58,100
Apportionment	8	9	9	9

era.[16] This stability allows one to trace geographic patterns in party support and other empirical indicators of development without the complication of county and district changes.

Table 4.1 presents the state populations, their potential electorates, and respective apportionments.[17] There is no need for a separate table detailing districts and counties. Maryland presents a larger gap between its population and potential electorate than the Middle Atlantic states. This is because of slavery. In 1810, for example, over 105,000 Marylanders, nearly one-third of the state's population, were enslaved. Several Maryland counties, principally those along the Potomac River and the Chesapeake's western shore, counted nearly as many, or even more, enslaved African Americans as free whites. In 1800 the number of African American Delawareans was 14,421. Of these men, women, and children, over 6,000 were slaves. This was roughly 10 percent of the state's population. Delaware's enslaved population declined during the era, but as late as 1820 approximately 6 percent of the state's population was still enslaved. Free African Americans could not vote in either state.

Border-state elections draw attention to certain markers while others are less informative. For example, stability in the states' districts and counties simplifies tracing the geographic distribution of party support. Since the region is the boundary between North and South, these states are especially informative for tracing national changes in party support. Delaware and Maryland provided few opportunities to leverage electoral rules for advantage. Delaware was simply a single-member district or dual-member district, depending on the year. While districting might have made a partisan difference, this would be difficult, indeed unthinkable, in a state with only three counties. Maryland, by adding a second representative to the already Republican Baltimore district, only reinforced its preexisting partisan orientation.

Evidence of Effective Nominations

The Maryland and Delaware parties developed formal nominations in the first years of the nineteenth century. By 1802 Delaware Democratic-Republicans used county-level mass meetings to select state convention delegates to nominate their congressional candidate. The Federalists soon followed suit by introducing state nominating conventions, and these remained in use for the remainder of the era.[18] The Maryland parties established delegate-convention nominations by the first years of the nineteenth century.[19] Here the parties developed and used formal nominations centered on counties and election districts. Fredrick County Federalists illustrate nomination methods for both Maryland's House of Delegates and House of Representatives elections. In 1803 they held a convention that nominated candidates for the House of Delegates. The meeting appointed a committee to meet with a similarly selected Montgomery County committee to settle on the district nominee for the upcoming election.[20] Similarly, in late April 1804 Republican electors in Prince Georges and Anne Arundel Counties met at their respective polling places to appoint delegates to committees to confer with other appointed committees to choose a district congressional nominee.[21] The Republican conferees for those counties justified formal nominations on the grounds that "it is necessary to collect the sense of the republicans, in order to concentrate their efforts against their political opponents, who on all occasions, act with unanimity. . . . This was done in most of the districts in both counties. If some of them were unrepresented, the fault was their own."[22] Formal nominations "were not fully acceptable to all," but party leaders understood their necessity.

In addition to organizing nominations, the meetings produced and distributed pamphlets, handbills, and printed ballots.[23] Figure 4.1 presents a Delaware Democratic-Republican nomination handbill. It captures how the emergent parties legitimized and broadcast nominations and endorsements.[24] In this case, it reports the outcome of an August 1807 Dover meeting that nominated Joseph Haslett for governor and

Meeting
OF THE
DEMOCRATIC REPUBLICAN
CONFEREES,
Of the State of Delaware.

At a meeting of the Democratic Republican conferees of the State of Delaware, convened in the town of Dover, on the 4th. of August 1807, in pursuance of previous appointment, for the purpose of selecting suitable characters, to be voted for and supported by the Democratic Republicans of the State of Delaware, at the ensuing general election, for the office of Governor and Representative to Congress; David Hall was called to the chair, and John Hamm appointed secretary.

Upon consideration,

It was resolved unanimously, That Joseph Haslett be and he hereby is selected by this meeting as a suitable character to be voted for and supported by the Democratic Republicans of the State of Delaware, for the office of Governor, at the ensuing general election.

Resolved unanimously, That John Dickinson be and he is hereby selected by this meeting as a suitable character to be voted for and supported by the Democratic Republicans of the State of Delawre, at the ensuing general election, as a candidate to represent this State in the Congress of the United States.

Resolved further, That this meeting do recommend the above named candidates to the citizens of the State of Delaware, as worthy of their suffrages and support, at the ensuing general election, and as possessing in an eminent degree, that patriotism, and those abilities, which are the sure pledges of a faithful discharge of public duty.

Resolved, That the foregoing proceedings be signed by the conferees from the several counties in this State, and be published in handbills, for the information of our fellow-citizens.

Signed,

DAVID HALL,
JOHN FISHER,
JOHN WAY,
JOHN MERRITT,
PETER WILLIAMS,
WILLIAM D. WAPLES,
FERDINAND CASSON,
REUBEN GILDER,
JOHN COLLINS,
JOHN HAMM.

GEORGE READ,
WILLIAM BELL,
JOHN ADAMS,
ROBERT JAMISON,
THOMAS LOWBER,
JOHN FARISS,
WALTER DOUGLASS,
JOHN CAREY,
MITCHELL KERSHAW.

Dover, August 4, 1807.

Figure 4.1. Delaware: Nomination Broadside, 1807

Constitutional Convention delegate John Dickenson for a special election to the Tenth Congress. The conferees included several party luminaries: Declaration of Independence signatory George Read, former Delaware governor David Hall, and Reuben Gilder, who served in the Revolutionary War as a surgeon and later became a well-established Baltimore physician. The conferees requested that copies of the handbill be distributed throughout the state to focus electors on the endorsed candidates. Unfortunately for the Democratic Republicans, Haslett and Dickenson both lost in close elections to Federalist candidates.

Nominations were effective.[25] Both parties almost always limited candidate entry, and formally nominated candidates were typically the only competitive candidates.[26] In Delaware each party overcrowded the field just once—the Democratic-Republicans in 1806, and the Federalists in 1816. In every other election they got it right: when Delaware's apportionment was one, each party stood a single competitive candidate, and when its apportionment was two, each party stood two candidates. Maryland enjoyed nearly comparably effective entry control. Of Maryland's seventy contested single-member district elections, the Democratic-Republicans and the Federalists fielded a single viable candidate in 90 and 86 percent of these elections, respectively. Only a handful of single-winner elections saw three or more competitive candidates. In addition, each party stood two candidates in four of the five contested dual-member elections. The historical record and the empirical evidence shows that the border states developed effective candidate entry barriers early in the nation's history.

The Number of Electors and Turnout

The number of men who voted in Delaware and Maryland differs because of their vastly different populations and potential electorates. In tiny Delaware about 6,500 men voted in a typical House election. This figure increased to an average of 7,500 after 1810. Even in Delaware's traditional Sussex County the number of electors roughly doubled between 1800 and 1810. These numbers were not inconsequential. The nearly 2,700 Sussex County electors that voted in 1810 accounted for nearly half of the county's voting-age white male population.

In Maryland about 30,000 men voted in a typical election year. It was not uncommon for Maryland counties to see upwards of three-quarters of the eligible electorate cast ballots. The number of electors differed across districts because of differences in population and the competitiveness of the district. Prior to 1812, single-member districts saw an average of about 2,800 electors, with some districts hosting fewer than 1,000 electors. Other districts saw nearly 6,000 men vote. From 1812 onwards the single-member district elections saw an average of roughly 3,900 electors. The dual-member Baltimore district recorded at least 5,000 electors in every election after 1804, and more commonly over 7,000. In 1824 Baltimore saw over 10,000 electors cast votes, and that was in a one-party contest. The city's electorate grew with its population, and these men turned out in force even though the city and county were safely Republican.

Delaware and Maryland saw some of the nation's highest turnout rates. The border states turnout rates often reached levels "that was seldom surpassed . . . even in the Jacksonian period."[27] Figure 4.2 shows that most elections had turnout rates greater than 50 percent and often over 60 percent. This owes to the competitiveness of these elections.[28] In Delaware the relationship between competition and turnout is especially clear. These elections were decided by razor-thin margins. Turnout was regularly greater than 50 percent of the potential electorate and often closer to 70 percent. The noticeable 1806 decline was anomalous and likely due to the one-time inability of Democratic-Republicans to control candidate entry. Three Democratic-Republicans challenged the incumbent Federalist James M. Broom. In the face of a split vote and Broom's strong support in Kent and Sussex Counties, Democratic-Republican electors stayed home. One sees this in the county-level vote. Only thirty Republican votes were cast ballots in Kent County, and a mere 293 votes were cast in Sussex County. Broom even won a plurality in the Republican's home turf in New Castle County. Here just over 1,200 Democratic-Republicans divided their support between two candidates. The Democratic-Republicans reestablished entry control in the following election, which featured one candidate from each party, and turnout rebounded.[29]

Few Maryland districts were competitive, but the statewide partisan balance was tight, and turnout was often high. Naturally, there were anomalous years. In 1810 turnout declined precipitously. This is not due to franchise expansion. The eligible Maryland electorate increased at the margins following an 1810 constitutional reform that rescinded properly qualifications. This produced only a modest expansion of an

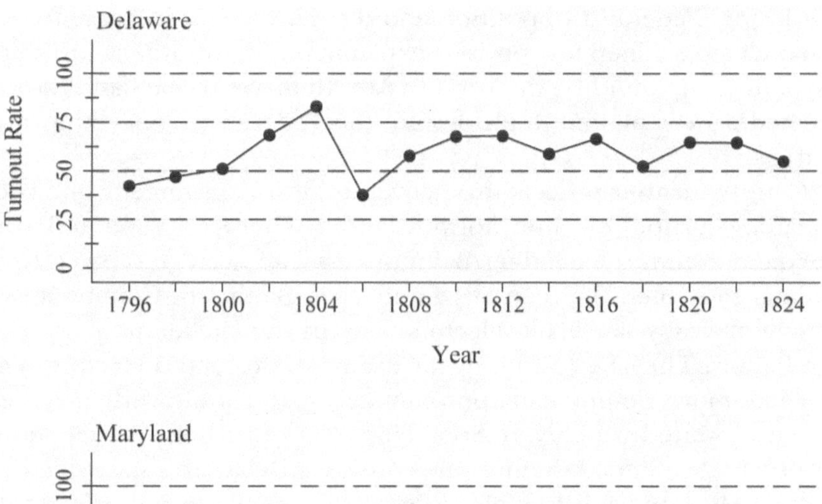

Figure 4.2. Delaware and Maryland: Turnout Rates

already large electorate. In 1810 only about 21,000 electors completed ballots, compared with approximately 35,500 in the preceding and following cycles. It is clear why participation decreased so steeply in this one election. Of Maryland's eight districts, the Federalists conceded four without a fight, and the Republicans did the same in two districts. The district centered on Fredrick and Montgomery Counties captures the effect of party competition on turnout. In 1808 this district saw over 4,000 voters in an election that Federalist Phillip B. Key won with two-thirds of the vote. Key won the following election unopposed with fewer than 800 votes. Similarly, in 1808 the Fourth District, comprised of Allegany, Fredrick, and Washington Counties, saw nearly 6,000 electors cast ballots. The Republicans edged out the Federalists by just over 200 votes. No Federalist sought election in the following cycle, and turnout plummeted by over half. The following cycle saw reemergent, albeit losing, Federalist opposition and district turnout increase to over 6,700 electors. The most obvious explanation for resurgent turnout is the politics surrounding the War of 1812. In this year Maryland turnout reached a near all-time high despite the Federalists conceding three districts.

County turnout reflects this active political engagement, the occasional low-turnout election notwithstanding. Between 1802 and 1820 Maryland counties excluding Baltimore saw an average of over 1,800 electors cast votes. Between 1812 and 1820 Baltimore County outside the city typically saw 2,400 electors vote. In the city about 4,200 men cast ballots. The 1820 turnout, for example, was 7,400 electors. That year Baltimore County had approximately 5,300 adult white men, and the city counted roughly 10,800. This level of turnout is exceptional for one-party affairs. Whether one considers Delaware's statewide elections or Maryland's district elections, mass participatory elections were well established by the first years of the nineteenth century. Only party-organized, competitive elections produce turnout of this magnitude.

Party Support

The border states were competitive, with both parties enjoying significant support in House of Representatives elections. This is especially true in Delaware, which may have been the most competitive state in the young nation. This is captured in the statewide general-ticket votes, which were always close. In Maryland the Democratic-Republicans were the dominant party, but much of this owes to Republican support in Baltimore city and county, and the large numbers of electors in this district. Baltimore was decidedly Democratic-Republican, but enough districts in other parts of the state voted Federalist to keep the state reasonably competitive through much of the era. The overall outstate vote saw more partisan balance, with the Federalists and the Democratic-Republicans each enjoying their own bastions of support. This is captured in the district and county votes. Maryland and, especially, Delaware present balanced party competition.

AGGREGATE PARTY SUPPORT. Figure 4.3 displays the Delaware and Maryland aggregate vote. In Delaware the Federalists averaged about 53 percent of the vote, a figure that remained quite stable throughout the era. While the Federalists won more elections, many of these were near ties. Perhaps the most interesting feature of Delaware elections is that three of the five dual-candidate elections sent split delegations to Congress. These were elected in 1816, 1818, and 1820. One resulted from Federalist inability to control entry. In 1816 the leading Federalist candidate, Louis MacLane, won with nearly 3,600 votes. However, two minor Federalist candidates each received a few hundred votes. This drew just enough Federalist votes to elect Democratic-Republican Willard Hall to the second seat. Ballot roll-off drove the 1818 and 1820 split delegations. In 1818 the second Federalist candidate enjoyed slightly less support than the frontrunner. A difference of 200 votes was enough to elect the leading Democratic-Republican. Even larger Federalist roll-off in 1820 also produced a split delegation. That ordinary and modest ballot roll-off could produce split delegations despite effective entry control speaks to the state's partisan balance. Delaware elections further demonstrate why won elections is a misleading measure of party support. Between 1796 and 1824 the Federalists won fifteen House seats while the Democratic-Republicans won three seats. This lopsided Federalist tally viewed in context of often absurdly close elections confirms that seats won often masks deeply competitive elections. The Delaware Democratic-Republicans were well supported, just not quite well enough.

Maryland Federalists averaged about 36 percent of the vote throughout the era and won a proportional number of elections. The party peaked at just over half of the aggregate vote in 1814, winning five of Maryland's nine seats. This was driven by the immense political tension generated by the War of 1812. That summer, riots targeted the Federalist Baltimore *Federal Republican.* These were sparked by anti-war articles published by the newspaper. The riots produced injuries and even deaths. George Washington Parke Custis, grandson of Martha Washington and future father-in-law of Robert E. Lee, led the funeral procession for one of its victims. The Baltimore riots were a galvanizing force for Federalists both in Maryland and nationally. The low point for Maryland Federalists came in 1822 when they won just a fifth of the statewide vote. They rebounded slightly in the next election, but the Democratic-Republican and Federalist era was over. The Federalists were Maryland's minority party, but they remained a political force through the era. This was because, as will be seen, their support was geographically concentrated.

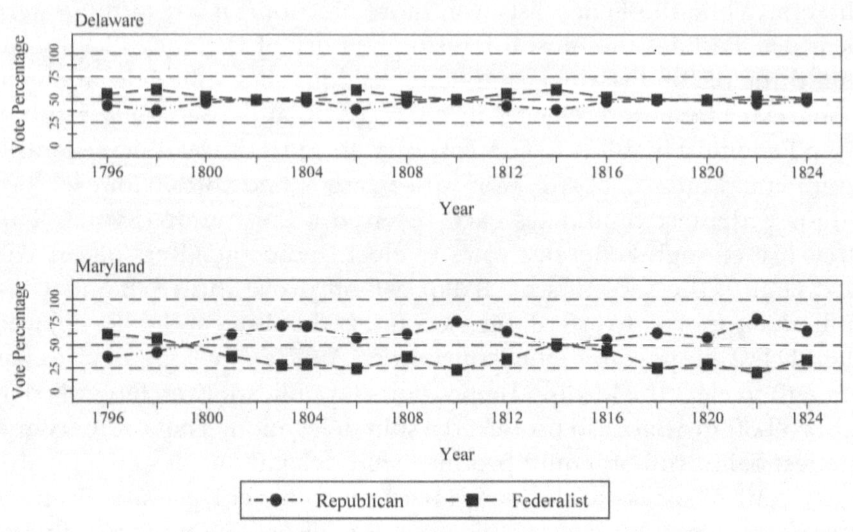

Figure 4.3. Delaware and Maryland: Aggregate Party Vote Shares

EVIDENCE OF PARTISANSHIP FROM BALLOTS AND GEOGRAPHY. Previous research argues that partisanship existed in the border-state electorate. Pollbooks from Maryland's Fredrick and Kent Counties from 1796 to 1802 provide such evidence. The books contained thousands of individually identifiable votes for presidential electors and representatives. These showed that the large majority of electors were stable in their voting preferences across time and office. Well over 80 percent of Fredrick County voters were "rigid" partisans, as were over 60 percent of Kent County electors, where "rigid" means voting for the same party across all elections and offices. Importantly, when the aggregate vote changed across elections, it was not because of vote switching but due to changes in turnout. Fredrick and Kent voters would rather stay home than vote for the other party.[30]

First party era Delaware held five two-winner elections, and Maryland hosted ten dual-member district elections. These reveal much about partisan attachments and provide strong evidence that partisanship anchored the electorate. In 1812 Delaware Federalists Henry M. Ridgely and Thomas Cooper won House seats with 4,193 and 4,183 votes, respectively. Their two Democratic-Republican opponents received 3,221 and 3,210 votes. This means of 7,414 electors, it is highly likely that about 4,200 voted the Federalist ticket and 3,200 voted the Democratic-Republican ticket. One cannot confirm that electors cast a straight ticket without individually identifiable votes. However, only ten votes separate Ridgely and Cooper, and the Democratic-Republicans are separated by eleven votes. These virtually nil within party vote spreads extend to the county level. In New Castle County only four votes separate the Federalists candidates and only a single vote separates the Democratic-Republican candidates. The likelihood that there are even a few split tickets in the presence of such tight intraparty vote differences is infinitesimally small.

Other Delaware elections display the same patterns. In 1814 there is almost no within party vote spread; the vote differences between the Federalist candidates, on one hand, and the Democratic-Republican candidates, on the other, are in single digits. In the aforementioned 1816 election only thirteen votes separate the two Democratic-Republican candidates. Fewer than 150 votes separate the two leading Federalists. In this election, the Federalist gap certainly owes less to roll-off than to spoilers siphoning votes from the ticket. Federalists were still voting the party, but a small number voted for the interloping Federalists. The 1818 Federalist gap was 196 votes, and the Democratic-Republican gap was 105 votes. This is out of a total of 11,910 distinct votes cast by about 6,000 electors. Again, the overwhelming majority of electors voted the party ticket.

The following election saw larger within party vote gaps. The Democratic-Republican gap is over 500 votes, while the Federalist difference is 418 votes. This, however, reflects the larger electorate. In 1820, 14,972 votes were cast by nearly 8,000 electors. The county returns show the origins of these gaps. The two Republican candidates, Caesar A. Rodney and Willard Hall, did equally well in Kent County, with fewer than twenty votes separating them. However, their vote differences in New Castle and Sussex Counties were larger, with 224 and 297 votes separating the leading Rodney from Hall. In these counties approximately 1,700 Federalists and 1,360 Republican voters cast ballots. The vote differences are small relative to the number of electors, but still sufficient to produce a split congressional delegation. Hall was the less popular candidate, and some Republicans apparently chose to return an incomplete ballot. This pattern is repeated for the two Federalists,

Louis MacLane and John Mitchell. New Castle and Sussex County Federalists were slightly less likely to vote for Mitchell. Overall, there is little credible evidence of ticket splitting.

The city and county of Baltimore was Maryland's only two-member constituency. This Democratic-Republican district never sent a Federalist to Congress. Here one sees larger vote spreads between the leading and trailing Republican candidates. This is certainly because electors are secure in the knowledge that only Republicans would be elected. Without serious party competition, one can express displeasure with a candidate without risk. In contrast, Delaware's state-level competitiveness minimized ballot roll-off. Both Baltimore and Delaware multicandidate ballots make clear that there was a pronounced level of party voting. Even the largest vote gaps are small relative to the number of electors and votes. Border-state electors voted the party, not the candidate.

The geography of support presents further evidence that partisanship resided in the border-states electorate. House districts and counties differ in important characteristics, including their economic foundations, settlement patterns, religiosity, and a host of other considerations that shape party support.

Delaware's geographic distribution of the vote presents a clear example of county-level differences in partisan leanings. The Democratic-Republicans were strongest in the north; the Federalists, in the south. Each party enjoyed a bastion of support. For the Democratic-Republicans it was New Castle County. The Federalist stronghold was Sussex County. To illustrate, the 1810 election to the Twelfth Congress saw Federalist Henry M. Ridgely defeated Democratic-Republican Richard C. Dale by seventeen votes out of the 7,251 that were cast statewide. Ridgely carried Sussex County by 655 votes, while Dale won New Castle County by 864 votes. The Federalist victory was owed to Kent County,

Table 4.2. Delaware County-Level Party Vote and Partisanship, 1796–1824

	Dem-Rep Median Vote	*Federalist Median Vote*	*Dem-Rep MAD*	*Federalist MAD*	*Contested Elections*
New Castle	62	38	3	4	15
Kent	45	55	3	3	14
Sussex	33	67	3	3	15

Table 4.3. Maryland County-Level Party Vote and Partisanship, 1800–1824

	Dem-Rep Median Vote	*Federalist Median Vote*	*Dem-Rep MAD*	*Federalist MAD*	*Rep/Fed Win*	*Contested Elections*
Allegany	44	56	6	6	3 / 6	9
Ann Arundel	58	42	5	5	7 / 2	9
Fredrick	45	55	12	11	5 / 8	13
Montgomery	35	65	7	7	2 / 5	7
Prince Georges	50	50	6	6	4 / 5	9
Somerset	28	72	11	11	1 / 6	7
Worcester	39	61	11	11	1 / 6	7

which favored Ridgely by 226 votes. The Federalists enjoyed a banner year two cycles later when they won both seats with a 61 percent statewide margin. The bellwether Kent County swung in the Federalist direction, giving the party over 60 percent of its vote.

To confirm these patterns, table 4.2 presents the median Federalist and Republican county-level vote and their deviations. These show that New Castle County was reliably Democratic-Republican and Sussex County was reliably Federalist. Each party won consistently on its home turf, receiving, on average, over 60 percent of the vote. Kent County displays more partisan balance. The Federalists won here eleven times. There is a temporal pattern in the Kent County vote. In 1812 and 1814 the Federalists won over two-thirds of the vote. In 1816 and 1818 the Federalist vote declined to the mid 50 percent range. By 1820 the Federalists won just under half of the vote. Simply, Kent County transitioned from majority Federalists to nearly evenly divided between the Republicans and Federalists. The vote in all counties is stable and retains its partisan orientation. Delaware electors were not easily moved by transitory political circumstances.

Table 4.3 presents similar information for Maryland's seven most competitive counties. These counties saw least seven contested elections with each party winning the county at least once.[31] Allegany, Ann Arundel, and Prince Georges Counties were especially competitive. Here the party votes often hovered near 50 percent, and typical deviations were in single digits. The tighter variation in the Ann Arundel Democratic-Republican vote advantaged that party's candidates. The Fredrick, Summerset, and Wooster votes display higher variation than the other counties. Prince Georges County was quite competitive and saw nine contested elections, with each party winning the county multiple times. Montgomery, Summerset, and Wooster Counties had more lopsided vote shares and fewer contested elections than the other counties. The Federalists won the county vote in most of these elections.

The less competitive Maryland counties inform much about geographic redoubts of party support. Baltimore city and county were firmly Democratic-Republican, as were Caroline, Cecil, Harford, Kent, Queen Annes, and Talbot Counties. The Federalists dominated Calvert, Charles, Dorchester, and St. Mary's Counties. The reliably partisan counties present geographic patterns. The Republicans did best in the northern Chesapeake Bay region, especially its eastern shore. Cecil County shares a boundary with Delaware's New Castle County. Kent, Queen Annes, and Talbot Counties are all on the northern end of Maryland's eastern shore. Outside the Chesapeake region the Republicans also did well in the panhandle's Washington County. Federalists fared best in the southern Chesapeake. Among these counties, St. Mary's at the southern end of the bay is the oldest settled part of the state and is bordered by Calvert and Charles Counties. Reliably Federalist Sommerset and Worchester Counties were on Maryland's southern Atlantic coast. These counties shared political affinity with Delaware's Sussex County. Finally, the most competitive Maryland counties were anchored on the southeast by Prince Georges and Ann Arundel Counties and continued north and west to Montgomery and Fredrick Counties.

Figure 4.4 shows the district-level party support for four election cycles: 1806, 1812, 1816, and 1820. Read in order, the maps show that the county patterns aggregate to the district level. One again sees two distinct areas of Federalist support: the lower Chesapeake and the upper-central region. The Federalists never lost a House election in the south Chesapeake district. The upper-central region centered on eastern Fredrick County and Montgomery County, while leaning Federalist, was more competitive. The Federalists only lost here once, in 1824. The southeast Chesapeake, including Dorchester, Somerset, and Worchester Counties, also leaned Federalist, but this support weakened toward the end of the era.

Maryland's handful of competitive districts included the eastern and western shore Second and Seventh Districts. The Second District centered on Anne Arundel County and was home to Annapolis. This district produced near ties in every House election between 1806 and

1818. For example, the 1816 election between winning Federalist John C. Herbert and Democratic-Republican Joshua Barney was decided by 46 votes out of 3,163 cast votes. Across the Chesapeake the Seventh District formed by Caroline County, Queen Anne's County, and Talbot County was equally competitive. In the same year, Democratic-Republican Thomas Culbreth won the eastern shore district with 51 percent of the vote. This is not to say that these two districts were hard fought every year. The Federalists occasionally failed to field a candidate. When this happened, two Democratic-Republicans often sought the seat. It does show that when both parties contested these districts, which was more often than not, both the western and eastern shore districts were competitive.

One can see the effects of population concentration on the aggregate vote by considering the 1810 Democratic-Republican high-water mark. This year saw the Republicans win about three-quarters of the approximately 26,000 Maryland cast votes. This translates to approximately 20,000 Republican votes. Baltimore alone provided about half of these votes. The remaining Democratic-Republican votes were spread among the state's seven single-member districts, as was most of the Federalist vote. The Federalists translated these votes into three districts won by wide margins. Two of these districts were in the southwest and southeast Chesapeake region. They also won a northern district centered on Westminster. Similarly, the Republicans claimed three unopposed victories. This pattern maintained itself across most elections. Maryland's single-member districts tended to be solidly Republican or solidly Federalist, and in roughly equal measure. The lopsided Baltimore Republican vote obscures that outside of the city and county of Baltimore, Maryland had fairly balanced party competition even if many districts did not.

The geographic distribution of party support tends to be stable over election cycles. This further indicates that partisanship resided in the electorate. In Maryland, Democratic-Republicans didn't seek votes in Saint Mary's County, and Federalists didn't seek votes in Baltimore, in each case because there were few to be had. It might be that in Delaware's counties, different electors voted Democratic-Republican and Federalist across elections, thereby producing the illusion of a core base of Federalist voters in its counties. But this strains credulity. The border-state electorate was partisan, and its electors consistently supported their preferred party.

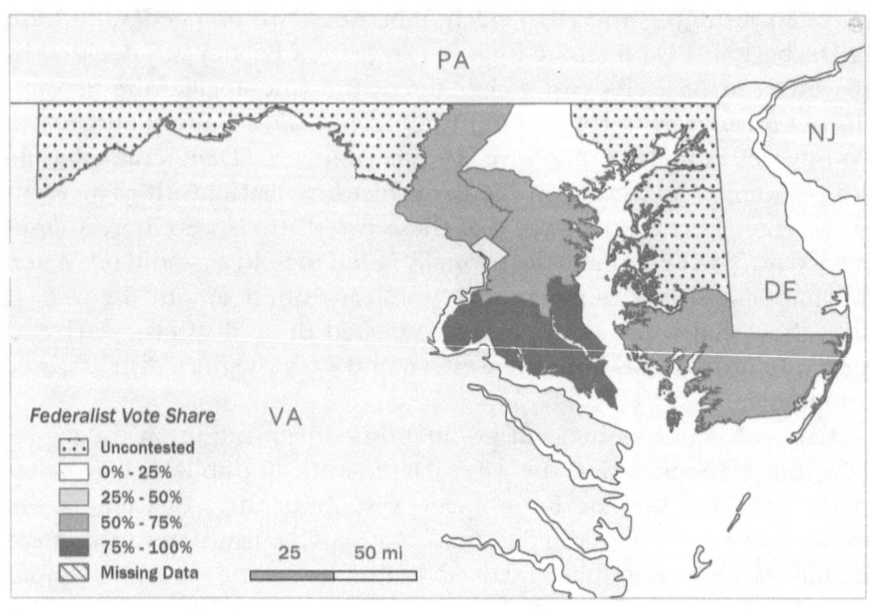

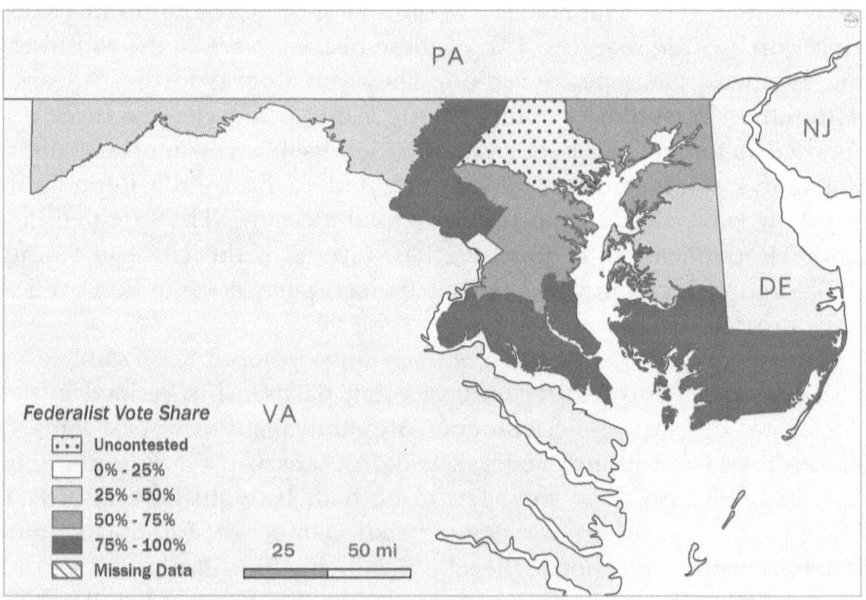

Figure 4.4. Maryland: Areas of Party Support in 1806, 1812, 1816, and 1820

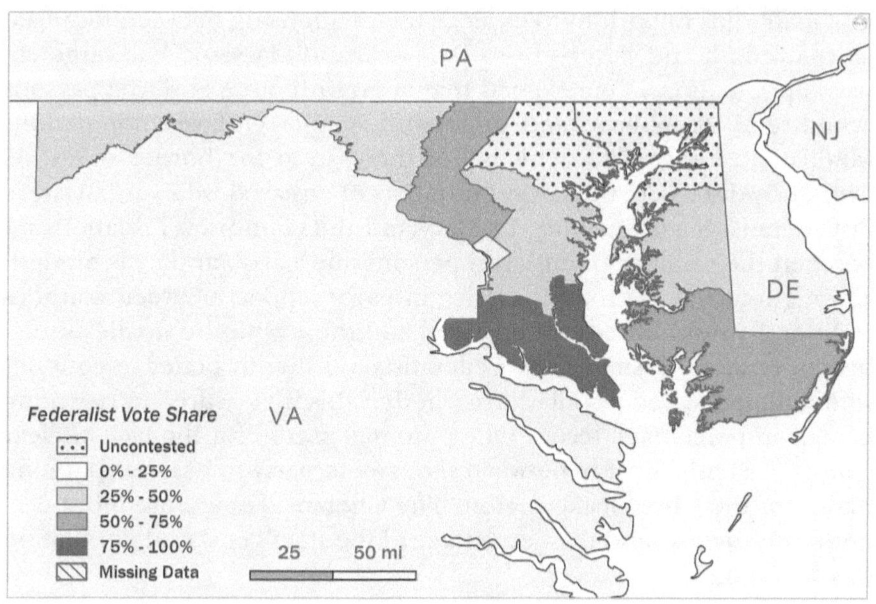
PA
NJ
DE
VA
Federalist Vote Share
Uncontested
0% - 25%
25% - 50%
50% - 75%
75% - 100%
Missing Data
25
50 mi

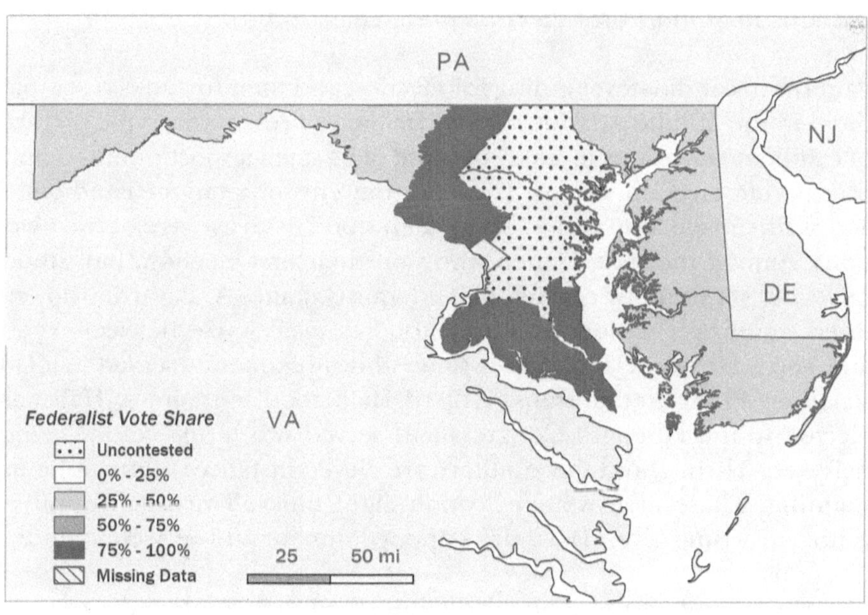
PA
NJ
DE
VA
Federalist Vote Share
Uncontested
0% - 25%
25% - 50%
50% - 75%
75% - 100%
Missing Data
25
50 mi

Finally, it is important to explore the relationship between localized party strength and slavery. Both Delaware and Maryland had large enslaved populations. One expects that areas with more enslaved persons would tend Republican and those with smaller enslaved populations would tend Federalist.[32] This is not the case in the border states. As previously discussed, the largest numbers of enslaved Delawareans were in Federalist Sussex County. In Maryland the county-level relationship between the number of enslaved persons and party support is modest. Throughout the era the difference in party support between counties with the largest numbers of enslaved and those with the smallest numbers of enslaved is small. The Federalists did slightly better in counties with larger enslaved populations, whether this is measured in raw numbers or in percentage terms. One potential reason for the lack of clear county-level relationship between slavery and party vote is the changing nature of the Chesapeake region. The Chesapeake became more economically diverse, and the percentage of the state's enslaved population was declining.[33]

Patterns in Standing for Election and Reelection

Patterns in candidates standing for election and their fortunes resemble those in the Middle Atlantic region. Delaware presents a simple picture of candidate decisions to stand because of its small apportionments and transparent election system. There were twenty-one unique candidates across fifteen election cycles. These men stood in an average of two elections. Among the sixteen men who won their first election, half stood once and six stood twice. Among Federalists, James A. Bayard, who enjoyed significant national stature, stood in every cycle between 1796 and 1804. He won election four times and subsequently served as a US senator. Among Republicans, Willard Hall stood four times. Hall was elected to the Fifteenth Congress and served two terms before being defeated. Throughout the era there are eleven instances of incumbents standing. These men won reelection eight times. This small number is not surprising given Delaware's apportionment and very competitive elections.

In Maryland 103 unique candidates stood in a combined 120 elections. Of these men, over half stood once. The large majority, over 80 percent, stood in three or fewer elections. Even among those who won their first election, approximately one-third chose not to stand again. Forty-eight of Maryland's 108 single-member district elections featured an incumbent. These men were usually reelected. This is weighted by Baltimore, which regularly saw two Democratic-Republican incumbents stand with near certainty of reelection. However, this pattern was broken in 1810 when four strong Republicans stood. Incumbent Nicholas Moore, who had served in the House since 1803, lost the second spot by a mere 124 votes. These candidates shared the Republican vote almost evenly. This election illustrates the difficulty of entry control in a multiseat district where one party dominates.

Typically, Maryland incumbents voluntarily stepped out of office. After winning their initial election, representatives served on average just shy of three terms and declined to stand thereafter. Since incumbents enjoyed relatively high second-term election rates, these men were most likely voluntarily leaving Congress. Among persistent and successful incumbents, Federalist Phillip Stewart, veteran of both the Revolutionary War and the War of 1812, was initially elected in 1810 from the southern First District centered on St. Mary's and adjacent counties. He was reelected to three successive terms, effectively unopposed each time. When he left office, the district elected Raphael Neale Jr. in a competitive election pairing Neale and fellow Federalist Nicholas Stonestreet. Stonestreet gave it another try in 1820, again losing to Neale in a close contest.

Democratic-Republican John Archer's congressional career illustrates that the electoral fortunes of Maryland incumbents were not always secure. Archer was a physician with an illustrious Revolutionary War service record. He was first elected to the Sixth Congress from a north Maryland district bordering Pennsylvania and Delaware. Archer was reelected to the Seventh, Eighth, and Ninth Congresses. However, he lost reelection to the Tenth Congress when he equivocated on his association with the Democratic-Republicans, a mistake not made by his opponent, John Montgomery.[34] Archer tried to rectify his mistake in the election to the Eleventh Congress, but the damage was done. He finished a distant third to Montgomery, who won, and to a strong Federalist candidate. Archer's defeat shows that even well-established incumbents were sometimes voted out of office. It also demonstrates that one reason voters might do so is if the candidate appears less than committed to the party.

Overall, border-state incumbents stood in few elections and were likely to win those that they contested. There is little in the way of discernable patterns in incumbent losses. From 1816 forward it was typical for three districts in each cycle to feature an incumbent, one of whom lost. These losses visited Republicans and Federalists in roughly equal measure. More often, incumbents left office of their own accord. Still, as Representative Archer discovered, there are things that even a well-established incumbent can do to lose an election. One of these is to equivocate on party affiliation.

Leveraging Electoral Rules for Partisan Advantage

Neither Delaware nor Maryland presented many opportunities for leveraging election rules for partisan advantage. Delaware's apportionment increased to two following the 1810 census. In the period, districts were typically created using counties as their building blocks. This means that for Delaware to district it would need to create two single-member districts from three counties; one each centered on New Castle and Sussex Counties. This would leave the question of where to place Federalist-leaning Kent County. Recalling that Kent County was the state's most competitive county, attaching it to either New Castle County or Sussex County would present risks for both parties. For the Federalists the rise of the Democratic-Republicans made pairing it with Sussex County dangerous. A modest shift in the vote could easily produce two Democratic-Republican districts. The safest course for both parties was to leave the electoral regime unchanged and strive to carry the statewide vote. Unlike in New Jersey, it is doubtful that either party thought the general ticket conferred significant partisan advantages.

Maryland also presented few opportunities to district for advantage. Even though the era predates constitutionally required population-based districting, there were norms of adjusting districts to account for population. The city and county of Baltimore together constituted the most obvious area for increased representation following Maryland's 1802 apportionment increase. Between the first and second census, the city of Baltimore's population nearly doubled to 27,000. By 1810 the city counted over 46,000 residents. There was little appetite for carving out Baltimore city from the surrounding county. Given that the Democratic-Republicans controlled the Annapolis statehouse in 1801 and were assured of winning any Baltimore-area congressional seats, the simplest and safest way to add an additional representative was to make the preexisting Baltimore district a dual-member district. The Democratic-Republicans never lost an election in it or even faced serious opposition.[35]

Maryland did gerrymander its presidential elector districts in 1816 in a manner that provided the James Monroe–led Democratic-Republican ticket a couple of extra votes. The Federalists were anticipated to win four of the Electoral College districts. The districting was intended to reduce this to two districts. Ultimately, the Federalists won three Electoral College votes. However, these were not cast and reflected in the national total because the Federalist electors did not arrive in Annapolis in time to cast their votes.[36] The importance of the Electoral College gerrymander is not its effect on the presidential election, but rather that it demonstrates that as late as 1816 Maryland Republicans knew the Federalists could win at least four of these votes.

The border states contribute only modestly to our knowledge of the early use of election rules for advantage. Both were cautious when apportionment increases presented opportunities to district. Maryland's Baltimore district ran the risk of packing too many Republicans in a single, albeit dual-member, district. The state's Democratic-Republicans appear to have preferred the sure bet by increasing the Baltimore city and county representation. Similarly, Delaware maintained the existing election process. It is impossible to know what the parties in these states would have done had opportunity arisen, but counterfactuals of this type are rarely informative. The fact is that both states were characterized by stability in institutions and processes. The creation of the dual-member Baltimore city and county district was politically necessary given the regional population growth. Delaware was so politically competitive that any districting brought more risk than potential reward. Parties in both states "played it safe."

Conclusion

Delaware and Maryland were politically competitive throughout the first party era. Delaware's Democratic-Republicans and Federalists vigorously contested elections. The Federalists remained not only competitive but also won the era's last two elections outright and most of the seats in the preceding two decades. The Democratic-Republicans were not shut out, and they too won seats in always-close elections. Maryland shows the secular decline of Federalist fortunes, but here too the Federalists remained competitive, even dominant, in several counties. Recognizing that the Democratic-Republicans controlled the two Baltimore House Seats, the Federalists and Democratic-Republicans enjoyed relative parity in many areas, with each party having its own areas of political primacy.

The border states contained some of the most electorally competitive and developed areas in the young nation. Campaigning and associated activities such as stump speaking were de rigueur. Markers of electoral development reflect these practices. The parties typically fielded the correct number of candidates given election methods in use. Delaware's parties rarely overcrowded the field, with votes confirming that they successfully focused voters on endorsed candidates. In larger Maryland, both parties were nearly as successful, overcrowding the field only a handful of times. In both states, House election turnout was well over 50 percent of the eligible electorate in most elections. Even in "low" turnout years the percentage of the electorate that went to the polls was considerable. The parties mobilized electors and did everything possible to get every voter to the polls. This is reflected in the thousands of electors in Delaware's at-large elections and Maryland's district elections.

Party efforts were driven by the competitiveness of the elections. This is especially true in Delaware, where almost all elections were decided by thin margins. Here the Federalists never diminished as an electoral force. In Maryland the Federalists declined toward the end of the era, but remained viable in some areas. Leveraging their regionally concentrated support, the Federalists continued to elect representatives. As late as 1824 the Federalists won three House seats. They would have won four seats, but they failed to control entry in one district, allowing the Democratic-Republicans a win despite the combined Federalist vote outpolling the Republicans by over a thousand votes. The Republicans held another district by 167 votes out of over 3,600 that were cast. Even at the end of the era, Maryland Federalists were still quite capable of winning elections.

Partisanship was well established in the border states from the earliest days of the republic. Delaware's five two-candidate elections display ballot discipline. The typical within party vote difference was only a couple of percentage points. Combining this with elector turnout presents a picture of a core partisan electorate that voted at about the same rate across election cycles and cast straight tickets. The evidence for Delaware's partisan electorate is further supported by the geography of party support. The Federalist and Democratic-Republican vote differs across counties; the north tended Republican, and the south, Federalist. This is a bit surprising because Wilmington was the state's only major city and a center for shipping and commerce. However, religion also shaped Delaware's regional partisanship. In the north the Quakers were friends of trade, commerce, and mercantile pursuits. Along the lines of "the enemy of my enemy is my friend," Paul Goodman argued that a "group's relationship to other groups . . . influenced partisan choice. . . . Thus local conditions in Delaware led Quakers to become Republicans."[37] The established Anglican families along with the Scots-Irish of the south kept this area in the Federalist orbit. The Anglican-Methodist order provided additional reason for the Quakers to align with the Republicans. This is evident in the returns.

Maryland too displays consistent partisanship patterns associated with territory. The Democratic-Republicans dominated Baltimore city and county to such an extent that Federalists seldom contested these elections. Baltimore's rapid growth, especially among recent immigrants, provided Democratic-Republicans a potential electorate far removed from the seemingly old politics of the lower Chesapeake. Federalist support in the lower Chesapeake and the north-central counties may appear to be the pairing of two disparate areas, but both shared an agricultural focus with smaller plot holders and a mutual feeling of being removed from the political influence of Baltimore and Annapolis. Maryland's pattern of solidly Democratic-Republican and Federalist districts may owe to the state's lack of an elected governor. Lack of elected, high-profile state offices tends to localize politics, in this case at the district and county levels. Had a governorship been at stake, it is likely each party would have expended more resources to organize in the other party's territory.

Delaware and Maryland present an emergent recognizably modern style of elections. The border states held party-organized elections by the first years of the nineteenth century, if not before. Delaware presents one of the nation's most developed electoral regimes. The parties were strong enough to affect structured nominations and control entry, and its candidates campaigned in the Jacksonian style. Reflecting this, electors turned out in large numbers and voted straight tickets for their party's candidates. Maryland isn't far behind, but its heterogeneity and significant geographic and intrastate regional differences temper some of these patterns. Nonetheless, in neither state do the results show anything that resembles the old deferential practices of previous generations. Border-state elections closely resemble those in the Middle Atlantic states and, as will be seen, differ from those in the South.

5 | New England

Scholars describe New England as a proto-democratic region dominated by political elites. The political egalitarianism of these states was partially a chimera. Regional political leaders, especially Federalists, were unashamedly elitist. If the politics of deference was waning, the Madisonian ideal of leadership by the "natural aristocracy" was still alive in New England. Despite its tradition of local meetings and corporate representation centered on the township, early New England politics was controlled by the old families, Congregationalist leaders, intellectuals, and wealthy merchants. Nowhere is this truer than in Connecticut's "Standing Order," but most New England states combined egalitarian rhetoric with patrician sensibilities.

This chapter evaluates electoral development in Connecticut, Massachusetts, New Hampshire, and Rhode Island. Massachusetts elected its representatives from single-member districts. New Hampshire, Connecticut, and Rhode Island elected theirs at-large.[1] In New England ballots were typically handwritten, although the parties published the names of nominated candidates. These states required a majority to win, which introduced the possibility of multi-round elections. Runoffs were sometimes required, but not often. For example, between 1796 and 1824 only thirty-two of nearly 250 Massachusetts House elections required multiple rounds to select a representative. General ticket runoffs were also rare.[2] The paucity of runoff elections points to electoral development. It indicates that the parties successfully limited entry so that only one candidate from each party stood in a single-member constituency and that parties contested at-large elections by presenting slates. This precluded spoilers from syphoning enough votes to force multiple rounds.

While New England leaned Federalist, it was more competitive than commonly recognized. Indeed, it was Federalist regional strength that spurred the Democratic-Republican organizational efforts that ultimately bore fruit. This relationship was reciprocal. By the 1810s both parties worked to get their supporters to the polls.[3] New England party organization was present, but for the most part it was decentralized. The parties relied heavily on local leaders who built on local practices and traditions. As elsewhere, electoral rules and processes greatly affected party fortunes. New England's general ticket elections often turned modest statewide majorities into electoral sweeps. Consequently, the minority party forfeited seats that would otherwise be won if the state districted. Federalists in Connecticut unashamedly used a variety of rules and processes (discussed below) to maintain their electoral dominance. Finally, a key feature of New England was the ubiquitous printed word in the form of handbills, broadsheets, and pamphlets. These transmitted political commentary and exhortations to vote to receptive audiences.

The first generation of New England Federalists maintained their party's distaste for soliciting votes. Here remained the vestiges of an old style of electioneering through the candidates' "friends." Despite the recalcitrant old guard, Republicans and a younger generation of Federalists brought New England a more recognizably modern style of elections. These practices developed in response to Republican inroads into the Federalist-dominated region. In Massachusetts and Connecticut, "Federalist political leaders . . . became preoccupied with getting a leg up on the Democratic-Republicans. They built a party machine aimed at mobilizing voters and winning elections. As they became 'more professional' they also became more adept at the types of electoral 'chicanery' that characterized the nineteenth-century urban machines."[4] Democratic-Republicans were more likely than Federalists to publish election lists and announce meetings in the newspapers. The initially reluctant Federalists organized mass meetings, taking care to ensure that electoral organization remained out of sight as much as possible. However, this changed as Democratic-Republican strength grew. By the first years of the nineteenth century, Federalists were hosting election meetings and directly soliciting votes, embarrassingly explaining that doing so was necessary because the Republicans started these practices.[5] For example, in 1804 the Federalists met in Boston's Faneuil Hall to accommodate the large crowd.[6] Campaigning, stump speeches, and mobilizing voters became commonplace.

New England's electoral development was uneven. Even within states there are ebbs and flows. Watershed moments seldom present themselves. The Jeffersonian Embargo Act of 1807 was deeply unpopular with seaport merchants and communities. Its 1809 repeal did little to revive Republican fortunes on the cusp of "Madison's War." The Hartford

Convention diminished the Federalist luster, but not immediately.[7] The immensely unpopular Compensation Act of 1816 had outsized effects in New England, forcing many representatives to disavow it, with several incumbents declining to seek reelection or experiencing defeat.[8] This disproportionately visited Federalists.[9] New England party competition with the partial exception of Connecticut was more competitive than commonly realized, with tight vote spreads and both parties electing representatives through at least the Seventeenth Congress.

Connecticut's electoral setting was very different from its regional neighbors. Prior to 1800 there was little in the way of modern political life, electoral or otherwise.[10] Connecticut's "Standing Order" consisting of Congregationalist ministers, leading families, Federalist politicians, and intellectuals ruled the state as an aristocracy not terribly distinct from that in England. In these days Connecticut's "preachers were politicians, and her politicians were preachers."[11] The Standing Order was threatened by the rising Jeffersonians and adopted electoral practices to preserve their standing. These elites maintained their authority "entrenched behind an impregnable barrier of statutes, patronage, and election devices . . . which laughed to scorn . . . platitude regarding a government popularly controlled."[12] Two of these devices were especially effective: nomination elections and the Stand-up Law. Connecticut used at-large elections to "nominate" candidates for the general election. The nomination election selected eighteen men to stand in the general election, of whom seven were elected. Electors received eighteen noncumulative votes to nominate candidates and seven noncumulative votes in the general election. The Federalist statewide majority ensured that their candidates enjoyed nearly exclusive access to the general election. The 1801 Stand-up Law required electors to stand and publicly declare their votes including before local clergy and elites. This eliminated all pretense of secrecy at the polls. And it was pretense. Previous voting by ballots still allowed the election judge to open these, and nominations of any other than candidates lacking the imprimatur of church and political elites "required a boldness only possible in men politically and financially independent."[13] The Stand-up Law was intended to intimidate, and it did.

Still, things were slowly changing. In the first years of the nineteenth century, party organization increasingly brought out the vote. The Republicans "organized and drilled" their supporters to vote for the party candidates. The "Jeffersonian party was educating the people to use the ballot and not to leave the business of governing to a professional class."[14] The Federalists responded, reluctantly perhaps, by organizing their supporters. Their exhortations included reminding supporters of "the hardships Washington used to undergo to attend an election."[15] For both parties the ballot increasingly became the primary vehicle through which supporters could influence government and its policies rather than serving primarily as a symbol of political standing. As such, its value was determined and enhanced through party politics and organization.[16]

The early Republican organizational successes forced the Federalists to further manipulate the rules to preserve their standing. To do so, the Connecticut Assembly passed additional laws to preserve the status quo. These included tightened existing property requirements by requiring new voters to hold local property for at least four months before the election. In 1804 an unknown Connecticut writer anticipated further increases in property barriers when he or she published the following in the Cheshire, New Hampshire, *Political Observatory*:

> It is whispered among the knowing ones here of the federal party, that in ripping up the old foundation established by Washington and the sages of the convention, relative to our national elections, the design is . . . to proceed from striking out negros, to striking off from the list of voters all white men not possessed of property to a considerable amount. . . . He pays a poll-tax equal to the richest man, is taxed for faculty, works at highways, does military duty &c. &c. yet for all this he cannot be a freeman nor have a voice in his rulers, unless he owns considerable quantity of properly, paid for and entirely unencumbered.[17]

The contributor was prescient, but off by about a decade. Sensing political momentum was not in their favor, between 1813 and 1814 the Federalist-dominated Connecticut Assembly disenfranchised African Americans, required mortgage-free property to obtain franchise, and imposed fines for misrepresenting one's qualification to vote. These measures only reflected the Standing Order's increasingly tenuous position. Regional electoral development was advanced by the emergence of a more forward-looking and less status-conscious clergy.[18] Republicans finally won the Connecticut nomination battle in 1818, after which these elections were discarded. Reformers broke many of the remaining barriers, and Connecticut's Standing Order was rendered even less politically relevant by the adoption of the state's first constitution. This was more consequence than cause of underlying political and electoral changes. Finally, the Panic of 1819 and the simultaneous rise of Boston's "Middling Interest" ultimately removed the Federalist leaders from power in that city.[19] These political moments, while important, leave many open threads. New England simply presents a complex electoral setting.

House Election Returns and Markers of Electoral Development

Massachusetts counted the largest share of the region's population by far. In 1800 over half of New Englanders lived in Massachusetts. Further, the region's population was growing, albeit at a slower rate than the large Middle Atlantic states. In 1810 Massachusetts's population, not including Maine, was just over 472,000. The next largest New England state, Connecticut, counted just over 260,000 residents. By 1820 Massachusetts had nearly 525,000 inhabitants. Even accounting for Maine and Vermont statehood, nearly a third of New Englanders lived in Massachusetts, and Boston was the nation's fourth-largest city.

Table 5.1 presents the state populations, their estimated voting eligible populations, and apportionments.[20] New England's population exceeded a million and represented about 20 percent of the nation's potential electorate. There were differences in regional franchise. New Hampshire approached universal adult male suffrage. Massachusetts imposed property restrictions, but these were modest and were rendered more so over time because qualifications were in nominal rather than real values. Connecticut and, especially, Rhode Island, granted a more restrictive suffrage, but even here the large majority of white men could vote.

Massachusetts presents 246 complete district returns. The New Hampshire and Rhode Island state-level at-large votes are complete. Connecticut's nomination elections complicate assessing returns. The nomination election determined the congressional delegation through 1818. After the Republican victory that year, nomination elections ceased and the general election was decisive. There are eleven complete nomination election returns and twelve complete general election returns. The latter are not particularly interesting because Federalists swept the field through 1816 and Republicans did so afterwards.

The New England county returns, excluding Connecticut, are largely

Table 5.1. New England Population, Potential Electorate, and Apportionment, 1796–1824

	Congress			
State	*5th–7th*	*8th–12th*	*13th–17th*	*18th–19th*
Massachusetts				
Population	378,787	422,875	472,040	523,278
Electorate	111,200	126,200	154,900	123,200
Apportionment	14	17	20*	13
New Hampshire				
Population	141,885	183,858	214,460	244,161
Electorate	34,350	38,880	46,020	54,050
Apportionment	4	5	6	6
Connecticut				
Population	237,946	251,002	261,942	275,248
Electorate	51,900	53,600	57,000	62,100
Apportionment	7	7	7	6
Rhode Island				
Population	68,825	69,122	76,931	83,059
Electorate	13,400	14,100	16,200	18,100
Apportionment	2	2	2	2

complete. There are twenty-two Massachusetts counties including the nine that became part of Maine in 1820. Fifteen of these counties present complete returns for all election cycles. The remaining counties provide complete returns across several cycles. In total, there are 301 Massachusetts county-level returns.[21] There were five, and later six, New Hampshire counties. In 1805 New Hampshire created Coos County from the northern part of Grafton County in the Connecticut River Valley in the western part of the state.[22] New Hampshire is only missing county votes from 1796 and 1800. There are seventy-six complete New Hampshire county returns. Connecticut's six counties only provide returns from the Sixteenth through Nineteenth Congresses. While these thirty-two returns are useful, this presents a deficit in our knowledge of Connecticut's electoral development. At the other end of the spectrum, returns from Rhode Island's five historic counties are complete.

This chapter follows the same format as previous chapters: nominations and entry, elector turnout, party support, evidence of partisanship, and candidate entry and standing patterns. I then discuss the effects of

New England election methods on party fortunes. Collectively, these measures argue for the development of New England party-centered elections, albeit a development that proceeded at different paces in and across states.

Evidence of Effective Nominations

The historical record confirms that New England parties developed effective nominations in the first decade of the nineteenth century. New Hampshire had these by 1804.[23] That year the Republicans held a state convention attended by "a large number of gentlemen from various parts of the State."[24] The New Hampshire Federalists followed suit using a caucus system.[25] About the same time, the Massachusetts parties organized. The Massachusetts Republican central committee was based in Boston, but county and town committees made district-level nominations. The Federalists eventually organized a similar system for their nominations.[26] Connecticut's Democratic-Republican Party contested the nominations elections through 1810 by formally nominating candidates for House and other elections. For example, in 1804 a general caucus of Republicans produced and circulated nomination tickets for statewide elections.[27] This was not lost on the Federalists, who responded by increasing their organizational efforts. Rhode Island nominations never fully formalized. Formal nominations outside of the state legislature did not emerge until 1808. In that year the Republicans held a convention to nominate House candidates. This system continued through the era.[28] The Federalists embraced tradition and would only admit that nominees emerged through the "free consultation and extensive communication" among freemen.[29]

The Massachusetts nominations were effective. Recalling that there were 246 single-member district elections, the large majority of these saw one Democratic-Republican and one Federalist stand for election. The Federalists declined to contest fifteen elections while the Democratic-Republicans absented themselves from forty-five elections. If one considers the 162 elections in which both party's candidates received at least 5 percent of the vote, only eighteen saw a party overcrowd the field. When the Democratic-Republicans contested the district, the Federalists overcrowded the field five times. The corresponding figure for the Democratic-Republicans is three. The few failures to control entry is impressive in majority winner elections. This is because spoilers had greater incentives to join the race. If a tertiary candidate could prevent a first-round winner, it was possible he would win in a subsequent round. In Massachusetts multiple-round elections were rare, attesting to party ability to control entry.

The general ticket presents parties with a more complex problem. The rewards for effective nominations are greater because of the likelihood of an electoral sweep, but nominations are more challenging because of the larger number of candidates. Between 1796 and 1800 New Hampshire's apportionment was four, and most competitive candidates did not embrace a party label. In no election did each party field four and only four candidates. This changed after 1800. Between 1802 and 1810 New Hampshire's apportionment was five. Both parties stood the proper number of candidates in four of the five elections. The Democratic-Republicans overcrowded the field in 1802, and the Federalists did so in 1806. Table 5.2 shows the anomalous 1806 election vote returns. Here two noncompetitive Federalists, John Wheeler and Timothy Farrar, received hundreds of votes. These were not enough to make a difference. The Republicans had sufficient support to sweep the election even if the Federalist spoilers did not enter the race. Still, the election captures the difficulty of entry control in multi-seat constituencies. In 1812 New Hampshire's apportionment increased to six, and each party fielded precisely six candidates through 1816. The 1819 election to the Sixteenth Congress saw the Federalists stand six candidates while seven Democratic-Republicans received substantial numbers of votes. Few candidates were identified by party in the remainder of the period. Overall, New Hampshire elections between 1802 and 1820 demonstrate that the parties understood the importance of limiting ballot access and were usually capable of doing so.

Perhaps because Rhode Island party labels were less meaningful, the state presents more complex candidate entry patterns. The election of 1800 saw two Republicans and three Federalists receive votes, but one of the Federalists drew little support. Parties appear to better appreciate the value of limiting entry in the following election. The Federalists only overcrowd the field in 1806. By 1808 the parties appear to have mastered the process. A Federalist announcement published in the *Newport Mercury* on July 9 in anticipation of the August election presents the nominations of Richard Jackson and Elisha Potter for the Tenth Congress. Jackson was simultaneously nominated to fill the un-

Table 5.2. New Hampshire Election Returns, 1806 (winners in italics)

Within Party Finish Order	*Republican*	*Votes*	*Federalist*	*Votes*
1	*Jedediah K. Smith*	5,789	Samuel Tenney	3,637
2	*Clement Storer*	5,712	Caleb Ellis	3,626
3	*Francis Gardner*	5,693	David Hough	3,616
4	*Peter Carlton*	5,690	Thomas W. Thompson	2,840
5	*Daniel M. Durrell*	5,144	Silas Betton	2,826
6			John Wheeler	934
7			Timothy Farrar	798

expired term of Representative Nehemiah Knight, who had expired. The nominators, whomever they may be, assure readers that "the nominations are the result of free consultation and extensive communication throughout the state:—they are the unsolicited dictates of public opinion." The announcement concludes with an exhortation to vote, reminding electors that "the exercise of the right of suffrage, affords the only constitutional means of redress: and that redress, if we will be true to ourselves, and prompt, zealous and steady in our endeavors, is in our power." There's no way to confirm whether these nominations are the "unsolicited dictates of public opinion." However, the fact that the Federalists were compelled to present the nominations as springing from broad public opinion says much about the development of elections in even one of the most recalcitrant New England states.

The Connecticut nomination election was *the* election. Both parties presented scrums through 1810, after which the Republicans temporarily stopped contesting these elections. Until 1818 only Federalists advanced to the general election. Sensing their time had arrived, the Democratic-Republicans contested the 1818 nomination election and trounced the Federalists. Far more Republicans received votes in the subsequent general election than the apportionment would support, but the party easily swept all seats. Republican discipline increased in the last two cycles of the era as only as many candidates as seats available won significant numbers of general-election votes. The Democratic-Republicans stood slates in the final years of the first party era and won all the seats.

New England displays generally effective entry control. This is especially true for Massachusetts and New Hampshire. In a large majority of elections, only the proper number of candidates stood. This is impressive given these states required majorities to win, and three of the states elected their representatives at-large. Only parties can effectively limit the number of candidates to avoid overcrowding the field.

The Number of Electors and Turnout

The nature of New England party politics affected turnout across states. In this respect, the New England states differed greatly. New Hampshire and Massachusetts saw high levels of participation through much of the era. Massachusetts Republicans created a county-level machinery that included town "managers" whose responsibilities included identifying qualified electors, determining their likely partisanship, and getting sympathetic voters to the polls.[30] The raw number of Massachusetts and New Hampshire electors is impressive. At its peak just over 70,000 men voted in Massachusetts House elections. This means that a typical single-member district election counted between 2,000 and 3,500 men. Even low turnout elections saw respectable numbers of electors. In New Hampshire low turnout elections saw about 9,000 men vote while the high-turnout 1812 and 1814 elections each saw just shy of 35,000 electors.

Figure 5.1 displays the Massachusetts and New Hampshire turnout rates. Both states display the same general pattern. Turnout increased from 1800 to about 1816, then began a precipitous decline. New Hampshire turnout was consistently higher than Massachusetts. In some years it approached 80 percent of the potential electorate. Massachusetts's highest rate is closer to 50 percent of the potential electorate. At their post-1816 low points both states saw about one-fifth of their potential electorates cast ballots. These declines most certainly resulted from the collapse of party competition in the era's final years. For example, in 1818 New Hampshire candidates from both parties contested the election. In 1820 party labels were not attached to candidates, and turnout was half of that in the previous cycle. The northern New England states were competitive and their parties well-organized. Here, regardless of whether turnout was low or high, men of typical means dominated these polling places.

Rhode Island and Connecticut display modest levels of participa-

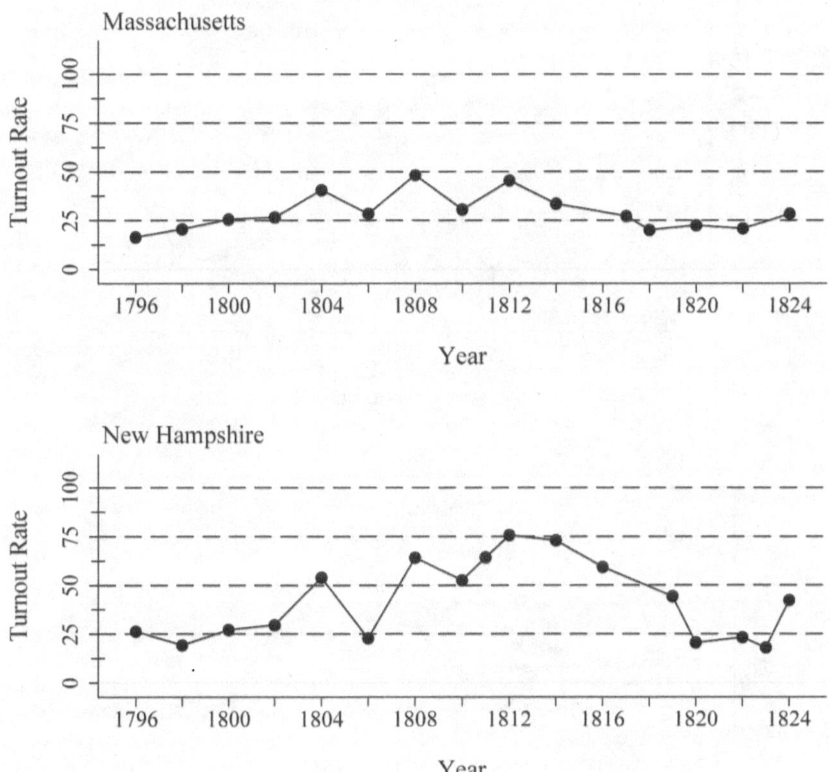

Figure 5.1. Massachusetts and New Hampshire: Turnout Rates

tion. This is not surprising. The southern New England states were dominated by powerful social orders and were less competitive. Rhode Island's small population, combined with a restrictive franchise, produced a limited potential electorate. The state clearly captured the effect of party competition on turnout. Rhode Island saw uncontested elections in 1804, 1816, 1818, 1822, and 1825. These elections display significant drops in turnout relative to the proximate contested elections. The 1804 election, for example, saw only a trifling 1,618 electors turn out to vote for the Republican ticket. The contested 1806 election saw twice as many electors because Federalists had a reason to vote. More generally, Rhode Island's contested elections typically saw about 5,000 men, or roughly a third of the potential electorate, cast votes. Indeed, between 1806 and 1814 Rhode Island turnout approached a

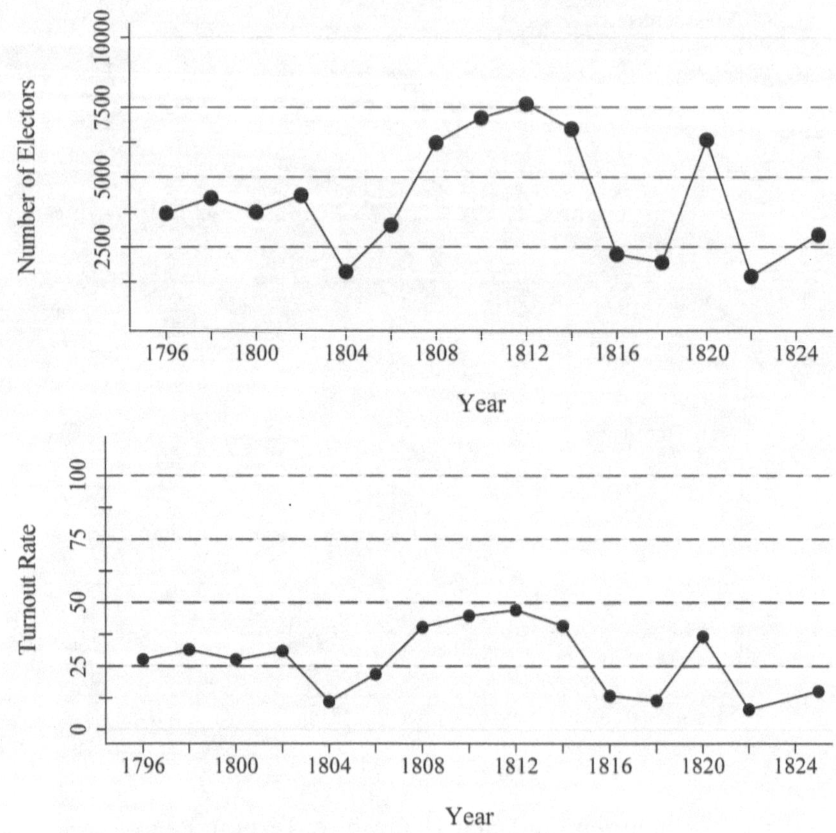

Figure 5.2. Rhode Island: Number of Electors and Turnout Rate

respectable 40 percent of the eligible electorate. The high point was in 1812, when just under half of the potential electorate, or approximately 7,600 men, voted. This high turnout captures the political agitation surrounding the War of 1812, which was declared two months earlier.

Connecticut raises the question of whether the relevant turnout figure is for the nomination election or the general election. Sometimes turnout was higher in nomination elections, and sometimes it was higher in the general election. Regardless, participation was always low in either election. Connecticut held eleven nomination elections through 1818. The returns for three general elections are missing.[31] This leaves eight cycles with complete returns for both the nomination and general election. These permit one to compare turnout in each type of election.[32] In both types of elections, turnout hovered in the 8–10 percent range of the potential electorate. Connecticut elections were not populated by typical men. In 1804 the Democratic-Republicans made a full-throttled effort to break the Federalist monopoly in nominations and won nearly 40 percent of the vote. This was not sufficient to advance any Republicans to the general election, but the effort motivated nearly a quarter of the potential electorate to vote. The general election with the highest turnout was in 1812, when 18 percent of the potential electorate voted. More generally, Connecticut's combination of nomination elections and one-party dominance guaranteed low turnout. While he is describing the twentieth-century American South, V. O. Key Jr. could have just as easily be charactering early Connecticut when he wrote that "since the primary determines the outcome, voters have no occasion to become excited about the general election."[33] The combination of a strong, elite order, at-large nominations, the standup law, and one-party dominance understandably discouraged Connecticut men from going to the polls.

Party Support

New England is thought of as the Federalist home. This is easy to understand. The Federalists won most of the House seats allocated to the New England states. It was New England Federalists that organized the infamous Hartford Convention to toy with the idea of regional succession in response to "Madison's War" and the perceived national dominance of the southern Democratic-Republicans. Not a single Connecticut Democratic-Republican was elected to Congress from 1796 through 1816, and the other states elected few Democratic-Republicans as well. Closer examination, however, reveals a more politically balanced and competitive region. Throughout the period the Democratic-Republicans won nearly 40 percent of the regional House seats. Republican strength resided in Maine, soon to be separated from parent state Massachusetts. In Massachusetts and New Hampshire, the Republicans won many elections, with each party enjoying clear bases of support. The state assemblies counted Federalists and Republicans, with neither party enjoying unchallenged supremacy. This balance and the partisanship that underlies it is captured in aggregate party support, ballots, and in the regional geography of support.

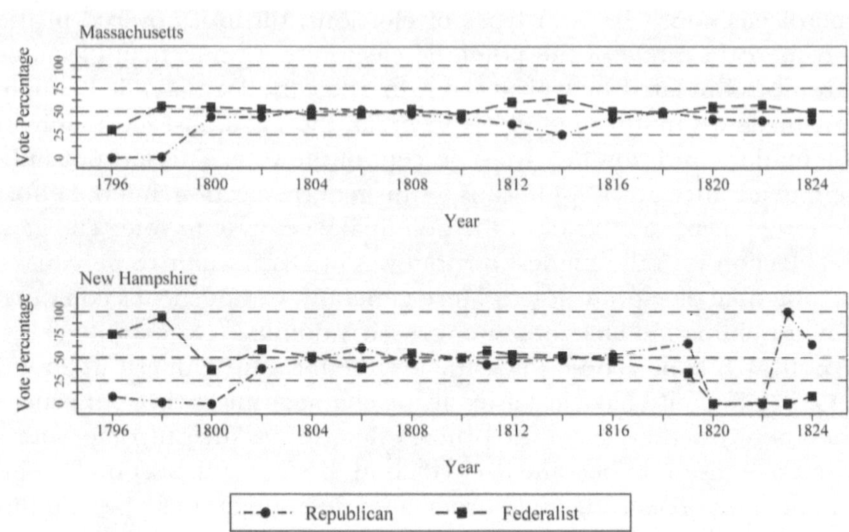

Figure 5.3. Massachusetts and New Hampshire: Aggregate Party Vote

AGGREGATE PARTY SUPPORT. Figure 5.3 presents the Massachusetts and New Hampshire aggregate party votes. To highlight how competitive these states were during the period, the figure graphs the aggregate vote from 1800 to 1820. In both states the Democratic-Republicans and Federalists competed on nearly equal terms for several election cycles. This is true in Massachusetts for much of the era. The only exception is the noticeable 1812 to 1814 disruption when the Republicans lost support. This is transient with the Republican vote rebounding in 1816. However, near parity in the aggregate vote does not necessarily translate to parity in seats. One way this can happen is that a party can win fewer districts by larger margins than its rival. This can result from population disparities across districts, gerrymandering, or other sources including geographic concentrations of support. New Hampshire maintained partisan parity from 1802 until 1818, after which the Federalist vote collapsed.[10] Here, the general ticket translates near partisan parity to electoral sweeps.

The early Connecticut nomination elections reveal a Democratic-Republican presence. The Democratic-Republicans were certainly the minor party, but their candidates won at least a quarter of the vote between 1802 and 1810. Thereafter, and especially in the wake of the War of 1812, it became clear that there was no Republican path to winning under the nomination system. The Democratic-Republicans simply deferred until their 1818 reemergence. The Rhode Island Democratic-Republican and Federalist Parties are evenly matched between 1806 and 1814. Both parties' vote shares range from over 40 percent to north of 50 percent across cycles. In 1816 the Republicans declined to field a ticket, while the Federalists followed suit in 1818. The Republicans were sure to win the 1820 election, which was contested only in the most perfunctory manner. The expected Democratic-Republican victory proved tempting to office seekers and attracted three Democratic-Republican candidates. The Republican Party's failure to control entry created a four-candidate contest that nearly cost it a House seat. Specifically, the fourth-place finisher, Republican Nathanial Hazard, received a significant number of votes that appear to have been siphoned from second-place Republican Samuel Eddy's tally. Eddy bested the third-place Federalist candidate, but only by a mere 118 votes out of over 11,000 cast.

The New England party vote presents two additional patterns. As in other regions, there is a post-1800 collapse of the "other" and nonaffiliated vote. Only rarely does this vote exceed 10 percent. In most states, most of the time it is in single digits. In Massachusetts the average party vote difference is about 16 percent across all years. In several cycles it is much closer. Between 1800 and 1810 the Federalists enjoyed about a seven-point advantage in the aggregate vote. This doubled in 1812 and 1814. In 1818 the Democratic-Republicans and Federalists ran even, while thereafter the Republican advantage was significantly larger. The New Hampshire Democratic-Republicans and Federalists competed on roughly equal terms between 1804 and 1816. Despite the perception of New England as a Federalist stronghold, the aggregate party vote was often close.

EVIDENCE OF PARTISANSHIP FROM BALLOTS AND GEOGRAPHY. Three New England states used the general ticket. However, Connecticut's elections, whether nominations or general, inform little about partisanship because these were one-party affairs. This focuses attention on Rhode Island and New Hampshire. Rhode Island is straightforward because it elected two representatives. Beginning with the Eighth Congress, the Rhode Island intraparty vote difference averaged about 1.5 percent. These differences are less than 1 percent in several cycles. The 1806 election is typical. In this year nearly 3,300 electors cast ballots.

The two Federalist candidates were separated by 27 votes while the two Republican candidates posted a difference of 164 votes. The tight Rhode Island intraparty vote spreads between 1802 and 1816 show that electors voted the ticket, and their propensity to do so was driven by these elections being contested.

New Hampshire presents a more robust test of partisan affiliation because electors cast five or six votes, depending on the apportionment cycle. The New Hampshire intraparty vote spreads were typically small and decreased as the era progressed. Recalling the 1806 returns presented in table 5.2, the Federalist top-to-bottom spread was 811 votes, or nearly 21 percent. The Democratic Republican figure is 645 votes, or about 13 percent. Such large differences are anomalous, especially as the era progressed. Recalling the 1816 return in table 1.1, the Federalist top-to-bottom difference is 123 votes, or less than 1 percent. The first-place Federalist, William Hale, and the last-place Federalist, Parker Noyes, received nearly equivalent votes. Likewise, the leading Republican, Josia Butler, received 15,569 votes while the sixth-place Republican candidate, Arthur Livermore, received only 338 fewer votes. The average New Hampshire intraparty vote differential between 1802 and 1810 is about 14 percent. This figure includes an anomalously large gap for the Republicans in 1802 (89 percent). The Federalists also had an unusually large vote gap in 1806 (29 percent). In contrast, the three elections between 1812 and 1816 typically saw only a few hundred votes separate leading and trailing party candidates. Only in 1819 did the parties again experience large intraparty vote differences.

Overall, New Hampshire ballots point to party organization and partisanship in the electorate. The parties ran slates, and electors voted the ticket. Most electors appear to have cast straight tickets. The within party top-to-bottom vote differences are ballot roll-off. This pattern required a few election cycles to emerge, and it weakened in the final years of the era. By 1820 the parties were under stress, and this is reflected in the larger gaps that emerge within the parties' votes. This is not surprising; the first party era was ending, and electoral coalitions were shifting.

The district and county-level returns reveal geographic patterns of party support and the stability of this support. This informs whether partisanship was present in the electorate. The regions, whether western Massachusetts or New Hampshire's Connecticut River Valley, differ from the coastal areas and its populated cities. The districts and counties present distinct economic and social foundations that shape partisanship. The regional political societies differ in their partisan attachments, just as they do in any age. That said, while geography indicates that partisanship resided in the electorate, it was more developed in some places than others. Again, the problem of ecological inference precludes stating with certainty that stability in geographic patterns of party support capture comparable stability in the individual-level vote, but as will be seen it is certainly suggestive.

Figure 5.4 maps the Massachusetts district vote. It displays four election cycles spanning the Tenth (1807–1809) to Seventeenth (1819–1821) Congresses. The shading represents Federalist support, but since the unaffiliated vote was typically modest, the maps capture the two-party vote. These show Federalist strength concentrated in the mid-state and northeast regions. This sharpens between the Thirteenth and Fourteenth Congresses, reflecting the party's strong 1812 showing. The Federalists owned the two districts that straddled Hampshire County. Here they won a combined twenty elections from the Eighth to the Seventeenth Congresses, typically by wide margins. The Federalists also won twenty-one of twenty-two elections in the two Worcester-area districts.

Several districts, whether competitive or not, displayed consistent levels of Federalist and Republican support. This indicates that each party enjoyed a core base of electors. Other Massachusetts districts were competitive. Bristol, south of Boston, was arguably the state's most competitive district. Here both parties averaged about 50 percent of the vote across several elections. Only rarely did either party's vote dip below 43 percent or exceed 57 percent. Some districts display gradual changes in the vote. The western district centered on Berkshire County, for example, was initially a Republican stronghold. However, it became more competitive as the era progressed and eventually saw the election of nonaffiliated candidates.[34]

The Massachusetts county vote provides more leverage in assessing partisanship. Seventeen of twenty-one counties saw at least seven contested elections between 1802 and 1820.[35] The Federalists enjoyed strong support in Massachusetts' northern tier. These counties included Cumberland, Essex, Hampshire, Suffolk, Washington, and Worcester Counties. Here the Federalist tally including elections the Republicans conceded is a combined seventy-two wins.[36] The Republicans did best in Middlesex, Norfolk, and Plymouth, and in Maine's Kennebeck River region.[37] Breaking down by apportionment cycles, between 1802 and 1810 the Republicans won the county vote in every election in Barn-

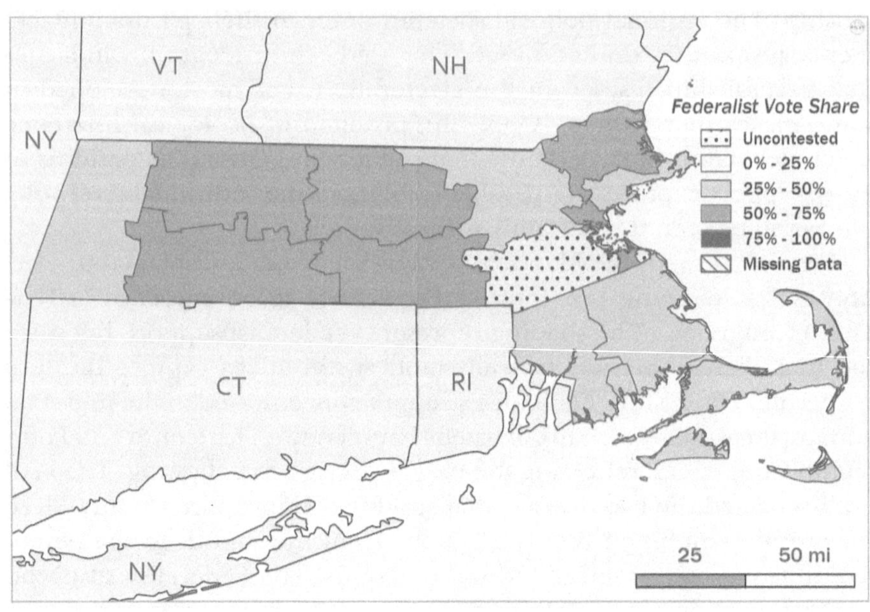

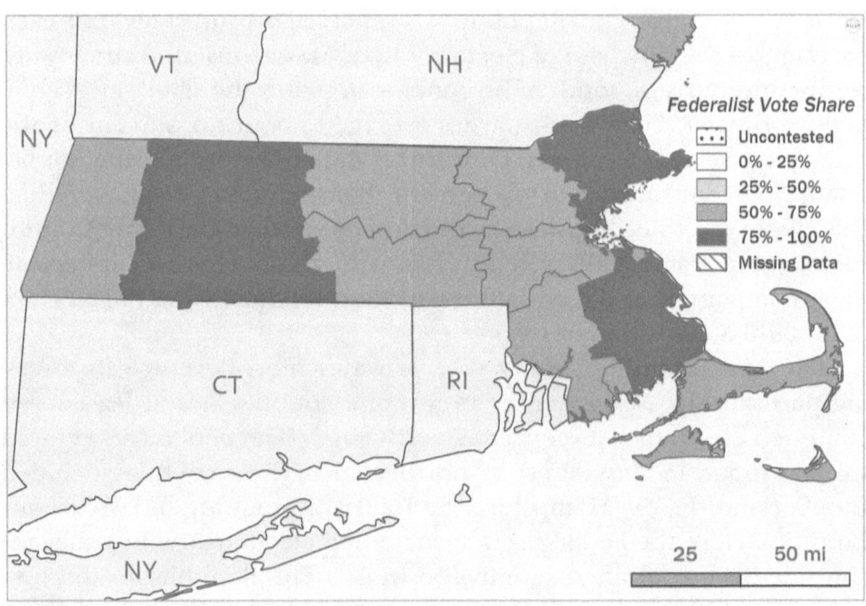

Figure 5.4. Massachusetts: District-Level Party Support in Tenth, Thirteenth, Fourteenth, and Seventeenth Congresses

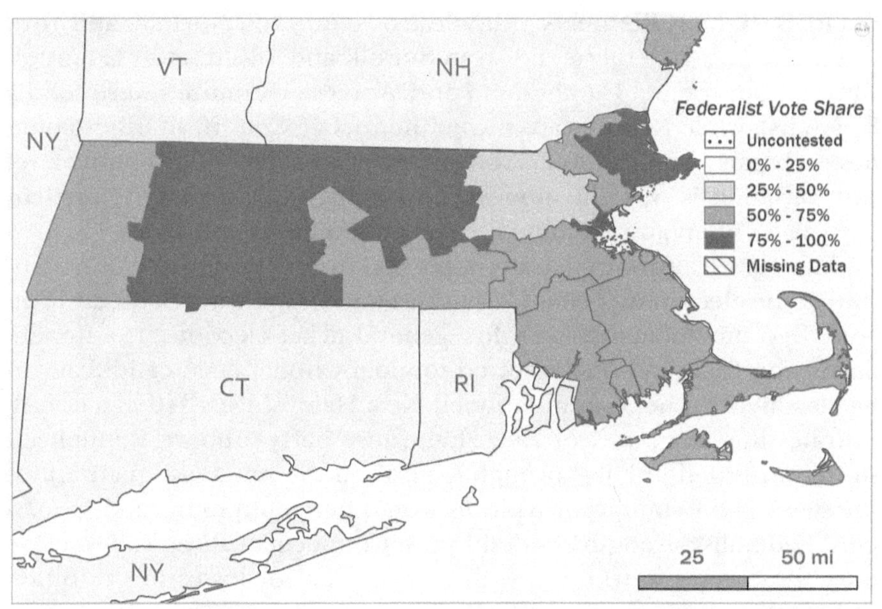
VT
NH
NY
Federalist Vote Share
Uncontested
0% - 25%
25% - 50%
50% - 75%
75% - 100%
Missing Data
CT
RI
NY
25
50 mi

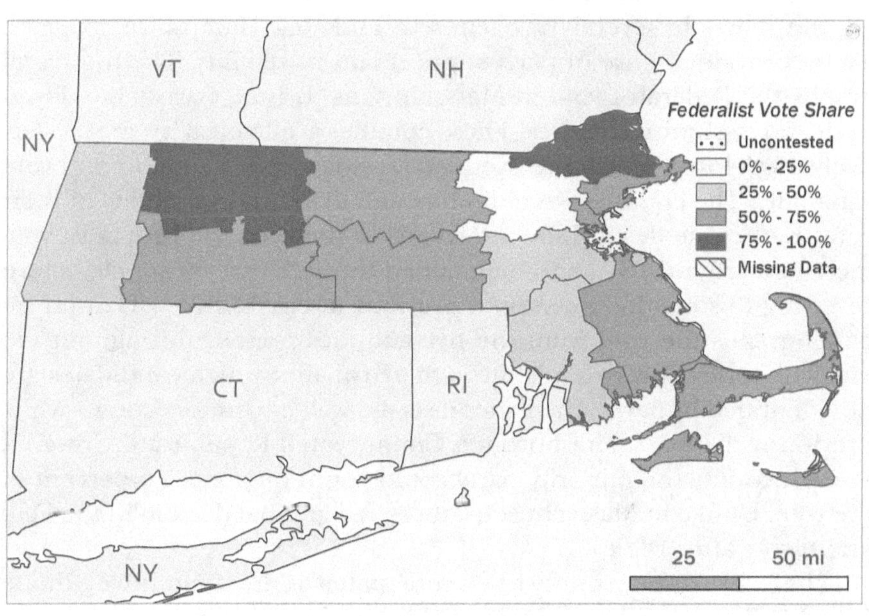
VT
NH
NY
Federalist Vote Share
Uncontested
0% - 25%
25% - 50%
50% - 75%
75% - 100%
Missing Data
CT
RI
NY
25
50 mi

stable, Berkshire, Kennebec, Middlesex, Nantucket, Norfolk, and York Counties. The Federalists did so in Suffolk and Washington Counties. Throughout the era Cumberland and Worcester Counties were solidly Federalist, while Republicans owned Kennebec County. In other counties each party won the vote at one point or another.[38] The county-level vote variation is typically modest. This helps explain why the median party votes often approximate the county-level wins and losses.

The New Hampshire county votes also display evidence of partisanship in the electorate.[39] New Hampshire was competitive. Between 1802 and 1820 the Federalists won five general ticket elections, the Republicans won four, and one featured too many nonaligned candidates to be classified.[40] The aforementioned New Hampshire 1816 election illustrates the geography of New Hampshire party support. Republican strength resided in Hillsborough County, in the southeast quadrant of the state. The Republicans typically won other counties by modest margins. Federalist strength resided in the Connecticut River Valley. However, these votes were too few to compensate for losses in the other, typically more populated, counties.

To further explore the county votes, figure 5.5 graphs the Federalist vote shares in several Massachusetts and New Hampshire counties. These provide a sense of party support and its stability. The top panel graphs the Federalist vote in Massachusetts' Bristol, Barnstable, Plymouth and Berkshire counties. These counties are "typical" in that collectively they closely match the overall county-level party support and vote variability. The counties were often competitive, and variability in their votes is often modest. There are trends in the vote; the Federalist vote increased around 1812 and maintained through the 1814 cycle before reverting to something closer to previous levels. The New Hampshire panel graphs the vote from the five counties present throughout the era. The series only extends through 1819, after which candidates are not identified by party. The Federalists did well in Grafton County while previously discussed Hillsborough County voted Republican. However, in each county the minority party could count on about 40 percent of the vote. Unlike in Massachusetts, there is a gradual decline in the Federalist vote after 1814.

There are even county-level vote patterns in diminutive Rhode Island.[41] These counties were established before the first party era and remained unchanged. Providence was the state's most populous county—and often its most electorally competitive. The Republicans

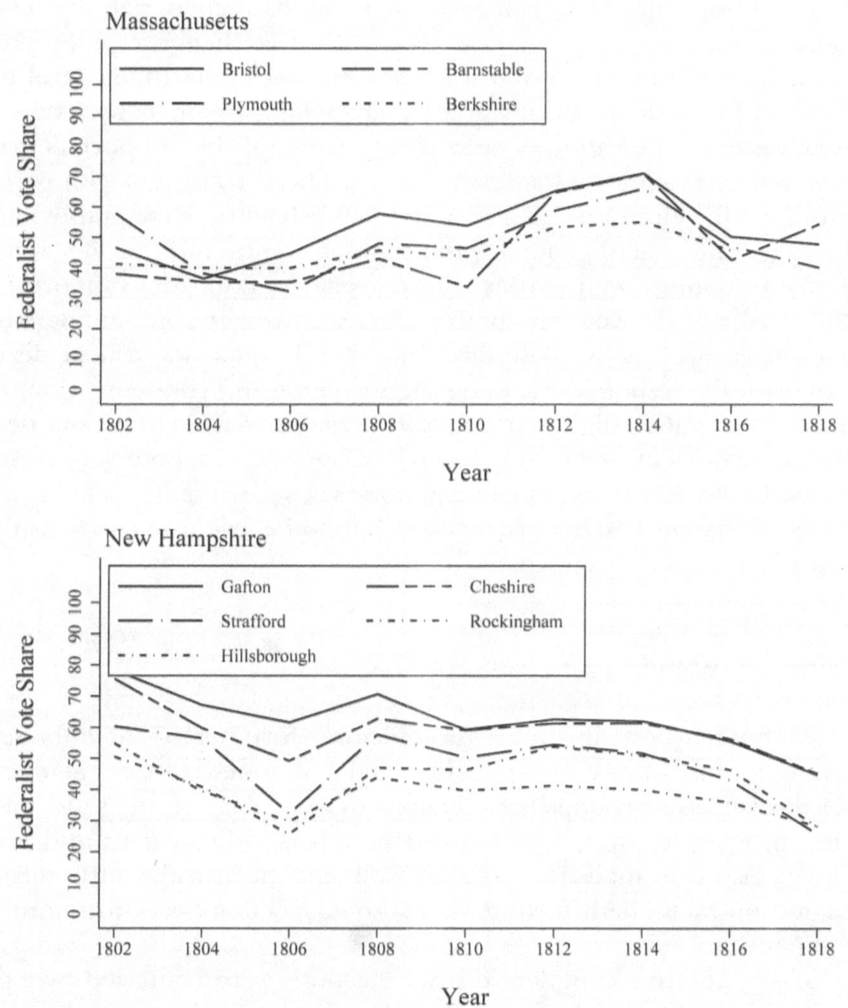

Figure 5.5. Massachusetts and New Hampshire: County Votes

were strongest in Bristol County while the Federalists did best in Kent and Washington Counties. The Washington County vote was less predictable. Bristol is on the eastern shore of Narragansett Bay, while Kent and Washington Counties form the southern border with Connecticut. That said, Rhode Island does not display the regional distinctiveness of New Hampshire; this is not unexpected given its size.

The most important feature of these series is their stability. The county-level votes, with few exceptions, did not change rapidly. The Massachusetts and New Hampshire parties' votes found their level by 1802, and experience mostly gradual changed through 1820. The series gives every indication of each party having reliable supporters that maintain their allegiance across elections. This is consistent with partisanship in the electorate. The second notable feature of the graphs and the aggregate vote in general is the competitiveness of these elections. In many counties both parties enjoyed reliable, nontrivial support. In Rhode Island, for example, both parties won respectable numbers of votes in each of its five counties. The 1810 election was a near dead heat, with the Republicans doing slightly better in Providence County and the Federalists slightly stronger in Kent and Washington Counties. The party votes in Bristol and Newport Counties were both very close. Rhode Island, like its regional neighbors, saw several quite competitive elections. Ballots and geography lead one to believe that partisanship resided in the New England electorate.

Patterns in Standing for Election and Reelection

Massachusetts best illustrates the electoral fortunes of incumbents. This is because of its large apportionment combined with single-member districts. New Hampshire elections were verdicts on the slate, and the outcomes cannot be easily attributed to individual candidates. This is also true for Rhode Island. Connecticut provides little information on incumbent fortunes because its elections were intramural competitions.

Massachusetts's complete district elections were contested by 244 unique candidates.[42] About half of these men stood once. Of those that won their first election, about 40 percent only stood once. However, when incumbents stood, they won about 80 percent of the time. Among those that lost their first election, over half declined to stand again. All of this means that in any given cycle, well over half of the seats were open. The 1806 election is fairly typical. These seventeen district elections featured eight incumbents. All won. Throughout the era only a handful of men stood four or more times, whether successfully or not. Among them, Republican Richard Cutts won five times in the district centered on York County, Maine. Likewise, Federalist

Samuel Taggert won six elections in the Hampshire South district near Springfield. Less successful was Republican physician Thomas Kittridge, who fought at the Battle of Bunker Hill. While this secured Kitteridge's place in history, his impressive résumé was less useful in House elections. Kittridge sought election six times between 1802 and 1814 and never won.[43]

New Hampshire and Rhode Island present similar patterns in standing and seeking reelection. There were eighty-eight unique New Hampshire candidates. Half of these candidates stood once. Of the remainder, twenty-six men stood three or more times. The competitiveness of New Hampshire elections meant that standing multiple times did not greatly enhance incumbent reelection success. Neither party won sufficient successive elections to insulate incumbents from being defeated after a couple of terms. Of the twenty-four incumbents that stood, over half were part of a losing ticket. The most successful incumbent as measured by successive wins was Federalist Abiel Foster, who was first elected in 1796, then reelected in 1798 and 1800.[44] The largest number of candidate wins, regardless of incumbency status, was three, an achievement shared by five men, both Republican and Federalist. Smaller Rhode Island saw twenty-six unique candidates, just under half of whom stood once. Nine men stood three times, but as in New Hampshire this was not necessarily a path to electoral success.[45]

Connecticut is more difficult to assess because of its nomination elections. Focusing on the general elections, these featured fifty-seven unique candidates. Twenty-six of these men stood once. Of the remainder, thirty-one stood two or more times, with a core of eight men that stood five or more times. These men were nearly unassailable, winning almost as often as they stood for office. This group included Benjamin Talmadge, the young nation's foremost Revolutionary War spy, and John Davenport Jr., who did nothing quite so swashbuckling but nonetheless was elected to Congress nine times. These electoral elite epitomized the political power of Connecticut's Standing Order.

The value of incumbency is best captured by Massachusetts elections contested in the two apportionment cycles between 1802 and 1820. In these years there were 175 observed House elections. Approximately half of these featured an incumbent. Approximately a quarter of the incumbents were defeated.[46] In 1804 there was an unusually large number of standing incumbents, eleven in total, and five lost. Four of the losing incumbents were Federalists. There are discernable patterns in incumbent defeats. The War of 1812 proved especially disadvantageous for Republicans, with four defeated.

Some years presented clear reasons for incumbents declining to seek reelection and for the defeats of those who stood. One of these is 1816, following passage of the Compensation Act, which established a congressional salary. Specifically, the act replaced the existing per diem system with a generous $1,500 annual salary. The House voted on the act on March 19, 1816, and the public backlash was harsh, especially for Federalists. Nineteen Massachusetts representatives voted, all but two of whom were Federalists. The delegation voted nearly unanimously in favor of the bill, with one nay and a handful of abstentions. Electors extracted their pound of flesh. Nine representatives declined to seek reelection. This may be partially accounted for by the brief congressional careers of the period, but there is good evidence that some declined to seek reelection because of their support of the bill.

Representative Timothy Pickering from the Essex South district provided such evidence. Pickering was an exceptionally prominent Federalist who held several important positions prior to serving in the House. He was President Washington's secretary of war, the nation's third secretary of state, and a US senator. He explained his decision to not seek reelection in a letter to the *Salem Gazette.* After reminding readers of his long public service and that he "was determined to serve the next two years if elected," he acknowledged that

> Two or three weeks ago . . . considerable dissatisfaction had manifested among some of my federal constituents, on account of my voting for what is called the "Compensation Law" which stipulated an annual salary of 1,500 dollars in place of the former compensation of five dollars a day to members of Congress. . . . Considering therefore, how nearly balanced was the federal by the opposite interest, in this district, I had concluded by public advertisement, to decline being a candidate.[47]

Pickering stood down to protect the Federalists in a competitive district. By voting for the bill, Pickering made his own defeat nearly inevitable. His instincts were right. The Democratic-Republicans won what should have been a safe Federalist district by the absurdly close margin of thirty votes out of the 2,866 that were cast. Of the ten Massachusetts incumbents that sought reelection, half were defeated. Only two Federalists who voted for the act were reelected. To place these figures in context, the previous election saw eleven Federalist incumbents seek reelection. One lost.[48] Two Massachusetts Republicans who voted for the act stood for election; one survived. The following year was also hard on Massachusetts incumbents when three of six, one Republican and two Federalists, were defeated.

The Massachusetts incumbency reelection rate, especially when interpreted along with the fortunes of regional general ticket slates, shows anything but a differential electorate. Incumbents enjoy electoral advantages, then as now. However, when the electorate is attuned to political issues or circumstances, voters could and did control their representatives. While any number of factors may contribute to forgoing reelection and electoral defeat, the numbers are far enough removed from the typical range as to provide evidence that incumbents were punished. This is not unique to Massachusetts; the five-point New Hampshire vote swing that removed the Federalists from power that same year likely owes to the same underlying source. Northern New England electors were prepared to clean house when the occasion merited it.

Leveraging Electoral Rules for Partisan Advantage

Gerrymandering is by far the best-known party-advantaging election process. The practice's name derives from Massachusetts governor Elbridge Gerry and the March 1812 election law that districted in a manner that bears his name. The law created a Boston-area senate district that advantaged Democratic-Republicans. It also affected House elections by dividing towns in a manner that manipulated districts.[49] One such instance centered on the town of Malden and raised the question of whether it was in the Middlesex district or the Essex South district. This confusion caused an "unfortunate blunder" when Malden Federalists voted for William Reed even though he stood in another district. Federalist electors were unaware that "Malden had been Gerrymandered into the Essex South District . . . and under that conviction they gave sixty votes for the Hon. Mr. Reed."[50] This misunderstanding gave Reed nearly sixty votes in a district that he did not contest and cost him votes in the district that he did contest. The error had little effect; the Republicans won Middlesex by a couple of hundred votes, and Reed won Essex South by an even larger margin. Despite having little tangible effect, the election shows that in an age when we tend to think electoral politics was more honorable, the Democratic-Republicans were none too anxious to correct the Federalist misunderstanding of the district boundaries. The districting law was quickly repealed, but gerrymandering remained a staple of Massachusetts politics through the rest of the era.[51] The practice did not originate or reach its fullest potential in Massachusetts, but New England is gerrymandering's spiritual home.

No state exhibited the effect of election rules on party fortunes more than Connecticut. Connecticut's nomination system was properly described as "rigged."[52] It simply eliminated the Republicans from the general election—this despite Republican candidates winning roughly one-third of the nomination votes between 1802 and 1810. These votes were never enough to advance Republicans to the general election. The returns show that a substantial number of Connecticut electors voted Democratic-Republican under what would have been immense scrutiny and with full knowledge that they would not be rewarded with House seats. The effect of the nomination system can be further seen by comparison to gubernatorial and statehouse elections. These reveal the Federalists were the dominant party, but there was some level of party competition. For example, the 1807 gubernatorial election saw multiterm incumbent Federalist Johnathan Trumbull defeat Republican William Hart with 60 percent of nearly 20,000 votes. In their 1808 rematch Trumbull defeated Hart by nearly the same ratio, but with about 1,500 more votes cast. Republican presence is also felt in the statehouse. Assembly elections between 1802 and 1816 saw the Republicans typically win about sixty of the approximately 200 seats. Some towns, including Lichfield, Fairfield, Danbury, and Newtown, hosted competitive elections.[53] The Republicans gained control of the Assembly in 1817, after which the electoral universe and the rules that supported it changed. The Republicans dominated Connecticut through the rest of the era.

The New Hampshire general ticket further demonstrates how vote aggregation rules can magnify the leading party's seat advantage. Between 1802 and 1819 the Federalists won five cycles, with an average vote share of 54.4 percent. They claimed every seat. In the same period the Republicans won three cycles, with an average vote share of 60 percent, again taking all the seats. Only the 1810 election, which was a virtual tie and went two rounds, produced a split delegation. The system disadvantaged the Federalists later in the era in part because New Hampshire's most populous counties, Rockingham and Hillsborough, leaned Republican, outweighing Federalist strength in less populated Cheshire and Grafton Counties.[54] This regional support indicates that

Table 5.3. New England: Effects of Electoral Rules, Eighth–Seventeenth Congresses

	1802–1810 (8th–12th Congresses)		1812–1820 (13th–17th Congresses)	
	Votes	*Seats*	*Votes*	*Seats*
New Hampshire				
Republican	220,416	9	373,619	18
Federalist	236,224	16	345,280	12
Other	1,812	0	67,887	0
Massachusetts				
Republican	115318	44	86,411	33
Federalist	118526	41	130,778	60
Other	6,375	0	13,536	0
Rhode Island				
Republican	24,707	6	24,564	4
Federalist	20,188	4	23,585	6
Other	382	0	77	0
Connecticut				
Republican	401,521	0	177,244	7
Federalist	890,270	35	491,093	21
Other	2,325	0	26,665	0

the state would have elected at least some mixed House delegations if the state had districted in a manner that respected county lines.

To more clearly see the effects of vote aggregation methods, table 5.3 displays the regional votes-to-seats translations. It shows the votes for each party in the two apportionment cycles and the number of seats each party won. The Massachusetts single-member district system is well-balanced throughout the era, with the party vote shares and seat shares matching well. The Federalists continued to win in northern and western Essex, Franklin, Hampden, Hampshire, and Worcester Counties, which remained in the Federalist camp until the Age of Jackson. Rhode Island also presents votes-to-seats translations that are roughly in alignment, although the Federalists win more seats that the Democratic-Republicans on slightly fewer votes over the second apportionment cycle. As expected, the New Hampshire general ticket translates modest majorities in the popular support to noticeable advantages in seats. Connecticut is in a class by itself. For most of the era, Republican votes are nearly meaningless, despite their sometimes respectable showings in early nomination elections. The large drop-off in Republican support in the second decade of the cycle reflects the party conceding elections until its 1818 resurgence. The table shows that the Land of Steady Habits was not as stable and reliably Federalist as supposed. The rules ensured stability of result.

The New England rules of the game affected party competitiveness and incentives to contest elections. Over the course of two decades, the effects of the rules tend to balance out, although this is surely cold comfort to the losing party in any given election cycle.

Conclusion

New England is central to the American storybook of republican government. In this understanding, freemen gathered at Congregationalist churches, taverns, and other places to express their political views and engage in self-government. This is only partially true. New England's governing elite consisted of gentlemen, ministers, and descendants of the old families. They did not give up power easily. However, there was an inexorable movement to party-structured elections and large-scale participation.

House of Representatives returns display this transition. The House returns point to effective, party-structured nominations. This is present in the hundreds of Massachusetts single-member district elections and in the New Hampshire general-ticket returns. The parties typically fielded the correct number of candidates given the available seats and the rules in force. Effective nominations gained less traction in Rhode Island, and none in Connecticut. Connecticut elites adopted election rules and processes to prevent change. Nomination elections, the Stand-up Law, and other restrictions protected the ruling elite, at least for a while. These laws, however, were intentionally created because of the rise of party politics and, in particular, the potential for a viable Republican opposition.

New England often saw high elector turnout and even low turnout elections display respectable levels of participation. These states, excluding Connecticut, display a similar pattern: turnout typically increased from 1800 to 1804, became stable and high from 1806 to 1816, and then declined. More importantly, the number of men voting often numbered in the tens of thousands. The state electorates were comprised primarily of men of average means. Whether at the county, district, or state level, party-organized elections engaged large numbers of electors.

The party vote was often competitive. This is seen in the numbers of votes received by each party across apportionment cycles. Vote margins were tight in New Hampshire from 1802 to 1816 and in Massachusetts throughout the era except for the short-lived Republican decline owing to the War of 1812. Rhode Island had competitive House elections between 1806 and 1812. The few futile attempts by Connecticut Democratic-Republicans to contest the nomination election demonstrates they had nontrivial popular support. This never materialized in the general elections, from which they were excluded by design. Multicandidate ballots and the geography of support argue that partisanship resided in the New England electorate. New Hampshire's general-ticket returns display ballot discipline. By 1808 the typical within party vote difference was quite small. Affiliated voters looked to nominated lists and voted the ticket.

The partisan electorate thesis is further supported by the geography of party support. The Federalists and Democratic-Republicans boasted concentrated support in some areas and less support in other areas. In Massachusetts the Federalists fared best in the midstate region and in the far northeast. Republicans did well elsewhere, while other districts were competitive. New Hampshire's Connecticut River Valley tended Federalist. Even Rhode Island reveals geographic patterns in party support. The regional voting patterns are sufficiently stable, and the social and economic foundations of the various areas sufficiently distinct, for one to conclude that partisan affiliation shaped the vote. This combined with high turnout argues for a partisan electorate.

Nowhere are the effects of voting processes more pronounced than Connecticut. Its nomination elections precluded meaningful party competition through 1816, after which the Republicans took charge of elections. Early Federalist domination does not owe entirely to their support on the ground. Connecticut's Standing Order relied on election processes to ensure their stranglehold on House elections. New Hampshire's general ticket also shaped the parties and their ability to elect representatives. Had New Hampshire districted, both parties would have elected representatives in most elections. However, New Hampshire was competitive, and both parties fielded competitive tickets, perhaps in the hope that organization and the political winds would work in their favor.

New England displays the transition to party-organized elections early in the nineteenth century. This development is slower than in the border and Middle Atlantic states. While the full features of Jacksonian electoral politics would not emerge for several years, New England elections bear stronger resemblance to these elections than the "deferential-participant" politics of the colonial period and the republic's first years. New England elections were maturing.

6 | The South

This chapter assesses electoral development in Virginia, North Carolina, South Carolina, and Georgia. The first three states elected their representatives from single-member districts. Georgia used the general ticket to elect its representatives. The South displays signs of electoral development, but this lagged other regions. Southern parties were slower to develop, and the old style of political leadership by elites and established families remained entrenched longer. Elites affiliated with the parties and advocated for them. They often did so, however, in their personal capacity and in a manner that preserved features of the old style of politics. Men often stood for office rather than sought office, and their "friends" worked for their election. Still, the South, or at least parts of it, display movement toward recognizably developed elections.

There are several reasons why southern electoral development was slower than in other regions. One is the distribution of wealth. Inequality contributes to political friction that manifests in party politics. Nationally, wealth was concentrated in the more established areas, and here resided the greatest income and wealth inequalities. The least economic inequality was in the "hinterlands."[1] A larger proportion of southern potential electorate lived in the hinterlands.[2] Southern inequality in and near towns and cities was greater than other regions, but there were fewer of these in the South. Further, southern wealth was deeply tied to slavery, which created a class of elites to whom deference was culturally slow to dissipate. An equally if not more important reason for slower southern party development was the lack of statewide elected offices. Gubernatorial elections were unknown. In all states the legislature selected the governor, and these governors enjoyed few powers. South Carolina and Georgia used the same method to select presidential electors.[3] A driving force for party organization was the need for statewide coordination of like-minded elites and electors. There was less to coordinate around in the South. This localized elections and slowed the development of mass parties.

This preamble on southern party development notwithstanding, the strongest version of the southern late development thesis is misleading. Parties and party-organized elections did emerge and develop. For example, in 1800, Virginia Democratic-Republicans created a Richmond-based standing committee and affiliated county committees. Virginia boasted twenty-one newspapers in the early nineteenth century. These were almost evenly divided between Republican and Federalist affiliation. As elsewhere, political issues shaped southern party development and competition. The unpopular 1807 Embargo Act energized southern Federalists from a Jeffersonian-induced lethargy. Its repeal did little to taper their efforts. Dissatisfaction with Republican management of the War of 1812 furthered Federalist fortunes, at least initially.[4] The downstream effects of the Hartford Convention were not particularly detrimental to southern Federalists, as none attended the meeting. Overall, one witnesses an emergence of political organization and party competition that reached its peak between about 1806 and 1816.

Southern politicking was well known and often quite creative. As elsewhere, the Republicans were the first to openly embrace electioneering. The Federalists soon became adept at these practices as well. Two essays published in period broadsheets illustrate this creativity and, more importantly, the substantive party politics that underlies regional electoral development. The first, published under the title "Strange Things," appeared in the *Alexandria Gazette* on April 3, 1810.[5] In it the unknown author details an extensive catalog of "strange things" including that "nominal Republicans fall in love with Hamilton schemes of banking" and "the majority in Congress can look at each other for three or FOUR months, meet, adjourn, pick the people's pockets, and do—nothing—without blushing for their degeneracy." The essay concludes with an exhortation that "democrats, at the next election, change the whole representation, excepting . . . thirty or forty members of the house of representatives—Nothing else can save the county, than the election of men of talents by the democratic party." Even in the first party era there were RINOs; Republicans in Name Only.

Perhaps less creative, but equally sincere, is "Cowpen's" letter to the Democratic-Republican Charleston *City Gazette.* The Charleston district was often competitive, with both Democratic-Republicans and Federalists winning here over the years. Cowpens, a self-described "plain unlearned man" who must "labor daily for my substance" and "cannot be expected to be elegant in diction," quite eloquently attacks the "enlightened" editor of the Federalist *Charleston Courier.* He presses hard, charging that the editor "apostatized from the republican cause." Cowpens asks why he previously considered W. L. Smith, Esq. the only person "fit to represent us in Congress," but has now "taken up another," one Mr. Lowndes, "in his stead"?[6] This change, Cowpens charges, reveals the "inconsistency of the [Federalist] party, and how little dependence is to be put in anything that comes from [it]." Worse, Cowpens alleges this change was made for "pecuniary" reasons. Cowpens reminds his fellow Republicans that regardless of the opposing Federalist candidate, "we have a candidate of our own, who is known to be firm, consistent, and truly patriotic, who has ever supported the genuine character of a true American . . . ROBERT MARION, the genuine republican."[7] Finally, Cowpens admonishes Democratic-Republicans to "sleep not, lest the enemy, thro' your apathy, gain an ascendancy, and a victory over you." One cannot know how much influence Cowpens's letter had on the election, but the Republican incumbent Robert Marion defeated Federalist Thomas Lowndes quite handily.

Southern Democratic-Republicans were not always in lockstep. This is evident in the case of "Madison's War." For example, Edwin Gray from Virginia's James River region, who served seven congressional terms including in the fateful years of 1812–1813, opposed the war and explained his opposition in a lengthy essay in the *Alexandria Gazette* that excoriated Democratic-Republican war efforts and defended his own congressional actions. In it he accused the Democrat-Republicans of hypocrisy in opposing Adams's efforts to establish a viable military but being now perfectly willing to burden their constituents with millions of dollars in taxes for a war with Great Britian. He doubted the United States had the military capacity to achieve its objectives, which allegedly included "taking possession of Canada." Gray knew that his opposition would likely cost his congressional seat. As such, he closed, "In addressing you now perhaps for the last time, I cannot forebear to the unfeigned sense of gratitude to those who have for fourteen years reposed their confidence in me—the impression on my heart will remain to the end of my life." In 1813 Gray lost decidedly to a fellow Republican, and the impression on his heart faded a few years later.[8]

While the South may have been Republican territory, Federalists held their own in several places. This is reflected in sometimes vigorous efforts to win House seats. For example, in 1813 Federalists contested sixteen Virginia districts in the elections to the Thirteenth Congress and won seven.[9] North Carolina was seen as so far removed from national political, economic, and social changes that it was given the derisive moniker "the Rip Van Winkle State." This characterization was more appearance than reality. North Carolina's elections to the Eleventh Congress present complete returns for eleven of twelve districts. Four of these were contested by one Federalist and one Democratic-Republican. Two were competitive. Overall, the Federalists won four seats. Importantly, North Carolina men turned out to vote. District turnout averaged nearly 4,300 electors, with over 5,400 men voting in one district. In 1813 the Federalists contested nine of North Carolina's thirteen districts and won four of them. The Federalists would have won five districts had they controlled entry in the western Thirteenth District. Here the combined vote of the two Federalist candidates out-polled the single Democratic-Republican by a wide margin, but internecine conflict cost the Federalists the seat. Federalist performance in the following cycle was comparable. South Carolina too shows signs of party competition.

None of this is to suggest that southern electoral development matched that in other regions. It did not. Its parties were less developed and less geographically extensive, and this situation lasted longer than elsewhere. There were, however, "hints" of development.[10] Party organization emerged in coastal areas such as Wilmington, but it struggled to reach other areas. The parties remained indistinct in the state interiors, at least early in the period.[11] Indeed, the sharpest political divisions tended to be between the coastal and established areas, in opposition to the western regions.[12] But neither was southern electoral development stagnant. Southern elections developed in their own pace and in their own way, but they developed. Recalling Virginian Henry Lee Jr.'s appeal to Virginia voters that concluded the second chapter, even in the South the old ways were passing.

House Elections and Markers of Electoral Development

As in previous chapters, this chapter uses district and county votes to evaluate markers of electoral development. These include nominations and entry, voter turnout, party support and evidence of partisanship, incumbency standing, and election patterns. I do not separate discussions of aggregate party support from partisanship as revealed by geography and multicandidate ballots. This is because there are fewer southern returns and only Georgia used the general ticket. I also present less

Table 6.1. Southern Population, Potential Electorate, and Apportionment, 1796–1824

	Congress			
State	*5th–7th*	*8th–12th*	*13th–17th*	*18th–19th*
Virginia				
Population	827,164	880,200	983,152	1,075,069
Electorate	98,900	104,800	116,000	129,300
Apportionment	19	22	23	22
North Carolina				
Population	444,362	478,103	556,526	638,829
Electorate	62,000	67,100	74,700	83,900
Apportionment	10	12	13	13
South Carolina				
Population	306,984	345,591	415,115	502,741
Electorate	34,600	39,200	43,400	48,900
Apportionment	6	8	9	9
Georgia				
Population	130,631	162,686	251,407	340,989
Electorate	16,300	21,900	30,800	44,600
Apportionment	2	4	6	7

discussion of parties using election methods for advantage, as this not as evident in the South. This is in part because, as will be seen, the fewer available southern returns make inferences on this question more tenuous. There is, however, evidence that Virginians districted for partisan advantage in some years.[13] The presence of gerrymandering in early Virginia should not be surprising, as demonstrated by the Monroe and Madison election to the First Congress.

To provide context, table 6.1 presents the state populations, their estimated voting-eligible populations, and their apportionments.

The figures obscure the large numbers of enslaved persons and their importance in understanding regional electoral development. The enslaved account for anywhere from a third to nearly half of the state populations. For example, in 1810 Virginia counted nearly 400,000 enslaved men, women, and children. Simply, 40 percent of Virginians were enslaved. The 105,000 enslaved Georgians account for 42 percent of the state's population. South Carolina's 169,000 enslaved people comprise nearly half of the state's population. About the same number of North Carolinians were enslaved, accounting for about 30 percent of the state's population.[14] This places the eligible electorates in clearer, but solemn, relief. Relative to other regions, the enfranchised are a smaller percentage of the state populations because of slavery. Slavery enters the discussion of southern electoral development in two ways. The first is the relationship between slavery and election turnout. Here one can ask whether areas of the state with greater or lesser enslaved populations participate at different rates. The second centers on the relationship between slavery and party support. Recall that this question was briefly explored in the chapter on the border states. The findings there were somewhat surprising in that the largest slaveholding counties were either more likely to vote Federalist or presented no discernible patterns. This chapter explores the question further because of slavery's centrality to the southern political economy. The southern counties provide leverage for understanding the implications of slavery for regional electoral development.

Virginia contained nearly half of the southern potential electorate. In 1810, for example, Virginia's free, almost entirely white, population was approximately 590,600. Just under one-fifth of this population was eligible to vote. By way of comparison, Georgia, which had nearly universal white male suffrage, presented a potential electorate that was a fraction of this number.[15] The Carolinas figures are similar. By the early 1820s some of the Virginia size advantage relative to the rest of the South narrowed. Still, culturally and in terms of its electorate, Virginia enjoyed an outsized influence on the southern political landscape.

Relative to other regions, there is a greater percentage of missing southern returns. While the extent of missing returns differs by state, it is not uncommon for only about half of all possible returns to be present. For example, between the Fifth and Nineteenth Congresses Virginia hosted 323 House elections. There are complete returns for 133 of these elections. Combined, the southern states present over 300 complete returns. The presence of hundreds of district-level returns is not inconsequential, but it increases the importance of the county-level returns for understanding regional electoral development. For this reason, the following discussion relies more heavily on the county returns than in other regions.

Table 6.2 displays each state's available district and county returns. The number of Virginia, North Carolina, and South Carolina district elections in any year is simply its apportionment. Virginia district returns are spotty. In the 1802–1810 apportionment cycle, for example,

Table 6.2. Complete District and County Election Returns

	Congress							
	5th–7th Returns		*8th–12th Returns*		*13th–17th Returns*		*18th–19th Returns*	
State	*District*	*County*	*District*	*County*	*District*	*County*	*District*	*County*
Virginia	21	102	35	184	55	237	22	107
North Carolina	21	96	47	239	44	201	21	95
South Carolina	14	29	22	0	20	2	13	0
Georgia	-NA-	65	-NA-	109	-NA-	112	-NA-	46

Virginia hosted 110 district elections; thirty-five of these returns are present. This is partially ameliorated by the 184 available county returns. North and South Carolina district returns are mostly available. North Carolina's returns are complete for 158 of 181 elections. The South Carolina figures are 100 out of 121 elections. Georgia used the general ticket, and these returns are complete.

The counties fill in many gaps left by missing district returns. These can be matched with the census to obtain estimates of turnout rates. The counties also provide a more fine-grained view of the geographic distribution of party support. Since districts are typically formed by counties, even if a district return is incomplete, one or more of its county returns may be complete. For example, in 1805 Virginia had ninety counties. The Eleventh District, southeast of the Rappahannock River, was comprised of four counties: Caroline, Essex, King and Queen, and King William. Only the Essex County return is complete. While just one county, Essex provides valuable information on this region. In this year the returns from thirty-six counties are present. From the Fifth to Nineteenth Congresses, there are 630 complete Virginia county-level election returns. North Carolina and Georgia also present hundreds of county returns. This is not true for South Carolina, which recorded votes by parish. There are very few South Carolina county returns.[16]

Evidence of Effective Nominations

In early southern elections, self-nominations remained common, as was nomination decided by gentlemen meeting in private.[17] As the era progressed, semiformal nominations emerged. Nomination announcements often came with the imprimatur of popular participation. Figure 6.1 displays nomination announcements from Virginia and South Carolina, respectively. For example, in Jefferson County, Virginia, in early 1811, Republicans called on fellow Democratic-Republicans to nominate a congressional candidate.[18] At a February 12 meeting following "public notice," Republican men met in a private residence to select nominees for the US House of Representatives, state senate, and assembly.[19] It is difficult to know the extent to which this meeting was truly "open." However, the Charles Town (Virginia) *Farmer's Repository* suggests it was. The *Repository* published the meeting's outcome that "a

CHARLES-TOWN, February 15.

In consequence of the badness of the roads we were unable to procure paper of the usual size for our whole publication this week.

At a meeting of a number of republicans of the county of Jefferson, on the 12th day of Feb. 1811, at the house of Henry Haines, in Charles-Town, (agreeable to public notice) for the purpose of nominating a fit person as a candidate, at the next election for a member, to represent this district in the next Congress of the United States—A fit person as a candidate at the next election for a Senator to represent this Senatorial district in the Senate of Virginia—And two fit persons as candidates at the next election for members to represent this county, in the next General Assembly of Virginia—John Dixon, Chairman, Robert C. Lee, Secretary.

On motion,

Resolved unanimously, That *Daniel Morgan*, Esq. of Jefferson county, be nominated as a fit person as a candidate at the next election for a member to represent this district in Congress.

Resolved unanimously, That *Charles Brent*, Esq. of Frederick, be nominated as a fit person, as a candidate, at the next election for a Senator, to represent this district in the Senate of Virginia.

Resolved unanimously, That *Jacob H. Manning* and *William P. Flood*, Esquires, be nominated as two fit persons, as candidates, at the next election for members to represent this county in the General Assembly of Virginia.

Resolved, That the proceedings of this meeting be published in the Farmers Repository.

JOHN DIXON,
ROBERT C. LEE.

Figure 6.1A. Southern Nomination Announcements.

number of republicans" unanimously nominated Daniel Morgan as "fit person" to stand for the House seat. Morgan was an experienced candidate who served several terms in the House of Delegates. However, fortune was not with him, as he lost to Federalist John Baker. Similarly, in 1812 a Charleston, South Carolina, circular announced that Federalist delegates nominated John Rutledge for Congress. The circular takes pains to assure readers that the attendees included representatives from the different wards of the city, indicating that it was not simply a cabal of a few leading men. It was not a good year for Federalists, and Rutledge lost badly. Still, he was the only Federalist to receive votes. This provides evidence that the nomination was effective, and the committee exerted their "best endevours . . . in promoting his election."

The returns show that these and similar nominations and endorsements were generally effective. Of the 360 southern single-member district elections for which we have complete returns, the Republicans contested 320, and Federalist candidates contested 229. In total, 218 elections were contested by candidates from both parties. Ninety-three of these elections were in Virginia. Each party fielded precisely one candidate nearly 80 percent of the time. When more than one Republican or Federalist stood, it was usually because the other party did not contest the election. In Virginia two or more Republicans stood in thirty-five elections, for example, but only eight of these saw a Federalist opponent. North Carolina Federalists conceded forty-eight elections, while the Republicans declined to contest twenty-five elections. In the remaining seventy-eight elections each party fielded precisely one candidate in fifty-six of these contests. Of South Carolina's sixty-nine observed district elections, forty were contested by both parties. Of these, just over half—twenty-four, to be precise—saw one Federalist candidate and one Democratic-Republican candidate. Although the missing returns make inferences tenuous, entry control appears noticeably better in Virginia and North Carolina than in South Carolina.

Regardless of whether nominations were determined in the parlors of the leading citizens or in formal, open meetings, the returns show that southerners understood the importance of limiting candidate entry. These efforts were often successful, but not as effective as in other regions. Overall, in all southern single-member districts contested by both parties, nearly three-quarters of these elections saw precisely one candidate from each party. Georgia general-ticket elections are harder to assess. This is because, as will be seen, these had less partisan identity

CIRCULAR,

Charleston, Sept. 24th, 1812.

SIR—At a meeting of Delagates, representing the *Federal Republicans*, in the different Wards, of this City and Neck; for the purpose of taking into consideration, the expediency of nominating and supporting a candidate, to represent the election District of Charleston, at the ensuing election, in the Congress of the United States, it was resolved by the meeting, to support Colonel JOHN RUTLEDGE; whose public service, talents, and political sentiments, are well known, to his fellow-citizens. We therefore, take the liberty of requesting you, to announce his name, at the usual places of election in your Parishe; and to use your best endeavours, to cooperate with us, in promoting his elections.

We remain respectfully, your obedient humble servant,

THOMAS ROPER, HENRY LAURENS, CHARLES FRASER, ROBERT SMITH,	*Committee of Correspondence.*

Figure 6.1B. Southern Nomination Announcements.

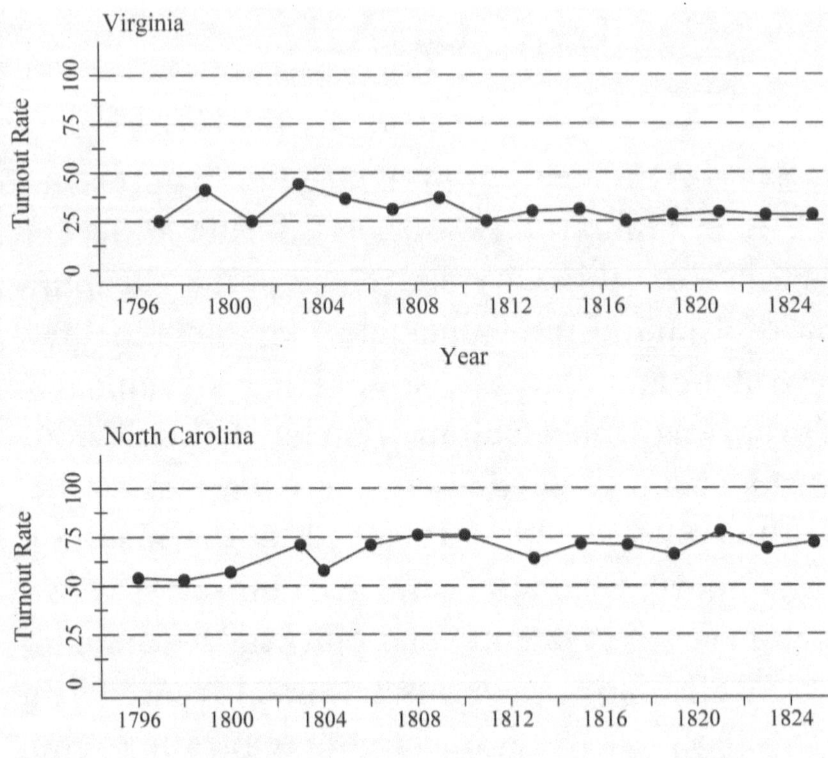

Figure 6.2. Virginia and North Carolina: County-Level Turnout

and because after 1806 they often turned into Republican scrums with more viable candidates than available seats.

The Number of Electors and Turnout

Robust electoral participation indicates electoral development. The raw number of electors is the proximate indicator. In the south, the larger number of missing district returns motivates calculating turnout at the county-level. One can use the decennial census to determine the county's adult white male population. I define the turnout rate as the proportion of adult white men that voted. Turnout rates may be compared across counties and districts, and these provide a good estimate of state-level turnout.[20]

Figure 6.2 graphs the median Virginia and North Carolina estimated turnout rates calculated from county-level data. It also displays the 25th and 75th turnout percentiles. The upper and lower percentiles provide a guide to the turnout range given lower- and higher-turnout counties and missing county-level returns. To illustrate, there are twenty-seven complete Virginia county-level returns for the 1811 elections to the Twelfth Congress. There appears to be nothing systematic about the counties present. These are from all regions of the state and differ in other characteristics. The median turnout rate is 25 percent. The 25th and 75th percentiles are 18 and 37 percent, respectively. Across elections, the median turnout rate is about 30 percent, and there is a slight downward trend toward the end of the era. The average number of county electors remained stable, at about 390, throughout the first party era. This masks growth in Virginia's electorate because the number of counties also increased.[21] Still, at the beginning of each apportionment cycle the census and extant counties coincide, providing a reliable estimate of state-level turnout in these years that likely extends through the apportionment cycle.

North Carolina's potential electorate is smaller than Virginia's, but "the Rip Van Winkle" state had considerably more county electors and higher turnout rates. This is not an artifact of different franchises or the number of counties, although North Carolina had fewer counties, befitting its smaller population.[22] This would be reflected in turnout rates. It is not. North Carolinians simply voted at higher rates than Virginians. As will be seen, this is because of North Carolina's more robust party competition.

In South Carolina only the city of Charleston presents extensive returns.[23] Prior to 1810 its potential electorate was approximately 2,900, with the number of electors ranging from several hundred to just over a thousand, depending on the year. Turnout increased between the Thirteenth and Seventeenth Congresses. From 1810 forward, Charleston averaged approximately 1,900 congressional electors and a 50 percent turnout rate. South Carolina's First District, centered on Charleston, typically saw about 1,700 electors, but participation dropped to fewer than 1,000 between the Fifth and Twelfth Congresses. After this, it increased and stabilized at approximately 2,400 electors.

Georgia's complete statewide returns simplify calculating turnout. This is because we observe the total number of electors and have good estimates of the state's voting-eligible population. Between the Eighth and Twelfth Congresses Georgia averaged nearly 15,600 House electors.

This corresponds to a 50 percent turnout rate. The rate dipped later in the era, with a typical election seeing between 12,000 and 15,000 electors and a turnout rate of approximately 35 percent. About 425 Georgia electors participated at the county level between 1802 and 1810. In 1810, for example, there are complete returns for twenty-three of the state's thirty-seven counties. Again, using medians to measure central tendency, the populations of these counties averaged 6,228, with over 40 percent of these populations enslaved men, women, and children. The typical number of electors was 417, and turnout was about 57 percent. This decreased to about 300 electors in the following cycle.[24] Importantly, the Georgia county-level turnout rates match the state figures closely. This provides a useful check on the whether county turnout allows one to make sensible inferences about state-level turnout. Assuming a reasonable number of county returns upon which to base inferences and nothing systematic about their availability, there is little reason to believe this would differ in the other southern states.

Some counties experienced noticeable changes in turnout. Virginia's Seventh District, formed by Loudoun, Fairfax, and Prince Georges Counties, saw about 20 percent turnout until 1809. After that, Loudoun County turnout was halved. This change owes to party competition. The Republican county was unable to elect a preferred candidate in the Federalist-dominated district. Federalist Joseph Lewis won the previous four district elections. In these elections Republican candidates turned in respectable, albeit losing efforts. This changed in 1811. As the *Alexandria Daily Gazette* explained, "No efficient opposition being expected to Mr. Lewis, the voters of Loudoun County did not turn out with their accustomed alacrity, which will account for the small number of votes taken in that county."[25] The *Gazette* was right: the Republicans threw in the towel.

There are counties that have consistently low or high turnout. In Virginia elections spanning the Eighth to Twelfth Congresses, Berkeley and Botetourt Counties typically saw turnout rates of 20 percent or less. All five of Fairfax County's elections are also in this range. In contrast, Norfolk County turnout often exceeded 55 percent. Five other counties counted two elections with greater than 50 percent turnout. The higher-turnout counties often combined to produce district elections counting a thousand or more voters. The median number of district electors across apportionment cycles ranges from roughly 1,400 to 1,700. Between 1802 and 1810, median district turnout is just over 1,400 electors, with lower and upper quartiles of approximately 1,200 and 1,700.

North Carolina saw very robust participation. A typical county election counted approximately 760 electors. This translates to turnout rates well over 60 percent. Turnout remained in this range throughout the era. Indeed, as will be seen in the following section, it is arguably the extent of party competition that accounts for much of the difference in turnout levels between North Carolina and its northern neighbor. In addition, North Carolina appears to have had fewer counties that displayed regularly high or low turnout relative to the state average. Higher-turnout North Carolina counties include Hyde, Cumberland, and Edgecombe, each of which returned at least seven elections with turnout exceeding the state's 75th percentile. Some counties, including Currituck, Granville, Mecklenburg, and Rutherford, saw eight elections where turnout was less than the state 25th percentile. However low these rates were, they were still relatively healthy, reflecting North Carolina's robust electoral participation. There is little geographic rhyme or reason to these patterns.

The county returns reveal the southern relationship between population and slavery. The turnout rate is highest in lower-population counties with a larger percentage of enslaved people. The turnout rate is lowest in larger-population counties with a smaller percentage of enslaved people. The Virginia figures are stark. In counties where the enslaved population exceeded 40 percent of the population, the turnout was nearly eight points higher than in counties in which the enslaved account for less than 40 percent of the population. This pattern becomes clearer if one overlays the county population on the comparison. Turnout averaged over 40 percent in counties with fewer than 10,000 people with the larger enslaved percentage. Turnout was approximately 25 percent in counties with more than 10,000 persons, fewer than 40 percent of whom were enslaved. Other southern states display a similar pattern. North Carolina's 124 highest-turnout county elections had populations averaging about 8,600 with the enslaved accounting for nearly 40 percent of these persons. In its ninety-seven lowest-turnout county elections, the median population was approximately 12,000 with enslaved persons accounting for one-fifth of these numbers. Georgia counties where enslaved persons were at least 40 percent of the population witnessed turnout about ten points higher than counties where less than 20 percent of the population was enslaved. The extent of slavery combined with the county population is a predictor of southern turnout rates.

Southern states sometimes display turnout approaching that of

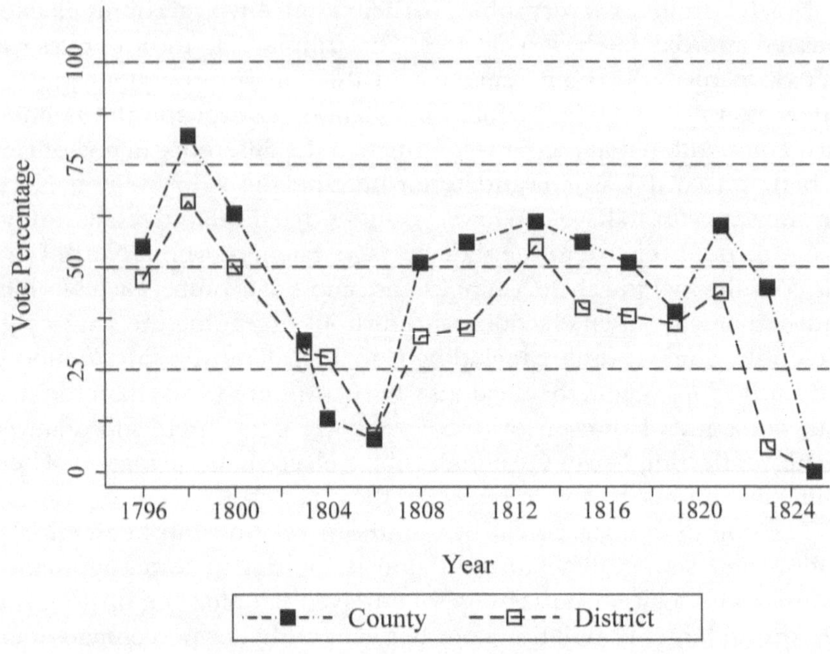

Figure 6.3. North Carolina: Federalist Party Support

other regions, but more often not. This most certainly reflects party development and the competitiveness of its elections. Social stratification and slavery are important components of this explanation. Here it is the more densely populated areas that have the lower percentages of enslaved persons that display the lowest turnout rates. More sparsely populated areas with high concentrations of slaves show fewer electors but higher turnout rates. Southern turnout often reflects the level of participation one expects in a more ad hoc electoral setting. This does not mean turnout was trivial. All states have counties in which hundreds of men vote, and these often aggregate to districts counting thousands of electors.

Party Support

The South was Democratic-Republican territory. Regionally the Democratic-Republicans won over 75 percent of the House seats, while the

Federalists won about 15 percent. These figures mask occasionally close elections and Federalist redoubts that are revealed at the district and county levels. To see this, consider Virginia elections spanning the two apportionment cycles from the Eighth Congress (1803) to the Seventeenth Congress (1821). These present ninety district-level returns that count a combined nearly 140,000 votes. Republican candidates won 65 percent of the vote and fifty-eight seats. The Federalists turned their 33 percent plurality into thirty seats.[26] Federalist strength remained constant or even increased slightly across the cycles. Between the Eighth and Twelfth Congresses, Federalist candidates won about 28 percent of the aggregate vote and twelve of thirty-five seats. In the following cycle the Federalists won 36 percent of the vote and eighteen of fifty-five seats. There are 421 county-level returns. The Republicans won over two-thirds of this vote while the Federalists won nearly all the remaining votes. This translates to 296 Republican county-level wins and 109 Federalist wins.[27]

The North Carolina returns at both the district and county levels show greater partisan parity in the aggregate vote. Figure 6.3 shows the aggregate district-level and county-level party votes. These match well.[28] There are some differences, especially around 1810, but overall the two series move in tandem. The graph shows that the Federalists were uncompetitive through 1806, but thereafter they were increasingly competitive and occasionally enjoyed near parity with their Republican rivals. In the first apportionment cycle, the Democratic-Republicans won about three-quarters of the county vote. In the second cycle, the Democratic-Republicans won about 60 percent of the district votes, with the Federalists taking the balance. The county tally is also closer. Throughout the period, the Democratic-Republicans won approximately two-thirds of this vote, producing 300 county-level wins. The Federalists took the remaining vote and 134 county-level wins. These ratios remain about the same at the district level, translating to eighty-five Democratic-Republican seats to the Federalist twenty-one. More importantly, other than their 1806 low point, the Federalists often won between 30 and 40 percent of the vote. They remained a viable political force. After 1822 the party votes collapsed, foreshadowing the opening stages of the Jacksonian period.

There are only forty-two complete South Carolina district returns. The Democratic-Republicans commanded 80 percent of this vote. This produced thirty-seven Republican wins to the Federalists' five. These ratios are largely unchanged across apportionment cycles. Unfortunately, the scarcity of county returns makes it impossible to evaluate party support at this level. The few that survive reveal that Charleston was competitive. Over the ten elections, the median Federalist and Republican vote shares were 43 percent 55 percent, respectively.[29] The Republicans won seven of these elections.

In Georgia, candidates often stood without party labels.[30] While many candidates, especially the successful ones, are identified by party—usually Republican—in biographical directories, here they are not assigned a party, in keeping with previous cautions about doing so. Recognizing this, the Federalists were never competitive. They seldom won votes after 1802, and the Republicans won large majorities in 1802, 1808, 1810, and 1812. The remaining elections saw nonaffiliated candidates win nearly all the vote. After 1812 there were few if any Federalist votes at the county level. Overall, Democratic-Republicans won over 85 percent of the county vote. Party labels largely disappeared after this cycle.

Two patterns emerge from the aggregate vote. First, while the Federalists may have been down, they were not out, at least in Virginia and North Carolina. In these states the Federalists were the minority party, but they still enjoyed considerable support. South Carolina Federalists remained viable in Charleston. However, their state-level fortunes quickly diminished, and they were nearly extinguished in Georgia. Second, the party vote is noticeably less structured as one moves south. Georgia elections have a perceptively ad hoc flavor.

It is more difficult to assess evidence of southern partisanship because of Democratic-Republican dominance in the region. Districts and their constituent counties appear similar in their political orientation. That said, the counties provide some leverage in this regard. Democratic-Republican domination of southern elections draws attention to those areas where the Federalists maintained electoral support. Such areas existed, although these were fewer. Some counties were regularly won by Federalists. In other counties, both parties completed on roughly equal terms.

Nearly thirty Virginia counties were competitive. These counted a combined 153 elections. In these the average party-vote shares were close, with the Republicans winning about 52 percent of the vote and Federalists the remainder. This translated to 83 Republican county-level wins, 69 Federalist wins, and, remarkably, one tie.[31] The most competitive Virginia counties were Bath, Botetourt, Fairfax, Ohio, and Southampton. Over the course of ten election cycles, each party won at least three times in these counties. However, the competitiveness of these counties may owe to high variability in the vote. There were significant vote swings, which cautions against inferring deep partisanship in these electorates. Fairfax County is different. Here the Republican median vote was approximately 55 percent, the Federalist vote averaged about 45 percent, and each party's vote deviation was typically modest. The Republicans and the Federalists had a predictable vote that was competitive enough for the county to be in play. The Republicans did better, but they had to earn their victories.

Other counties were less competitive. The Virginia Republicans carried fourteen counties at least seven times in elections between 1802 and 1820. These included Lancaster County, which voted Republican ten times. Not far behind were Essex, Fredrick, and Powhatan Counties, which were carried by the Republicans nine times. The Republicans typically won these counties in walkaways. The Federalists did best in the north-central and the western regions of the state. These counties include Berkeley, Hardy, Loudoun, Monongalia, and Ohio. In these counties the Federalists won at least half of the vote between 1803 and 1821. Federalists were also competitive in the eastern shore's Accomack and North Hampton Counties. The Federalists increased their presence in the Roanoke area after 1810, winning Botetourt County in three of five elections prior to 1822. They also carried Loudoun County in every election from the Eighth to Seventeenth Congresses. Here the median Federalist vote was approximately 70 percent, with only modest variation in this vote. This points to a core group of supporters who voted their party regardless of the candidate. The Federalists were also competitive in nearby Fairfax and Prince William Counties.

North Carolina Democratic-Republicans notched 300 county-level wins. Their support was strongest in Gates, Granville, Randolph, and Rutherford Counties. Here Republicans took each county's vote at least eight times. There was no effective Federalist opposition. In comparison, the Federalists won at the county level 134 times, mostly in the state's interior bordering South Carolina. This region ran roughly from Fayetteville in the east to the western hamlet of Charlotte. Anson, Cumberland, and Montgomery Counties were strongholds, with the Federalists taking the vote at least nine times in each county. Federalists also did comparably well in Cabarrus and Rowan Counties, north of Charlotte,

Table 6.3: Select North Carolina County-Level Votes, 1808–1821

County	*Federalist Median Vote*	*Republican Median Vote*	*Federalist MAD*	*Republican MAD*	*Federalist Wins*	*Republican Wins*
Chatham	35	65	4	4	0	5
Craven	41	59	1	1	1	4
Jones	60	40	4	4	4	1
Mecklenburg	31	69	1	1	1	4
Orange	44	55	1	2	2	3
Rowan	66	32	4	4	5	1
Wake	48	52	6	6	2	4
Wayne	48	52	9	9	2	3

and they won multiple elections in the eastern Greene, Jones, and Martin Counties.

To see county-level partisanship more clearly, table 6.3 shows eight of these counties and their votes in the competitive years between 1808 and 1821. These counties present at least five complete returns. In these cycles both parties obtain median vote shares of at least 30 percent with modest variation in the vote. While not conclusive, this indicates that each party has a core group of electors that maintain their allegiance across elections. This doesn't mean each party won. Chatham County, for example, was not especially competitive, but the Federalists consistently won about a third of its vote. In 1813 the Federalists surged, and the Democratic-Republicans won only a slim majority of the county vote. Other counties were weighted to one or the other party, but even the subordinate party won the county on occasion. Orange, Wake, and Wayne Counties were in play in almost every election. The table shows that regardless of how competitive the county was, each party could count on a certain number of votes from election to election. These electors could not be ignored by either party. If one expands to the 1800 to 1820 period, the list of competitive North Carolina counties grows. For example, the Federalists won the Carteret vote four times, and the Republicans twice. In addition, both parties won multiple times in Cumberland, Hyde, Iredell, Johnston, Moore, Person, and Richmond and Washington Counties. Closer examination of the county votes indicates that there were two types of competitive North Carolina counties; those where the partisan balance and tight margins were held in place by each party's core electorate, and those where the vote fluidity enabled each party to win on occasion. This indicates that partisanship was emerging in North Carolina, but not yet solidified.[32]

In South Carolina from the Eighth to Seventeenth Congresses, Federalist candidates competed in only twenty-six of forty-two observed elections. They won nine times. Overall, the Federalist vote was anemic. Few elections saw Federalists win or even come close. Importantly, the Federalists were usually competitive in Charleston. Here Federalist candidates averaged 42 percent of the vote and won three of nine elections. The two most competitive contests were in 1818 and 1820. In the former election two Federalists split the party vote, thereby electing Republican Charles Pinkney. In 1820 the Federalists were better organized and won in a tight race. Federalists also made respectable showings in the nearby Fourth District, centered in Collington County, and in the west-central areas near Abbeville, Laurens, and Newberry. After 1812 there were also close contests in the coastal region between Marlborough and Georgetown. Here the Federalists averaged about 45 percent of the vote and won one of three observed elections. Still, South Carolina Federalists did noticeably less well than their fellow partisans in North Carolina and Virginia. In Georgia this dissipation of Federalist strength is evident to an extreme. It simply dissolved after 1802.

Finally, southern party support is tied to slavery, but unlike turnout this support is unrelated to county population. As one expects, Democratic-Republican strength was concentrated in counties with the greatest proportions of enslaved persons. The Federalists did best in counties with a smaller percentage of enslaved persons. Virginia illustrates this pattern. Between 1801 and 1821, the Republicans won 296 times, and the Federalists did so 109 times. In counties won by Republicans the median proportion of the population that was enslaved was 42 percent; in those won by the Federalists, the median was 21 percent. To see this another way, consider the counties won by each party five or more times. The Republicans won thirty-three counties five or more times. The median percentage of enslaved persons in these counties was 48 percent. The Federalists did so in seven counties. The median percentage of enslaved persons in these counties was approximately 15 percent.[33] North Carolina displays a similar, albeit weaker, pattern. The Republicans won at the county level 273 times, and the median proportion of the enslaved population in these county-years was 32 percent. The Federalists won at the county level 77 times, and the median percentage of enslaved people in these county-years was 21 percent. South Carolina and Georgia are harder to assess in this regard. This is because the South Carolina county returns are missing and therefore cannot be matched to the census tabulations of the enslaved population. Party is less meaningful in Georgia. Nonetheless, Virginia and North Carolina show that county-level party support and slavery are deeply intertwined.

Patterns in Standing for Election and Reelection

Virginia, North Carolina, and South Carolina single-member district elections most clearly illuminate candidate propensity to stand for election and incumbent fortunes. Few Virginians stood for election multiple times. Of the 168 unique candidates in these returns, 114 stood once. Approximately three-quarters of these men lost. Of the remaining candidates, thirty-two stood twice, and twenty-two stood three or more times. Among those who stood in two or more elections, all but a handful won at least once. These men averaged nearly four elections and just over two victories. John Randolph led this group, contesting eight observed elections and winning six times under both Democratic-Republican and Federalist labels. Randolph aside, almost all candidates who won multiple elections ran consistently under a single party label. Indeed, of the ten candidates who won three or more elections, only two—Randolph and John P. Hungerford—switched affiliation; Hungerford did so only after his first election in 1811, when he stood as a Republican, before joining the Federalist camp.

North and South Carolina men sought election and reelection more often than did their Virginia counterparts. They also enjoyed greater electoral success. The observed North Carolina elections were contested by 137 unique candidates. Seventy-seven of these men stood once, thirty stood twice, and thirty more stood three or more times. Nearly three-quarters of those who won an election ran three or more times. Indeed, twenty-two candidates stood in at least four elections, and these men averaged three wins. Federalist John Culpeper was the most tenacious candidate, standing ten times between 1808 and 1825. He won half of these elections. Willis Alston compiled a remarkable record by standing eight times between 1798 to 1813—the first two times as a Federalist, then as a Republican. He won each of these elections, and one more for good measure in 1825. The sixty men who stood in multiple elections typically contested just over four elections and averaged nearly three wins. Most North Carolina elections from 1806 onward saw multiple incumbents stand for office. Overall, incumbents stood in fifty-three observed elections and won thirty-seven of these contests. Eight of these observed elections were in 1825, and half of the eight incumbents that year were defeated.

In South Carolina 106 unique candidates contested sixty-nine observed elections. As in Virginia and North Carolina, about half of these men stood once, with most losing. Among those who won their first election, about two-thirds stood in two elections, with the balance standing in three or more elections. These candidates averaged about two wins. Federalist Benjamin Huger from the coastal Georgetown district and Republican William Butler of the south-central region were the most persistent candidates. These men contested seven and eight elections respectively and won about as often as they lost. Here winning candidates seldom switched parties. The South Carolina returns present thirty-three incumbents who sought reelection. As with its northern neighbor, these men were successful about three-quarters of the time. Beginning in 1810 South Carolina electors became noticeably kinder to incumbents—except in 1816, when over half were defeated.[34] As in Massachusetts, these defeats likely owe to elector reaction to the Compensation Act. Georgia general-ticket elections from the Fifth to Nineteenth Congresses saw forty-six unique candidates. Approximately one-third of these men stood once. The thirty men who stood two or more times fared well. These men averaged just over three elections and won almost at will.

The southern returns confirm that few men sought a congressional career. That said, at least eight Virginians sought election to the House five or more times. One is the aforementioned John Randolph, who began his career as a political ally of Thomas Jefferson and ended it as President Jackson's minister to Russia, was elected to the House five times. Norfolk representative Thomas Newton Jr. served a remarkably long House tenure beginning in 1801 and continuing into the 1830s, but is otherwise remembered for little. In North Carolina Joseph Culpepper of Anson County stood in ten consecutive elections, winning four of them as a Federalist, and then for good measure stood twice as an "Adams Man," winning once. Republican Richard Stanford stood seven times between the Sixth and Fourteenth Congresses, never lost, and died in office in 1816. He was buried in the newly established Congressional Cemetery. In Georgia, Connecticut-born physician Joel Abbott stood five times and, after initial defeat in 1814, was elected in four successive elections. Alfred Cuthbert was also elected in four of five elections, before his tenure as a US senator beginning in the Twenty-Third Congress. Princeton-educated John Forsyth served continuously from 1812 forward. Given the high success rate for incumbents, one can surmise that most voluntarily declined to seek office. Men such as Randolph, Culpepper, and Abbott are the exception to the rule.

Finally, it appears that in the second decade of the nineteenth century, southern incumbents were more likely to stand and electors more likely to decline to reelect them to Congress. Of course, the more incumbents seek reelection, the more opportunities for electors to defeat them on election day. Still, that some of these men were defeated suggests that incumbency was a factor, but not the decisive factor, in many elections. These data are too few to make definitive statements, but they suggest that electoral competition was often robust and that office holders could not count on their status as an incumbent to ensure continued congressional service.

Leveraging Electoral Rules for Partisan Advantage

Only Virginia presents evidence of districting for partisan advantage. The Madison–Monroe contest notwithstanding, districting for advantage was present following the 1810 reapportionment. The apportionment increased Virginia's congressional delegation by one member, necessitating the formation of twenty-three districts. Most of the previous districts were unaltered, but at least three districts were changed for apparently partisan purposes.

The clearest of these partisan changes is reassignment of Hardy County from the Fourth District (1803–1811) to the Second District (1813–1821).[35] This advantaged the Democratic-Republicans in the increasingly competitive Fourth District. The three Hardy County returns from 1803 to 1811 show that these voters overwhelmingly supported Federalist candidates in an increasingly competitive district. Indeed, for the first and only time in the period, a Federalist, Jacob Swoope, won the district in 1809. More concerning to Democratic-Republicans was that Hardy County, in present-day West Virginia, was rapidly growing. This meant that if it remained in the Fourth District it would eventually provide enough Federalist votes for the party to regularly win the district. The election law of 1813 placed Hardy County in the already solidly Federalist Second District. One gerrymandering strategy is "packing"—that is, to place as many of one's political opponents as possible in as few districts as possible. The Hardy County reassignment was textbook "packing." It ensured the Fourth District elected Republicans with little hinderance and the Second District elected Federalists with far more votes than necessary.

A second way of districting for advantage was to simply do nothing; specifically, make no district adjustments to account for population change. An apparent example of this is Virginia's Twelfth (1803–1811) and Thirteenth (1803–1821) Districts, which were geographically the same district across both apportionment cycles. This district included solidly Federalist Accomack and Northampton Counties on the Delmarva Peninsula. It also included several mainland counties that voted Democratic-Republican.[36] By 1810 the Thirteenth District's adult white male population approached 5,100, and 40 percent of them lived on the peninsula. In total, the district's potential electorate was roughly a third larger than that in surrounding districts. These electors tended Democratic-Republican because of the mainland counties. Following reapportionment, there was no obvious way to place either Accomack or Northampton in other districts because of its larger potential electorate while maintaining any pretense of contiguous districting. However, three of the district's smaller counties on its southern boundary—Elizabeth City County, James City County, and Warwick County—were natural candidates to add to the Twentieth or Twenty-First District to balance regional district populations while respecting contiguousness. However, such a change would likely deliver the Thirteenth District to the Federalists and leave the Democratic-Republicans little better off in amended districts. It is difficult to determine whether inaction, especially in an era before equal population districting, constitutes purposeful districting. While there was often no formal requirement that districts contain approximately equal population, it was a norm that was generally respected. What is clear is that the regional districting remained unchanged despite significant differences in sizes of their potential electorates, and this advantaged the Democratic-Republicans.[37]

Conclusion

The South presents a mixed picture of electoral development. The northern tier states of Virginia and North Carolina display more signs of development than does South Carolina. Georgia barely registers on the scale. The turnout and party competition markers point most clearly toward development. Party competition is robust in Virginia and, especially, North Carolina. The Federalists won more at the county level than the district elections reveal. Even when the Federalists lost, they often obtained respectable support. The Virginia Federalists often secured about one-third of the vote but were rewarded with few House seats. For them one-third of the vote translates to 20 percent of the seats, whereas the Republicans received a seat bonus in these elections. The North Carolina pattern is similar. It also appears in South Carolina, although one cannot parse this to the county level. Georgia party competition is largely unstructured.

Election turnout was sometimes robust when measured as a percentage of the adult white male population. This is especially true in North Carolina. Counties saw hundreds of men vote, and this often aggregated to the thousands at the district level. This points to electoral politics being accessible to men of typical means, although this may differ in some areas. Sometimes higher turnout indicates the presence of at least some level of party organization. Still, only North Carolina turnout approaches that seen in other regions of the United States.

The South presents less clear evidence of developed elections with respect to nominations and candidate entry. Evidence of parties controlling entry is present. A significant proportion of contested elections feature one candidate from each party. This is the case in Virginia. At other times there were notable and costly failures to control entry, such as in North Carolina's Thirteenth District in 1813. There is little entry control in South Carolina, where nearly half of the contested elections saw one party or the other overcrowd the field. There is little sense in evaluating Georgia elections on this metric given the large number of elections contested by candidates with no party affiliation. As elsewhere, representatives seldom served more than a term or two. When they did seek reelection, they were often reelected. However, incumbent defeat was not unknown. Virginia and North Carolina saw incumbents defeated, especially in the second half of the era.

On balance, the returns show that southern congressional elections were noticeably less structured than in other regions. This certainly owes to political culture, the lack of statewide elected offices, and slavery. Republican support was strongest in the areas most deeply tied to slavery. This translated to sufficient political strength to preclude the need for developing strong organization. Since slavery and wealth coincided, this meant that the Republicans were largely unassailable, even with strong Federalist showing in some counties. This is most evident in Virginia but also in North Carolina. South Carolina's lack of county returns cautions against definitive statements, but the district-level distribution of party support suggests this pattern holds here too. On balance, the returns show that the Federalists maintained support in several locations. These, however, were insufficient to force greater efforts to develop the extent of party organization present in other regions.

7 | National Electoral Development and Party Systems

The remaining task is to craft a synopsis of the empirical analyses and what these tell us about early American elections. This includes exploring whether there is evidence of the development of a regional and national party system. That is the purpose of this chapter. Here it is worth reminding ourselves that House of Representative elections are the central pillar in national electoral development. The House of Representatives is the primary elected office that connects Americans to their national government.[1] Historically, governorships and Electoral College voters were not always elected, and the franchise in statehouse upper-chamber elections was sometimes different from that for the lower chamber and House. It was lower-chamber elections, both state and national, that legitimated and encouraged mass political engagement for most Americans. House returns interpreted in light of theories of party development provide immense leverage in assessing early US electoral democratization. If there is to be an emerging understanding of American electoral development, House elections do not just need to be part of it, House elections must be the foundation of it.

There is a debate among historians and historically minded political scientists over whether early elections were the province of the "natural aristocracy" or the "natural democracy." Did the deferential-participant electoral politics persist through most or all of the first party era? One can dispense with this quickly by returning to the definition of deferential-participant political culture. Its key element is "the *acceptance* of the view by the whole society that . . . people would naturally delegate power to a select minority. . . . [In such a society] it was possible for the broad mass of the people to *consent* to a scheme of government in which their own share would be limited."[2] A key underpinning of deferential-participant politics is that it was a *culture*, one shared by the high and mighty and low and modest. One doesn't need to manipulate election rules in the presence of a shared culture; one only does so if the culture is not shared. The Connecticut Standing Order maintained its electoral privileges not because of cultural norms or custom—at least, not shared ones—but because the rules were rigged in its favor. When Connecticut changed its voting method from written ballots to the "stand up" rule it did so precisely because there was not a shared political culture, certainly not a deferential one that depended on a shared acceptance of political stature and roles.[3] Here one could hardly vote for an "'atheistical' Republican with the minister present, under the eyes of local officers, and men of wealth."[4] Elites made this change precisely because this was the best means available to ensure their position. If a culture is indeed shared, there is no need to rig the rules to ensure one's political survival.

This is evident in other states. By the first years of the nineteenth century, New Jersey elections were little short of bare-knuckle politics. Indeed, nationally, polling places became so unruly that the men in control thought these no places for women.[5] The Virginia in which John Marshall was forced by necessity to announce his positions on policy issues and endure sitting at the polls in front of a rough crowd was an act hardly befitting a gentleman. The Anne Arundle County Democratic-Republicans held barbeques complete with liquor because they sought to entice electors to listen to campaign speeches. For an understanding of politics that is predicated on average citizens having a limited role, an awful lot of men showed up.

Granted, one can overemphasize such a sharp distinction between the old and new. Elements of both political universes resided in the early United States. However, the old style of elite-driven politics was in rapid decline. There remained vestiges of it, but these were few and centered in a handful of places. It lasted longer in the South but passed quickly in the Middle Atlantic states, if it even existed. From the founding, the politics of personality and patron-client relationships contended with a new electoral politics centered on parties, newspapers, and organizers.[6] This hybrid political culture consisted of a tapestry of "town meetings, county committees, petitioning, popular parades, [and] election campaigns," and was linked nationally by a partisan press and an efficient postal system. To work, this culture depended on local actors.[7] Does this mean elections were modern in the Jacksonian sense? No. The early republic represented a transitional period where the norms and practices of Jacksonian politics were present, but full expression of Jacksonian-era elections required the transportation, communication, and demographic transitions of the third and fourth decades of the nineteenth century.

This interpretation of congressional elections and the analyses that sustains it is informed by the so-called new political history. The "new" political history is neither overly centered on national-level elites nor entirely on the ground level. It instead brings to the forefront the middle range of party supporters whose names are not familiar, but who organized elections. Neither does this scholarship overlook the role of women, African Americans, and others on the periphery of elections. These histories draw from ballots, turnout, speeches, broadsheet appeals, and other considerations relevant to typical electors. This is the political history that is most supported by the book's empirical findings.

There are connections, sometimes unseen, between these histories and political science. Some connections are clear, such as Walter Dean Burnham's writings on electoral development, which are well-known in both disciplines. Other political science scholarship has not crossed into the historical literature, but greatly increases our understanding of what the vote returns say about early elections. These include why nominations and entry barriers are so important for the development of electoral parties. This also includes how vote aggregation methods affect party characteristics and their viability. Most important, but less known, are connections to recent political science scholarship on political parties. This refines and extends the standard definition of parties by conceiving of parties as "long coalitions" organized by midlevel functionaries. These men and women reconciled, held together, and advanced the interests of "intense policy demanders," various groups and electors. In the early republic, political elites including politicians were important, but the heavy lifting was done by others. This scholarship sees parties from a midlevel perspective, with organizers motivated more by ideas and policies than by patronage and pecuniary rewards. This bears a striking resemblance to how many historians describe the early United States. In both cases, party functionaries and associated groups contest elections to advance policy, ideals, and visions of good government.[8] In this sense, the early republic was as "modern" as later eras.

So, what remains to be said? It turns out there is much. There remains disagreement over the extent to which partisanship reached the electorate. The new political history notwithstanding, the received understanding is that "there is little persistent evidence of party loyalty election to election."[9] Others argue that not only did mass partisanship exist, but it was strong, stable, and reinforced by the network of presses and editors. Scholars also question the organizational capacity of parties. Did parties have sufficient capacity to supplant traditional elites? Other questions center on the extent of the Federalist demise. Was this as complete as thought? Historians agree that early republic election turnout was often robust. There is no dispute here. What is in dispute is what role parties played in structuring turnout, and whether high turnout signifies electoral development. Finally, did a national party system emerge before the Age of Jackson? Simply, questions about the source, breadth, meaning, longevity, and effect of these observations persist.

The previous chapters speak to these questions by extracting as much information as possible from House election returns and interpreting these considering the scholarly debates over the development of US elections. Collectively, this study is distinguished from previous scholarship, in part, by the sheer volume of returns upon which these analyses are based. Rather than inferring from a handful of elections contested at particular times and places, the book builds on a large inventory of elections. More importantly, it is distinguished by the theoretical lens through which these returns are interpreted. Turnout, the number of standing candidates, and related considerations take on meaning because of the importance that political science theory imparts to nominations, party and partisanship, and other foundations of electoral development.

The extent to which elections became recognizably modern depends on the emergence of political parties. These must have sufficient reach to organize elections and the electorate. Political parties are comprised of three elements: party in government, party organization, and party in the electorate. The first, party in government, is not in dispute. Nobody questions whether parties existed in Congress. They did. This leaves party as organization and party in the electorate. The press was the central element of party organization, and I primarily used entry control to assess the efficacy of party organization. This is one indicator of party organization, but it is an important one. Indeed, it is arguably the most important indicator of party advanced in the theoretical understanding of parties that underlies this book. The historical record confirms the existence of formal nomination process. The evidence here shows these were effective. In single-member districts it was uncommon for more than one candidate from each party to stand. The same pattern existed in multimember districts and general-ticket elections. In contested elections, the number of candidates from each party almost always equaled the number of available seats. Of course, then as today, parties could not hold off an occasional insurgent. However, these occurrences were rare. The primary challenge for parties was understaffing when the outcome was a forgone conclusion. Overall, the parties almost always stood the proper number of candidates in contested elections. Proper staffing was not limited to one or two regions. One observes this pattern nationally, with few exceptions. Among the exceptions is the Connecticut nomination elections. However, the failure to limit entry in these elections caused no harm to the party, only to individual office seekers.

One might ask if these entry patterns represent party organizational capacity or norms, perhaps "norms" enforced by elites. It may be that those who aspire to office willingly give deference to more established and stature-bearing candidates. This explanation is at variance with much of the historical record that documents the emergence of formal nominations and the creation of party lists. If norms are effective, one does not need formal processes, even if just for appearance's sake. Formal processes can be buttressed by norms, as they are today. Additionally, this explanation must account for why a decentralized network of midlevel party functionaries play along. If the understanding of political parties that underlies this book has purchase, then it is unlikely that these empirical patterns reflect norms and pressure. Instead, they are driven by rules and process. Early nominations, if merely window dressing, were very elaborate dressing for a very large window. This is not plausible.

Establishing whether party existed in the electorate centered on assessing voting patterns in multicandidate ballots, geographic voting patterns, and the volatility of the vote. Convincing evidence comes from all of these considerations. Multicandidate ballots, whether these be from statewide general-ticket elections or elections in multicandidate districts, show that electors vote the party, not the candidate. The within party vote distributions in general-ticket elections routinely display minimal differences. This is true even when some party supporters disapprove of a candidate, such as New Hampshire's Republican Arthur Livermore in 1816. One sees this elsewhere in the early United States. Historian Donald J. Ratcliffe's study of Ohio elections presents similar patterns. These ballots capture "the extent to which [electors] perceive national politics and legislative control in essentially partisan terms." In Ohio's first elections, electors voted the party, not the candidate.[10]

Partisanship in the electorate is further indicated by the district and county votes. These were often relatively stable over time. All regions presented some districts and counties that consistently voted for one party or the other.[11] This might be confused with voting for a particular candidate, perhaps because of his social stature. However, this explanation is questionable because few candidates seek multiple terms. Office seekers come and go, but the party vote remains. Except for the rare exception of surviving pollbooks, we cannot peer behind the veil of district and county borders to know if the same people voted Democratic-Republican or Federalist in successive elections. However, these patterns were often so stable, especially at the county level, as to make this argument implausible. It's hard to conceive a story that maintains large numbers of district or county electors switch parties across elections and yet produce aggregate vote stability. The often modest vote variation combined with relatively predictable levels of party support indicate partisanship in the electorate.

Of course, not all districts and counties fit this description. Some had larger election-to-election variation in the vote. This is likely because partisanship was still developing in some areas. This was a transitional period. There are other reasons why one might see higher variation in the vote. One of these is changing demographics from immigration and population growth. This may also reflect candidate quality or any of the myriad of factors that produce vote changes. Again, it is hard to know with certainly without information at the level of the individual voter. Local circumstances include means of livelihood, religion, ethnicity, and any number of other attributes that affect local party support and its stability. All this said, there are many areas characterized by stable support for one or both parties. The weight of evidence from multicandidate elections and geography is that partisanship resided in the electorate.

Turnout is the most studied marker of electoral development. This is for good reason. Voter participation is a key indicator of political system legitimacy. This understanding dates to the ancients, as reflected in Pericles's famous funeral oration. In it he reminds the Greeks that they fight and die for a civic life in which participation both enriches the individual and confirms the political order. The moderns, most famously Rousseau, agreed and thought free and meaningful participation was the foundation of political legitimacy. As theorist Richard Katz observes, all "democratic theories regard spontaneously high turnout as desirable."[12] These ideals deeply influenced the founding generation and resonated widely in the early United States. This is not to suggest that typical men discussed Pericles and Rousseau over a pint at the local tavern. Rather, these ideas were embedded in the way that the Americans thought and talked about government. Voting is not costless. Electoral participation signals that citizens accept the political system and understand that their participation sustains it. Turnout means that citizens believe it is worth their time to participate in elections.

Early United States election turnout was high. Hundreds of men voted at the county level, thousands at the district level, and tens to hundreds of thousands at the state level. The turnout rate regularly approached or even exceeded 50 percent or more of the potential electorate. As noted, this finding is not new. What is no longer in question is whether turnout regularly reached these levels in national elections. It did. The figures here show that previous findings are not unusual or episodic. More important is the question of whether turnout levels have anything to do with political parties and party competition. Many historians link high participation to party organization. However, there is debate. For example, a recent historical monograph on early elections argues that "party competition does not appear to have provided the stimulus for mass participation in politics; indeed, it seems to have had the opposite effect."[13]

Any electorally minded political scientist would view this statement with deep skepticism. High turnout is unequivocally a sign of strong parties, both as organization and as party in the electorate. Parties promote turnout in three ways: first, as mobilizer of electors; second, through partisan identification; and third, through party competition. When all three of these elements are in place, turnout is higher. When they are not, turnout is lower. Party isn't the only factor that drives turnout. A sense of civic duty, social pressure, and community norms matter. However, these factors and others are not sufficient to generate turnout at levels witnessed in early House elections.

The reason party is necessary to generate turnout is because voting is costly. It requires time and effort, and this was especially true in the early nineteenth century. Yet, even if one supports a particular party, one's vote matters little in determining the election outcome. The outcome will likely be the same regardless of whether one votes. There are few instrumental reasons to vote. This presents a collective action problem that must be solved by organizing like-minded electors. Elections are decided by groups acting in concert, a fact not lost on party organizers. Thousands of men do not show up to vote without exhortations to vote, prodding, incentives, provision of necessary resources such as transportation, and all the other things that foster turnout. The parties get their supporters to the polls. These organizers count men and women such as the Virginians that cajoled Pastors Blair and Buchanan to the poll in John Marshall's election. These are precisely the unknown "midlevel" functionaries that made parties work in the early United States.

Partisanship also promotes turnout.[14] It does so by reducing the costs of political participation and increasing the perceived rewards of participation. Partisanship reduces the costs of voting by simplifying an otherwise complex political world. One cannot easily understand the nuances of foreign policy or how a national bank might affect one's economic well-being. In contrast, one can easily understand that the Republicans and Federalists embraced different visions of the United States, and which vision one prefers. The traditional understanding that men could judge the characters of those who aspired to represent them, but not policies, contains its grain of truth. However, typical men were more than capable of judging different conceptions of the United States and its future. Then as today, this is more than sufficient to care which party controls the government. Electors are more likely to show up at the polls when they think something meaningful is at stake and that it matters which party wins the seat. Early US electors clearly thought something important was at stake in these elections.

The closeness of elections also drives turnout. The theoretical literature provides good reasons to expect close elections to generate higher turnout than less competitive elections. There are at least two reasons why one expects closeness to shape turnout. The first is that the potential value of one's vote is greater in a close election. One's vote is rarely decisive, but it is certainly closer to decisive in a close contest than a landslide. Second, parties expend more effort mobilizing electors when an election is expected to be competitive. There is little sense in expending scarce resources mobilizing supporters when one's party will win or lose with near certainty. However, these resources are well spent on competitive contests. That close elections see higher turnout is observed empirically.[15]

This expectation is confirmed in the early republic as well. The first elections saw high turnout in competitive contests that the parties vigorously contested. Turnout was low in uncompetitive and uncontested elections. New Jersey makes this patently clear. Here one sees high turnout when the Federalists contest the general ticket, and turnout collapses when they do not. Nothing of importance changed in proximate elections. For example, between 1808 and 1810 turnout dropped from 72 percent to 30 percent. Nothing happened in New Jersey in these two years that accounts for the loss of half of the electorate except for the Federalist decision to concede the election. As statistically oriented folks are apt to say, one can't explain change with a constant. In the fourteen contested New Hampshire general-ticket elections, turnout is tied to the closeness of the party vote. In perpetually competitive Delaware turnout is always robust. The relationship between closeness and turnout is confirmed at the county and district levels. Even in states that are tilted toward one party, such as North Carolina, turnout is higher in counties that see robust two-party competition than in those counties that do not. There is good reason to be confident in these assessments. The turnout statistics here are based on a large inventory of returns obtained at the county, district, and state levels. It is not a census, but it is as close as possible given the available historical records.

The turnout rate is important, but more important is the number of electors. Whether at the county level, district level, or state level, the number of men who voted is impressive. County-level electorates numbered in the hundreds, districts in the thousands, and states in the scores of thousands to hundreds of thousands. The numbers of voters confirm that elections were the province of typical men. It is not plausible that so many electors could be pressured, much less coerced, by their economic and social superiors in most places at most times. These men are far too many to be organized by anything other than parties. Pennsylvania provides one of the more entertaining examples of the difficulty of coercing potential electors. Here an election judge sought to preclude some ex-militiamen from voting because they had "no will of their own." The men responded that "we have fought for the right of voting and we will now exercise it."[16] As a matter of principle, this argument was difficult to deny. As a practical matter, the potential risk of turning determined young men away from the poll was probably not lost on local elites. The judge wisely backed down. Numbers carry a force of their own, and this could not be easily dismissed by those who did not care to count the political voices of average men. The evidence here clearly links turnout levels to party organization, party in the electorate, and party competition.[17] Civic duty alone is weak sauce for getting potential electors to the polls.

Evidence of party organization, partisanship in the electorate, and robust turnout encourages one to ask about aggregate party support. The received understanding is that the Federalists ceased to be a viable political force in the early nineteenth century. This is apparent if one solely focuses on congressional seats. The Federalist congressional delegation nearly evaporated. The story is more nuanced if one considers party support. That the Federalists maintained a presence in many places throughout the period is confirmed and extended by the present analyses. Delaware, New Hampshire, North Carolina, Pennsylvania, Maryland, and Massachusetts consistently saw the Federalists win 30 percent or more of the aggregate vote. Even in states where their support was softer, such as Virginia, the Federalists did well in several counties. None of this is to suggest that the Federalists competed on even terms with the Democratic-Republicans. They did not. The Federalists were the minor party. It means that although the Federalists controlled few House seats, this greatly understates their popular support.

This returns us to the relationship between turnout and party support. The Federalists enjoyed more support, and turnout was higher, than is often recognized. These observations are linked. An important reason why turnout was high in the young United States is precisely because Federalists were not eliminated as a viable party. They retained a base level of support in many areas that was too significant to safely ignore. The Democratic-Republicans had to maintain electoral momentum. When and where Federalist support diminished, so did turnout. One sees this in New York, where turnout was high when both parties ran aggressively, and turnout fell when the Federalists abandoned the party label. Delaware's partisan balance consistently drove high turnout. Turnout was lower in Maryland because, although the outstate was competitive, individual districts were not. Federalist strength in North Carolina likely contributed to that state's high turnout rate. The relationship between competitiveness and turnout even existed in Connecticut. One sees this by comparing turnout in the few nomination elections that the Republicans contested to that in the corresponding general election. The former elections saw a higher turnout than the latter. This is because Democratic-Republicans showed up to vote in the early nomination elections, then abstained from the general elections. This provides further evidence of party in the electorate.

Finally, the returns highlight the effects of election methods on electoral development. The rules under which elections were contested had significant implications for party fortunes. It is an exaggeration to say that the paucity of Federalist congressional representation owes primarily to election methods. However, election methods magnified the effects of their diminished popular support. In this way, election methods had something—indeed, something very important—to do with the Federalist inability to win congressional seats. For the Federalists, the playing field was often tilted in a manner that exacerbated the normal challenges of extracting as much representation as possible from their smaller pool of popular support.

Before discussing electoral processes that sometimes engineered the Federalists out of contention, it is useful to understand that the single-member district system, even in the absence of gerrymandering, advantages the majority party. This is simply the votes-to-seats translation in single-member-district, plurality rule elections. For the losing party, 49 percent of the vote might as well be 10 percent. The score is still 0–1. In the presence of national-level partisan parity and many elected seats, this translation tends to be balanced. Close losses in one district are offset by close wins in another district. This is why in the late twentieth century and the early twenty-first century the United States often saw national House of Representatives vote-seat shares that were proportional, meaning that the national party vote shares and House seat shares often matched closely.[18] However, the Federalists did not compete from a position of parity; they were the minor party. The number of available seats was also modest. The 1810 census apportioned 109 seats among the original thirteen states and 181 nationally, too few for close losses to be offset by close wins. This imbalance between votes and seats hurt the Federalists. In the three cycles between 1812 and 1816, the Democratic-Republicans won a small majority of the national House vote yet claimed two-thirds of the House seats.[19] The Federalists could not translate their national vote share into anything approximating a comparable seat share.

The general ticket and multimember districts further diminished trailing party fortunes, especially Federalist fortunes. New Jersey speaks for itself. The Federalists were significantly disadvantaged by the general ticket. This election method was largely responsible for the near complete demise of the Federalist Party in state-level elections even though it maintained support in several counties. Pennsylvania's multimember districts favored the Democratic-Republicans well beyond their vote shares. Between 1812 and 1820, Republicans turned roughly 55 percent of the vote in these districts into forty-five seats, while the corresponding Federalist figures were 42 percent and twenty-three seats.[20] Things did not always cut against the Federalists. They won most of New Hampshire's general-ticket elections through 1814 in generally close elections, while Republicans won just a handful of seats. Afterwards, the Federalists could not win a seat under the system, despite their strong effort in 1816. Connecticut nominations removed Republicans from contention before the general election even though they enjoyed the support of a substantial minority of the electorate.

The use of election methods for advantage is a bipartisan activity. It can also prove dangerous unless one has great confidence in the political future. It was the Federalists that initially brought the general ticket to New Jersey. New Jersey Federalists knew how badly the general ticket turned on them and how to district for advantage when given the opportunity. This opportunity came in 1813 when they adopted dual-member districts and won four of six seats. A contributor to the New Jersey *Centinel of Freedom* reminded readers of the origins of the general ticket.[21] Complaining that it was the Federalists who initially championed the general ticket and now hypocritically districted because it no longer worked in their favor, the unnamed contributor wrote, under the banner "Our Election Law":

> It is not more surprising than true that the federal legislature of New Jersey, now in session, has repealed the law authorizing the PEOPLE to choose members of congress . . . by a general ticket. . . . The state will be laid off into Congressional Districts; and according to this arrangement, we understand the federalists to calculate to succeed in electing four of the six members.
>
> What will the PEOPLE say to this highhanded . . . outrageous proceeding? Will they not rise in the majesty of their strength and clip the strength of men who have usurped their power and abused their confidence? Do they forget the mode of choosing members of congress by a general ticket is the mode which the FEDERALISTS adopted in 1800 and continued by the Republicans ever since?

That it was the Federalists that initially imposed the general ticket for their own advantage reminds one of the old saw about living and dying by the sword.

While assessing the full extent of districting for advantage is beyond this book's scope, as the term "gerrymander" make clear, nefarious districting was well-known in the era. While creating advantageous districts is a bipartisan activity, most statehouses were controlled by the Democratic-Republicans. This did not bode well for the Federalists. The 1802 creation of Pennsylvania's multimember south-central district is a less-remembered form of districting for advantage. By placing a concentrated Federalist electorate in an even larger Republican electorate, the Republicans won three seats—and in doing so, deprived the Federalists of two seats. This net gain of two Republican seats was produced by an impressive feat of electoral engineering that would make any modern political consultant proud. Virginia's eastern shore districts in 1810 achieved the same objective without lifting a finger. What is important is that districting for advantage provides strong evidence that partisanship resides in the electorate. This practice only works if one knows the number of one's supporters and opponents, knows where they are located, and is confident that their votes are reliable. If not, strategic districting is, at best, ineffective. At worst, it can backfire.

Finally, electoral development does not depend on a congressional career. The election and reelection patterns of early republic incumbents are consistent with studies of the congressional career, namely that there wasn't one. There wasn't one in the Jacksonian era, either. The congressional career emerged in the post-bellum era.[22] In most states, candidates stood for a couple of elections, and even the most successful candidates typically served only a handful of terms. There are exceptions, but these are few. That said, there are episodes of electoral responsiveness to events. The Compensation Act led many Massachusetts incumbents to decline to seek reelection and resulted in a higher defeat rate for those who stood. Effects of other major political events, such as the Hartford Convention, are apparent in the aggregate vote, even if its effects were regional. The convention did not initially adversely affect New England Federalists. Nor did it have any perceptible consequences for southern Federalists since these were few, and none had anything to do with the convention. However, it seems to have diminished the prospects of Middle Atlantic Federalists.

Overall, the vote returns point to established political parties and mass partisan politics. The exception is the South, especially the Deep South. Here electoral development lagged the rest of the nation. In other regions, party as organization and party in the electorate appeared to be developing, if not established. Elections were often characterized by high turnout, evidence of partisan loyalty, and party organization. This agrees with recent histories that provide a more generous and participatory understanding of the early republic. By the early years of the republic, the parties were highly organized and stable. The task now is to ask if these are localized observations, or nationalized party politics. The development of a party system raises the threshold further by requiring these ideas and programs to extend beyond the immediate reach of one's district, state, and region.

Evidence of a Developing National Party System

The next step is to assess the extent of regional and national party-system development. The historical record shows that party organizers of the several states communicated and shared political objectives. These were often combined with mutual participation in celebrations and other political activities. An illustrative example comes from an 1816 description in the Albany, New York, *Advertiser* of a local Federalist celebration of Washington's birthday.[23] The Federalists promulgated a resolution in honor of Washington, then:

> In Conformity with this resolution, the society convened on the 22d of Feb. ultimately at the house of J. Stiles in Granville at 10:00 O'clock, A.M. It was then duly announced that our federal friends of Fairhaven Vt. who had been invited to unite in the festivities of the day were approaching with an ingenious display of *naval* architecture as exhibited in a first rate frigate, highly emblematical of wise *federal* policy, which alone has sustained the honor of the nation.

The frigate's docking was celebrated by cheers, cannon fire, and a combined New York and Vermont Federalist parade complete with banners and flags. The men marched to the Congregationalist meetinghouse for a celebratory dinner. The meal was followed by fourteen formal toasts and, later, several less formal toasts. Among the former was one expressing the hope that Virginia understood that "her sisters are very weary of nurturing her children" and one expressing the hope that James Madison's "political days be few." Other toasts addressed the role of the judiciary, trade policy, foreign affairs, and other substantive issues. While entertaining, the anecdote is just one of innumerable examples of how decentralized and midlevel political organizers met, coordinated, and pursued common political objectives.

Party-system development requires multiple parties. In the early republic there was no reason for the Democratic-Republican vote to be connected across states if the Federalists were not viable. In a one-party federal system, party politics is intrastate, not interstate. It is centered on people and factions, and is free of political ideals and issues around which elites and electors might organize. If a national party system was developing, this should be reflected in the Democratic-Republicans and Federalists competing across states and regions.[24] Further, each party should be affected similarly by political events regardless of location. Two indicators of nationalization are useful here. This first is whether each party enjoyed reasonable levels of support across regions. Second, each party should have been affected similarly by political events and trends across regions. As political scientist E. E. Schattschneider asked, "Does the same trend appear throughout the country[,] or do conflicting trends appear?"[25] If the former is true, then the parties are linked nationally. If not, then there are few connections among them.

There are several indicators of party-system nationalization. Two of these are well-suited for the early republic and the returns at hand. The first is the number of contested and uncontested elections across states and regions. If both parties contest elections across regions, this provides evidence of nationalization. If a party bypasses elections in a particular region, then this indicates the opposite. The second is the extent to which the parties' electoral fortunes are connected across states and regions.

Beginning with the former, table 7.1 presents the number of observed elections in each state and the number of these that were contested by candidates from each party. For example, fifty-two observed Pennsylvania elections span the Eighth to Twelfth Congresses, thirty of which were contested by candidates from each party. Overall, the table shows that both parties stood candidates in most states and regions through the Eighteenth Congress. There are exceptions, but excluding New Jersey, Connecticut, and Georgia from their respective regions, candidates from both parties contested 70 percent of more than a thousand elections. New Jersey and Connecticut are rightly excluded because their election rules throttled party competition. Georgia is excluded because the party labels were not regularly applied. Maryland is a bit of an anomaly because it displayed fewer contested elections. This,

Table 7.1: Contested and Observed Elections

	Congress			
	5th–7th Contested/ Elections	*8th–12th Contested/ Elections*	*13th–17th Contested/ Elections*	*18th–19th Contested/ Elections*
Pennsylvania	30/33	30/52	60/74	23/36
New York	26/30	67/76	66/106	0/60
New Jersey	7/7	2/5	3/7	0/2
Maryland	13/24	19/45	20/45	8/18
Delaware	3/3	5/5	5/5	2/2
Massachusetts	12/42	81/85	71/93	19/26
New Hampshire	1/3	5/5	4/5	0/2
Connecticut	1/3	0/5	0/5	0/2
Rhode Island	2/3	4/5	3/5	0/2
Virginia	20/21	21/35	37/55	15/22
North Carolina	18/21	22/47	31/44	1/21
South Carolina	14/14	16/22	10/20	0/13
Georgia	1/3	0/5	0/5	0/2

as previously noted, is because while the state was typically competitive, many districts were not. That said, regionally, the Democratic-Republicans and Federalists contested about three-quarters of the observed elections in the Middle Atlantic and New England states, nearly 70 percent of southern elections, and about half of the border-state elections. Recalling that the NNV only attaches party affiliation to a candidate if the contemporary press did so, this provides evidence that the Democratic-Republican and Federalist labels had currency nationally. These labels were used nationally and had meaning at time of election.

As expected, the number of contested elections diminished in elections to the Eighteenth and Nineteenth Congresses. This signals the end of the first party era. Still, even in these cycles there were states that retained two-party competition. One might ask if the number of contested elections is related to the likelihood that these returns survived. There is no indication that there is a relationship between surviving records and contested elections. It is not easy to test this formally, but it seems unlikely. There is no obvious pattern that distinguishes Virgina, where fewer returns survived, and Pennsylvania and Massachusetts, where surviving records are plentiful. The returns show that Democratic-

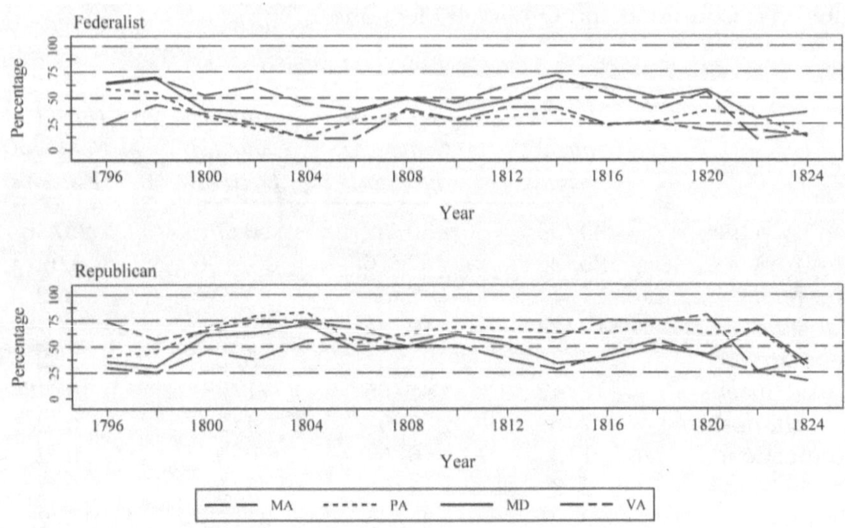

Figure 7.1. Party County-Level Vote Shares

Republican and Federalist office seekers contested seats nationally throughout the first party era.[26]

The second approach is to assess the extent to which a party's vote across states and regions is connected. The national-level relationships are best presented graphically. Figure 7.1 shows the mean Federalist and Democratic-Republican district-level vote shares from Pennsylvania, Massachusetts, Maryland, and Virginia. This is not total party support, although it's closely related. Previous chapters presented state-level party total support. The figure presents the average district-level support for the parties in these states. Recognizing that districts may be missing in any given year, this arguably best captures each party's underlying electoral support. This is because in these states, representatives were elected from districts. The figure presents additional advantages for understanding party linkages across states and regions. Since these are large states, with one in each of the nation's four regions, they collectively account for a significant portion of the nation's population.[27] The averaging strategy reduces the influence of outliers, allowing one to smooth out some of the noise to obtain a clearer picture of "typical" party support. Collapsing district returns into a single statistic also simplifies comparisons across states. This is because states have different numbers of complete district returns. These figures can be compared across time and place to assess whether each party's support was regionally and nationally connected. If party support across states and regions bears no relationship, then this indicates little party system development. On the other hand, if there was a developing national party system, one expects each party's vote share, within reason, to move in tandem. No approach to measuring state, regional, and national party support and their connections is bulletproof. This approach arguably presents the best balance of assets and liabilities.

The figure highlights important aspects of early American party politics and electoral development. First, while the Federalists were the minor party, they maintained respectable support nationally. Except for 1804–1806 in Pennsylvania and Virginia, the Federalist vote was often in the 30 to 40 percent range, or greater. Equally important, the vote shares track reasonably well. There are some differences in their trajectories, but quite often each party's support moved in tandem across states. The Democratic-Republicans gained in all states between 1800 and 1804, while the Federalists lost comparably. The Federalists gained support almost continuously from 1806 to 1814, while the Republicans held steady or lost support in the same period. The Federalists vote shares do not show a sustained decline until about 1822, signaling the end of the era. The important point is that these series largely move in tandem across states. This is further suggested by the series correlations over time. Federalist support is strongly correlated across all states except for Maryland and Massachusetts. Likewise, as previously suggested, the Maryland and Virginia Republican support is not strongly related, while the Maryland and Pennsylvania Republican vote is highly correlated. This provides further evidence that Maryland was politically more like its northern than its southern neighbor. Read in total, the series show that whatever affected Federalist or Republican fortunes in one state often did so in other states. This points to the nationalization of congressional elections.

Read in conjunction with the regional analyses, the returns reveal that a party system first developed in the Middle Atlantic and border states. This transition was slower in New England. Massachusetts became competitive and remained so as New Hampshire did, at least until the last years of the era. Connecticut stands out as an anomaly. This is because its electoral rules and institutions slowed this progression. The South, however, never fully developed in the same manner as the rest of the young nation. Virginia and North Carolina moved in this direction, less so in South Carolina, and Georgia did not. This slower southern progression likely resulted from the strength of the Democratic-Republicans in their home territory. It was also a consequence of institutions that, while perhaps not specifically intended to frustrate electoral development, did so. The lack of elected southern governors combined with their weak powers provided few incentives to create parties capable of large-scale organization. This localized elections. The slavery-based agricultural economy inhibited the development of centers of commerce and manufacturing, and the population density that accompanied such development. This too slowed party competition and development.

The picture of national party development that emerges is best understood as emanating from the Middle Atlantic and border regions outward. Development moved northward to New England, and never quite reached the South. This federalism-based interpretation, however, does not fully capture early party-system development and organization. If population is one's measure, then most Americans lived under something approaching national party organization by the end of the first decade of the nineteenth century. By 1820 Pennsylvania, New York, Maryland, and Massachusetts alone accounted for about half of the population in the original thirteen states and over a third of the US population. National party-system development is best understood as a balance of federalism focused on state-level parties and a national perspective that focuses on the numbers of persons whose electoral experiences were shaped by national political forces. If one's focus is on the federal structure, this presents a cautious assessment, while if one's focus is on population, this recommends a more generous assessment.

Finally, some scholars point to regional patterns in Electoral College votes to argue that no national party system existed in the early United States. Regional patterns in the Electoral College should not be overinterpreted. This is not only because some states did not use the popular vote to select presidential electors, but also because there have always been regional patterns to US presidential voting. Then, as today, the Electoral College is not the most robust indicator of popular support in presidential elections. There is no substitute for votes on the ground for assessing party-system development.

What can be said is that the weight of the American electorate resided in states that had achieved considerable levels of party and electoral development before the Age of Jackson. The things that affected

Democratic-Republicans fortunes in Pennsylvania were also felt in Massachusetts. Similarly, the things that defined Federalists and their electoral fortunes in New Hampshire were similar to those in Maryland. This is plausible. There was a national party press and there were national political issues.

Conclusion

Early congressional elections developed into recognizably modern form and the emergence of a national party system. This assessment is based on a large inventory of House election returns. Combined, these total well over 1,200 district returns, more than 3,500 county-level returns, and most general-ticket returns. These confirm that early US elections were more party structured and participatory than commonly recognized. Elections transitioned from ad hoc and elite-dominated, to processes organized by, if not professional administrators, those whose institutional responsibilities and loyalties extend beyond allegiance to individuals. Traditionally, the motivation for party organizers is thought to center on patronage or national-level policy, especially fiscal policy. This too quickly discounts the power of ideas to achieve the same outcome. These combined with political rhetoric secured the allegiance of midlevel organizers and constituencies. In the early republic these organizers created committees and communication networks that connected party leaders and "rank and file" supporters at the community, state, and regional levels.

The extent to which this system had national reach can be debated. The judgment of the reader prevails. However, in doing so, recall that there has always been a territorial component to US national politics. Party strength ebbed and flowed at different levels in different regions across history. A glance at current national politics confirms this fact. Assessing any empirical analysis of early republic elections, whether it be turnout, partisanship, or electoral linkages across states and regions, one must keep in mind that the bar for such assessment should be relative to historical patterns, and not some idealized notion of turnout, partisanship, or party system.

The two features of early American elections that receive the most attention, turnout and the party vote, support this assessment. Americans turned out in large numbers, and the Federalists enjoyed nontrivial support throughout much of the era. While existing scholarship provides evidence of high elector turnout, the present work confirms this feature of early elections based on very large numbers of elections to the nation's central republican institution. High election turnout, combined with often competitive, disciplined elections, was a broad feature of early American electoral development. These patterns are the norm, not the exception. This agrees with received theories of electoral development. Vibrant party competition produces high turnout. Noncompetitive, one-party-dominated elections produce low turnout. The Federalists retained a core electorate in many areas that the Democratic-Republicans could not afford to overlook.

Early House elections point to the effect of electoral rules, especially vote aggregation methods, on party development and competition. This is an aspect of early US political development that has received insufficient attention. The effect of election methods on party fortunes is especially clear in general-ticket and multimember district elections. Election methods inform our understanding of early American political culture. Again, at the risk of repetition, advantageous electoral rules and processes were adopted precisely because the old political culture dissipated. Connecticut is an extreme example, but here political elites were aware of what would happen if they allowed free and fair elections.[28] If the deferential-participant culture was truly sustained, it wouldn't have to be supported by the capricious use of rules that limited legitimate political opposition. The Connecticut approach to electoral politics wasn't viable elsewhere, as John Marshall experienced in Virginia and the anonymous election judge did in Pennsylvania when confronted by young men determined to vote. Other rule changes reflect rising party politics. New Jersey enfranchised not only some women, but also some African Americans. The Federalists enjoyed the support of women, while free Blacks supported the Democratic-Republicans. In a "Faustian" bargain, both parties supported the joint disenfranchised of each group, ensuring that elections remained the province of white men, with few implications for the party balance.[29]

Martin Van Buren is only slightly offstage in any discussion of the emergence of modern parties and elections. President Van Buren is "accorded the distinction of establishing permanent party competition in the United States."[30] He is credited with providing both a theoretical meaning and a constitutional defense of party competition that recognized the importance of legitimate opposition. He also contributed immensely to the modern mechanics of party-organized elections.[31] On the theoretical side, Van Buren identified clear differences between "parties" and "factions," with parties committed to general principles and enjoying long lifespans, while the factions were of short duration and narrow purpose. This purpose often benefited a correspondingly small number of persons.[32] Van Buren recognized that party competition kept political conflict within bounds.[33] He understood better than most the value of a two-party system for organizing and legitimizing national-scale politics. He saw the fragmentation of the Republican Party in the last years of the era as the product of Federalist electoral weakness. This led to the novel and perhaps counterintuitive argument that his own party's strength hinged critically on the viability of the other party. This is evident here. Party-system development depends on two-party competition, even if the Federalists were unable to often win office. Van Buren was also the archetype professional party organizer. Despite being from the Hudson Valley and of Dutch ancestry, he was not part of its elite. Van Buren was born to a tavern keeper in modest circumstances. He may have been the leader of the Albany Regency, but he was not a member of the established, wealthy Dutch aristocracy. Rather, Van Buren was the antithesis of the elites to whom deference was expected.

All of this recognized, there are two key considerations that temper one's assessment of Van Buren's contributions to the intellectual and practical foundations of party politics in the United States. At a theoretical level, many of the intellectual and constitutional arguments such as distinguishing between parties and factions were made by the founding generation. As early as 1792, James Madison, in his "A Candid State of Parties," observed that in the second great period of US parties, the first being for or against independence from Great Britian, among the supporters of the Constitution, "the great body were unquestionably friends to republican liberty," while among the opponents of ratification, "the great body were certainly well affected to the union and to good government." That is, political supporters and opponents of the Constitution were men of good faith and honest differences.[34] This intellectual legitimation and encouragement of party politics, as distinct from factional politics, at a theoretical and constitutional level, dates from the first years of the republic. Its most prominent advocates, including Madison, counted those who previously warned most forcefully of the dangers of faction.[35] As established early in this work, by the first years of the nineteenth century the "spirit of party" no longer carried a negative connotation. Parties enjoyed legitimacy as a means of political organization. Second, Van Buren framed advocacy of party politics and the importance of opposition in response to the perceived corrosive effects of one-party politics in the wake of the Federalist demise and the so-called Era of Good Feelings. However, as I hope the reader is now convinced, that era really didn't exist, at least in the storybook version.

A more realistic understanding of Van Buren's contributions starts with his early political career and his promotion of Thomas Jefferson's election in 1800. As he came of age, Van Buren recognized the importance to party building of the spoils system, caucuses, orderly leadership succession, and, above all, party discipline.[36] Van Buren, like other political leaders of his generation, did not come to define modern parties and the devices to build them in the waning days of the first party era. Rather, he saw elections develop over the course of his political life. The practices and devices that present themselves in congressional elections including nominations, stump speeches, getting electors to the polls, the effects of election rules, and other considerations, were the curriculum of his political education. He saw these practices used to greater or less effect in various locations. Van Buren knew that the "Old Federalist" obstinacy toward formal nominations produced overcrowded fields and that the "New Federalists" used these effectively.[37] He saw nominations and stump speeches that were decidedly not "window dressing." He understood that building partisanship in the electorate required contrasting visions of the United States and could not be based on the personal attributes of office seekers and the favors they might convey. He saw that organized parties mobilized voters, and turnout was highest in the face of two-party competition.

The second party era and Van Buren's contributions to it do not present a departure from a proto-democratic first party era. Rather, Jacksonian elections are an acceleration, refinement, and institutionalization of customs that emerged soon after the founding. As one historian succinctly put it, "The argument that partisan democracy began between 1828 and 1840 is simply no longer tenable."[38] Martin Van Buren did not invent modern party politics; he adapted existing ideas, practices, and norms for a nation where immigration and population growth, advances in transportation and communications, and the possibility of centralized national organization brought these practices to fruition.

Notes

1. *The Development of Congressional Elections*

1. James Madison, *Federalist*, no. 39, "Conformity of the Plan to Republican Principles," *Independent Journal*, January 16, 1788, http://www.constitution.org/fed/federa39.htm.

2. Philip J. Lampi, A New Nation Votes: American Election Returns, 1787–1825, American Antiquarian Society, 2007, https://elections.lib.tufts.edu/. See also Caroline F. Sloat, "A New Nation Votes and the Study of American Politics, 1789–1824," *Journal of the Early Republic* 33, no. 2 (Summer 2013): 183–186.

3. This regional political and cultural division is also proposed by Ronald P. Formisano, "Federalists and Republicans: Parties, Yes—System, No," in *The Evolution of American Electoral Systems*, ed. Paul Kleppner et al. (Westport, CT: Greenwood Press, 1981), 37–76.

4. The New Jersey Assembly generally elected three members from each county, although this number was occasionally adjusted to account for population changes. See Richard P. McCormick, *The History of Voting in New Jersey: A Study of the Development of Election Machinery, 1664–1911* (New Brunswick, NJ: Rutgers University Press, 1953), 101–103.

5. Jeffrey L. Pasley's *The First Presidential Contest* makes this point abundantly clear in the context of presidential elections. See Jeffrey L. Pasley, *The First Presidential Contest: 1796 and the Founding of American Democracy* (Lawrence: University Press of Kansas, 2013).

6. Andrew W. Robertson, *The Language of Democracy: Political Rhetoric in the United States and Britian, 1790—1900* (Charlottsville: University of Virginia Press, 1995), 23–30.

7. A sample of relevant works include J. R. Pole, *Political Representation in England and the Origins of the American Republic* (Berkeley: University of California Press, 1966), 150 and app. II; Jeffrey L. Pasley, "The Cheese and the Words," in *Beyond the Founders: New Approaches to the Political History of the Early American Republic*, ed. Jeffery L. Pasley, Andrew W. Robertson, and David Waldstreicher (Chapel Hill: University of North Carolina Press, 2004), 46–47; Andrew W. Robertson, "Jeffersonian Parties, Politics, and Participation," in *Practicing Democracy: Popular Politics in the United States from the Constitution to the Civil War*, ed. Daniel Peart and Adam I. P. Smith (Charlottesville: University of Virginia Press, 2015); and Daniel Peart, *Era of Experimentation: American Political Practices in the Early Republic* (Charlottesville: University of Virginia Press, 2014), 6–8.

8. Nelson W. Polsby, "The Institutionalization of the US House of Representatives," *American Political Science Review* 62, no. 1 (1968): 144–168.

9. John H. Aldrich, *Why Parties? The Origin and Transformation of Party Politics in America* (Chicago: University of Chicago Press, 2007).

10. John F. Hoadley, *Origins of American Political Parties: 1789–1803* (Lexington: University of Kentucky Press, 1986), 189, see also 19.

11. William Nisbet Chambers, "Party Development and the American Mainstream," in *The American Party System: Stages of Political Development*, 2nd ed., ed. Walter Dean Burnham and William Chambers (New York: Oxford University Press, 1975), 5.

12. Marty Cohenet al., *The Party Decides: Presidential Nominations Before and After Reform* (Chicago: University of Chicago Press, 2008), 20.

13. Cohen et al., *The Party Decides*, 20.

14. Cohen et al., *The Party Decides*, 31.

15. Cohen et al., *The Party Decides*, 31.

16. Richard Hofstadter, *The Idea of a Party System: The Rise of Legitimate Opposition in the United States, 1780–1840* (Berkeley: University of California Press, 1969, 1972), chapter 6, esp. 212 and 219–226. See also Jeffrey S. Selinger, "Rethinking the Development of Legitimate Party Opposition in the United States, 1793–1828," *Political Science Quarterly* 127, no. 2 (2012): 263–287.

17. Robert E. Ross, *The Framers' Intentions: The Myth of the Nonpartisan Constitution* (South Bend, IN: Notre Dame Press, 2019), 5.

18. Ross, *The Framers' Intentions*, 10.

19. Gary W. Cox, *The Efficient Secret: The Cabinet and the Development of Political Parties in Victorian England* (New York: Cambridge University Press, 1987), 56–57, 128–132.

20. The ideas that I discuss in the following section owe to Gary W. Cox, *Making Votes Count: Strategic Coordination in the World's Electoral Systems* (New York: Cambridge University Press, 1997), x, 3–7, 38, 56–57, 128–132.

21. Cox, *Making Votes Count*, 4.

22. Cox, *Making Votes Count*, 38.

23. Cox, *Making Votes Count*, x.

24. Cox, *Making Votes Count*, 7.

25. Cox, *Making Votes Count*, 5–6.

26. David W. Houpt, "Contested Election Laws: Representation, Elections, and Party Building in Pennsylvania, 1788–1794," *Pennsylvania History: A Journal of Mid-Atlantic Studies* 79, no. 3 (Summer 2012): 257–283.

27. For a survey of electoral rules used to elect the early Congresses, see Jay K. Dow, *Electing the House: The Adoption and Performance of the US Single-Member District Electoral System* (Lawrence: University Press of Kansas, 2017), tables 4.1 and 4.2.

28. Houpt, "Contested Election Laws," 269.

29. Houpt, "Contested Election Laws," 278.

30. Robertson, *Language of Democracy*, 53

31. David A. Bohmer, "The Maryland Electorate and the Concept of a Party System in the Early National Period," *The History of American Electoral Behavior*, ed. Joel Silby, Alland G. Bogue, and William H. Flanigan (Princeton, NJ: Princeton University Press, 1978), 146–173.

32. Bohmer, "The Maryland Electorate," 169.

33. Rosemarie Zagarri, "Festive Nationalism and Antiparty Partyism," *Reviews in American History* 26, no. 3 (September 1998): 504–509, esp. 507.

34. Formisano, "Federalists and Republicans: Parties, Yes—System, No," 33–76.

35. Cox, *Making Votes Count,* 186–193.

36. Cox, *Making Votes Count,* 186–193.

37. The nationalization of party systems has spawned an immense literature. For detailed discussions of party system nationalization in the United States, see William Clagget, William Flanigan, and Nancy Zingale, "Nationalization of the American Electorate," *American Political Science Review* 78, no. 1 (March 1984): 77–91; and Scott Morgenstern, Stephen M. Swindel, and Andrea Castagnola, "Nationalization and Institutions," *Journal of Politics* 71, no. 4 (October 2009): 1322–1341. For early approaches to measuring nationalization, see Donald E. Stokes, "Parties and the Nationalization of Electoral Forces," in *The American Party Systems: Stages of Political Development,* ed. W. N. Chambers and Walter Dean Burnham (New York: Oxford University Press, 1967), 182–202; and James L. Sundquist, *Dynamics of the Party System: Alignment and Realignment of Political Parties in the United States* (Washington, DC: Brookings Institution, 1973), esp. 332–340.

38. Gary Cox and Mathew McCubbins, "The Institutional Determinants of Policy Outcomes," in Stephan Haggard and Mathew D. McCubbins, eds., *Presidents, Parliaments and Policy* (Cambridge: Cambridge University Press, 2001), 21–63.

39. Formisano, "Federalists and Republicans: Parties, Yes—System, No," 37.

40. Scott C. James, "Patronage Regimes and American Party Development from 'The Age of Jackson' to the Progressive Era," *British Journal of Political Science* 36, 39–60. 40.

41. Pradeep Chhibber and Ken Kollman, "Party Aggregation and the Number of Parties in India and the United States," *American Political Science Review* 92, no. 2 (June 1998): 329–342.

42. Aldrich, *Why Parties?,* 65.

43. See Nobel E. Cunningham Jr., "Who Were the Quids?," *Mississippi Valley Historical Review* 50, no. 2 (September 1963): 252–263.

44. Throughout, I use the district designators in the NNV returns. These district numbers generally correspond to those in *The Historical Atlas of Political Parties in the United States Congress, 1789–1989.* The NNV sometimes designates districts geographically, such as "Essex South," which is one of several geographically named districts in Massachusetts. Kenneth C. Martis, *The Historical Atlas of Political Parties in the United States Congress, 1789–1989* (New York: Macmillan, 1989).

45. I define a competitive candidate in a single-member district as one who receives at least 5 percent of the vote. In at-large elections electing two or three candidates, I define a competitive candidate as one who receives 2.5 percent of the vote. In at-large elections that elect more candidates, I define a competitive candidate as one who receives at least 1 percent of the total votes cast.

I sometimes refer to higher votes shares as "nontrivial" and lower shares as "trivial." These bars are roughly equivalent: a single-member district candidate who receives 5 percent of the vote enjoys as much support as a candidate in a general ticket election who receives 1 percent of the total vote when electors cast five votes.

46. This rule leaves some candidates listed as nonaffiliated when the historical record disagrees. For example, Joseph Story, one of the early nation's foremost jurists, received votes in the Massachusetts Essex South district between 1806 and 1810. The NNV codes Story as unaffiliated in 1806, as a Democratic-Republican in 1808, and as unaffiliated in 1810. He was a Democratic-Republican—and a well-known one, as reflected in President Madison's decision to appoint him to the Supreme Court in anticipation that he would counterbalance John Marshall's Federalist jurisprudence. Story was an utterly uncompetitive congressional candidate; indeed, he probably received votes without his knowledge or consent. This likely accounts for the newspapers ignoring his candidacy and partisanship in two elections. In a very few instances, I recode the affiliation of a candidate when it is clear the data are wrong. One of these is Virginia Representative Edwin Gray, who is coded in some elections as a Federalist. He was a Democratic-Republican, and a high-profile one at that. That said, and despite its limitations, changing this coding convention risks substituting modern knowledge for understandings at the time. The NNV coding convention would have to be superseded for many candidates less prominent than Story and Gray. Preservation of the NNV party assignments also facilitates replicability.

47. These are Federal Information Processing Standard (FIPS) codes. The codes uniquely identify counties. New codes are assigned to counties as these are created. For example, in 1803 New Hampshire separated the northern part of Grafton County to form Coos County. Prior to 1803 this landmass known as Grafton County was assigned FIPS 33009. The new Coos County was assigned FIPS 33007, and Grafton County with its new boundaries retained FIPS 33009. For maps I use the year-appropriate county boundaries from the Newberry Library Atlas of Historical County Boundaries, https://digital.newberry.org/ahcb/index.html.

48. These are found in the Newberry Library Atlas of Historical County Boundaries. The electronic shape files for GIS mapping also are available on the Newberry Library website. Atlas of Historical County Boundaries, edited by John Hamilton Long (Chicago: Newberry Library, Dr. William M. Scholl Center for American History and Culture, 2012), https://www.loc.gov/item/2018487899/.

49. For a discussion of population-based representation in the early United States, see Rosemarie Zagarri, *The Politics of Size: Representation in the United States, 1776–1850* (Ithaca, NY: Cornell University Press, 1987), 57–60.

50. See, for example, Harry Marlin Tinkcom, "The Republicans and Federalists in Pennsylvania, 1790–1801" (Harrisburg: Pennsylvania Historical and Museum Commission,), 139–140.

51. The state-level and district-level estimates of the voting eligible popula-

tion come from Walter Dean Burnham, *Voting in American Elections: The Shaping of the American Political Universe Since 1788* (Bethesda, MD: Academica Press, 2010), table 2.1. For the county level I use the census to determine the number of adult white men. Therefore, county turnout should be interpreted as the proportion of this population that votes. I use linear interpolation to arrive at estimates of county adult white male population in subsequent years in the apportionment cycle. I check these against Burnham's yearly estimates of voting eligible population. There are typically only minor differences between the Burnham and census estimates of the potential electorate.

52. I prefer Burnham's term "potential electorate" to "voting eligible population" because of the latter's connotation of meeting de jure franchise requirements. As will be argued in chapter 2, the de facto voting population was often significantly larger than the de jure requirements allowed. Burnham's figures present a more accurate estimate of the voting universe and correspond to my own census-based estimates quite closely. The state-level eligible electorate figure is from Burnham, *Voting in American Elections,* table 2.1.

53. The early census recorded population in age groups. The relevant ones are 16–25, 26–45, and 46 and older. One must determine how many men in the 16–25 group are 21 or older. The received national estimate is approximately 43 percent. Following this, I calculate a county's potential white male electorate as follows: PE = .43*(16–25) + (26–45) + 46+. See J. D. Hacker, "Decennial Life Tables for the White Population of the United States, 1790–1900," *Historical Methods* 43, no. 2 (April 2010):45–79. These figures match well with Burnam's estimates of the state-level voting eligible population. Between censuses I use linear interpolation to estimate the potential electorate in any given election year. For the general ticket I calculate state turnout using Burnham's (2010) estimates of the state-level voting eligible population. The county-level census is obtained from IPSR study 2896, cited in Michael R. Haines and Inter-university Consortium for Political and Social Research, Historical, Demographic, Economic, and Social Data: The United States, 1790–2002 (Hamilton, NY: Colgate University, 2010), https://doi.org/10.3886/ICPSR02896.v3.

54. V. O. Key Jr., "A Theory of Critical Elections," *Journal of Politics* 17, no. 1 (1955): 3–18.

55. The press described these respective conventions as consisting of members of the legislature and "gentlemen from other parts of the state."

56. *New Hampshire Patriot* (Concord), October 29, 1816.

57. *The People's Advocate* (Portsmouth, NH), October 5, 1816, 1.

58. Michael J. Dubin, *Party Affiliations in the State Legislatures: A Year by Year Summary, 1796–2006* (Jefferson, NC: McFarland, 2007)

2. *Elections in the New Republic*

1. In addition to Orange County, Virginia's Fifth Congressional District included Amherst, Albemarle, Louisa, Culpeper, Spotsylvania, Goochland, and Fluvanna Counties. This district consisted of five Anti-Federalist-lean-

ing counties, two that supported the Constitution's ratification, and one that was divided. See Elmer C. Griffith, *The Rise and Development of the Gerrymander* (Chicago: Scott, Foresman, 1907), 35–41. Throughout the text I use period county names and boundaries. Over the years counties were regularly changed through boundary adjustments, division, augmentation, and elimination.

2. Letter from James Madison to Thomas Jefferson, December 8, 1788, reprinted in Gordon DenBoer, ed., *The Documentary History of the First Federal Elections: 1788–1790*, vol. 2 (Madison: University of Wisconsin Press, 1984), 324–325.

3. For an excellent account of this election, see Richard Labunski, *James Madison and the Struggle for the Bill of Rights* (New York: Oxford University Press, 2006), chap. 7. See also Thomas Rogers Hunter, "The First Gerrymander?: Patrick Henry, James Madison, James Monroe, and Virginia's 1788 Congressional Districting," *Early American Studies, An Interdisciplinary Journal* 9, no. 3 (Fall 2011): 781–820.

4. Labunski, *James Madison and the Struggle for the Bill of Rights*, 152.

5. Edward Carrington to James Madison, December 30, 1788, reprinted in DenBoer, *Documentary History*, 384.

6. See, for example, "Letter to the Freeholders of the Several Religious Denominations . . . ," *Virginia Herald* (Fredericksburg), January 15, 1789, reprinted in DenBoer, *Documentary History*, 336–337. Madison established his religious toleration bona fides by opposing taxes to support the Established Church and by supporting the Virginia Statute for Establishing Religious Freedom.

7. Labunski, *James Madison and the Struggle for the Bill of Rights*, 186.

8. Hunter, "The First Gerrymander?" Hunter casts doubt on whether the 1788 districting was a gerrymander. This assessment is supported by Griffith, *The Rise and Development of the Gerrymander*, 40–41. However, others disagree, including Zagarri, *The Politics of Size*, 122–123. Importantly, Madison and his contemporaries including George Washington thought the districting was designed to ensure his electoral defeat. See letter from Burgess Ball to James Madison (December 8, 1788), James Madison to Thomas Jefferson (December 8, 1788), George Lee Turberville to James Madison (December 14–16, 1788), and other correspondences. These letters are reprinted in DenBoer, *Documentary History*. It is clear that there were attempts to gerrymander Virginia in the various iterations of the districting bill, but most of these did not survive final passage. See Griffith, *The Rise and Development of the Gerrymander*, 31–41.

9. George Washington, "On Recruiting and Maintaining an Army," in *The Writings of George Washington*, vol. 4, *1776*, ed. Worthington Chauncey Ford (New York: G. P. Putnam's Sons, 1889), http://oll.libertyfuld.org/titles/2402/.

10. Ronald P. Formisano, "Deferential-Participant Politics: The Early Republic's Political Culture: 1789–1840," *American Political Science Review* 68, no. 2 (June 1974): 473.

11. Formisano, "Deferential-Participant Politics," 483.

12. J. R. Pole, *Political Representation*, 149.

13. Hofstadter, *The Idea of a Party System*, 47.

14. Formisano, "Deferential-Participant Politics," 484.

15. Richard L. McCormick, "The Party Period and Public Policy: An Exploratory Hypothesis," *Journal of American History* 66, no. 2 (September, 1979): 279–298; Joel H. Silbey, "Beyond Realignment and Realignment Theory: American Political Eras, 1789–1989," in *The End of Realignment? Reinterpreting American Electoral Eras*, ed. Byron E. Schafer (Madison: University of Wisconsin Press, 1991), 2–23; Joel H. Silbey, "The Origins and Development of U.S. Political Parties, 1790–1861," in *CQ Press Guide to U.S. Political Parties*, ed. Marjorie Randon Hershey (Washington, DC: CQ Press, 2014). See also William Nisbet Chambers, Walter Dean Burnham, and Frank Joseph Sorauf, eds., *American Party Systems: Stages of Development*, 2nd ed. (New York: Oxford University Press, 1975); Formisano, "Federalists and Republicans: Parties, Yes—System, No"; and Formisano, "Deferential-Participant Politics."

16. Hanna Fenichel Pitkin, *The Concept of Representation* (Berkeley: University of California Press, 1967), 172.

17. Edmund Burke, "Letter to Sir Hercules Langrishe (1792) from the *Prose of Edmund Burke*, ed. Sir Philp Magnus (1948), https://www.ourcivilisation.com/smartboard/shop/burkee/extracts/chap18.htm, accessed January 17, 2025.

18. John B. Kirby, "Early American Politics—The Search for Ideology: An Historiographical Analysis and Critique of the Concept of 'Deference,'" *Journal of Politics* 32, no. 4 (November 1970): 808–838; Robert E. Brown, *Middle-Class Democracy and the Revolution in Massachusetts, 1691–1780* (Ithaca, NY: Cornell University Press, 1955); Robert E. Brown and B. Katherine Brown, *Virginia 1705–1786: Democracy or Aristocracy* (East Lansing: Michigan State University Press, 1964).

19. Formisano, "Deferential-Participant Politics," 479.

20. Kirby, "Early American Politics," 816.

21. Pasley, "The Cheese and the Words."

22. Andrew W. Robertson, "Voting Rites and Voting Acts: Electioneering Ritual, 1790–1820," in *Beyond the Founders: New Approaches to the Political History of the Early American Republic*, ed. Jeffrey L. Pasley, Andrew W. Robertson, and David Waldstreicher (Chapel Hill: University of North Carolina Press, 2004), 57–78.

23. Kirby, "Early American Politics," 816.

24. Pasley, "The Cheese and the Words," 46.

25. Philip J. Lampi, "The Federalist Party Resurgence, 1808–1816: Evidence from the New Nation Votes Database," *Journal of the Early Republic* 33, no. 2 (Summer 2013): 255–281.

26. John F. Hoadley, "The Emergence of Political Parties in Congress, 1789–1803," *American Political Science Review* 74, no. 3 (1980): 757–779; John H. Aldrich and Ruth W. Grant, "The Antifederalists, the First Congress, and the First Parties," *Journal of Politics* 55, no. 2 (May 1993): 295–326; Aldrich, *Why Parties?*; William T. Bianco, David B. Spence, and John D. Wilkerson, "The Electoral Connection in the Early Congress: The Case of the Compensation Act of 1816," *American Journal of Political Science* 40, no. 1 (February 1996): 145–171; Jamie L. Carson and Jeffrey A. Jenkins, "Examining the Electoral Connection Across Time,"

Annual Review of Political Science 14, (2011): 25–46; Jamie L. Carson and Erik J. Engstrom, "Assessing the Electoral Connection: Evidence from the Early United States," *American Journal of Political Science* 49, no. 4 (2005): 746–757; Charles J. Finocchiaro and Jeffery A Jenkins, "Distributive Politics, the Electoral Connection, and the Antebellum US Congress: The Case of Military Service Pensions," *Journal of Theoretical Politics* 28, no. 2 (2016): 192–224; Samuel Kernell, "Toward Understanding 19th Century Congressional Careers: Ambition, Competition, and Rotation," *American Journal of Political Science* 21, no. 4 (1977): 669–693.

27. Bianco, Spence, and Wilkerson, "The Electoral Connection in the Early Congress."

28. See, for example, "Address of the District Delegates to the Democratic Citizens of the County of Philadelphia," Worchester, MA: American Antiquarian Society, 2018.

29. Jerrald G. Rusk, *A Statistical History of the American Electorate* (Washington, DC: CQ Press, 2001), table 5-16.

30. Polsby, "The Institutionalization of the US House of Representatives," table 2.

31. Carson and Engstrom, "Assessing the Electoral Connection."

32. Robertson, *The Language of Democracy*, ix.

33. Daniel Peart and Adam I. P. Smith, *Practicing Democracy: Popular Politics in the United States from the Constitution to the Civil War* (Charlottesville: University of Virginia Press, 2015), 7.

34. Formisano, "Federalists and Republicans," 38–39.

35. Richard P. McCormick, *The Second American Party System: Party Formation in the Jacksonian Era* (Chapel Hill: University of North Carolina Press, 1966), 27.

36. Formisano, "Federalists and Republicans," 38–39.

37. Formisano, "Federalists and Republicans," 35.

38. Formisano, "Federalists and Republicans," 35.

39. David Hackett Fischer, *The Revolution of American Conservatism: The Federalist Party in the Era of Jeffersonian Democracy* (New York: Harper & Row, 1965), xviii–xix.

40. Lampi, "The Federalist Party Resurgence"; Peart, *Era of Experimentation.*

41. Hoadley, *Origins of American Political Parties*, 190.

42. Aldrich, *Why Parties?*, 81. See also Aldrich and Grant, "The Antifederalists."

43. Aldrich and Grant, "The Antifederalists"; Aldrich, *Why Parties?*, 80–82.

44. See, for example, Selinger, "Rethinking the Development."

45. McCormick, "Political Development," 94–95.

46. McCormick, "Political Development," note 6.

47. Donald J. Ratcliffe, *Party Sprit in a Frontier Republic* (Columbus: Ohio State University Press, 1998).

48. Likewise, at-large House of Representatives elections, or the election of a strong governor, motivates party development because these are significant "all or nothing" electoral prizes. Joseph A. Schlesinger, "Political Party Organization," in *Handbook of Organizations*, ed. James G. March (Chicago: Rand McNally, 1965).

49. Schlesinger, "Political Party Organization," 767–769, 774–786.

50. Hoadley, *Origins of American Political Parties,* 46.

51. Hoadley, *Origins of American Political Parties,* 45–46.

52. Jeffrey L. Pasley, *The Tyranny of Printers: Newspaper Politics in the Early Republic* (Charlottesville: University of Virginia Press, 2001) 12.

53. Pasley, *The Tyranny of Printers,* 13.

54. William David Sloan, *The Party Press: The Newspaper Role in National Politics, 1789–1816* (PhD diss., University of Texas at Austin, 1981). The number of American newspapers tripled between the late 1790s and the first years of the nineteenth century. These papers were especially abundant in the northern states, where party competition was strongest, but extended throughout the nation. See Sloan, *The Party Press,* 38.

55. Literacy rates in late colonial America and the early republic were quite high, especially among whites. In New England literacy approached universality for both men and women, while literacy rates modestly declined as one moved through the Middle Atlantic to the South. However, in all regions the large majority of white men and women could read and write. Literacy further expanded in the early nineteenth century with increased availability of primary schooling. For a discussion of early republic literacy, see Robert A. Gross and Mary Kelly, eds., *A History of the Book in America,* vol. 2 (Chapel Hill: University of North Carolina Press, 2010), 286–295. See also Kenneth Lockridge, *Literacy in Colonial New England* (New York: W. W. Norton, 1975).

56. Pasley, *The Tyranny of Printers,* chap. 3.

57. Pasley, *The Tyranny of Printers,* 3.

58. Robertson, *The Language of Democracy,* ix.

59. Pasley, *The Tyranny of Printers,* 13.

60. Pasley, *The Tyranny of Printers,* 13.

61. Robertson, *The Language of Democracy,* 53.

62. Robertson, *The Language of Democracy,* 51–52.

63. *Oxford Gazette* (Oxford, New York), May 6, 1818.

64. Robertson, *The Language of Democracy,* 47.

65. Robertson, *The Language of Democracy,* 52.

66. McCormick, *The SecondAmerican Party System,* 23.

67. McCormick, *The Second American Party System,* 24. See also William Nisbit Chambers, *Political Parties in a New Nation: The American Experience, 1776–1809* (New York: Oxford University Press, 1963), 21–23.

68. McCormick, *The Second American Party System,* 25.

69. William G. Shade, "Political Pluralism and Party Development: The Creation of a Modern Party System: 1815–1852," in *The Evolution of American Electoral Systems,* ed. Paul Kleppner et al. (Westport, CT: Greenwood Press, 1981), 79.

70. Chambers, *Political Parties in a New Nation,* 22.

71. Nobel E. Cunningham Jr., *The Jeffersonian Republicans: The Formation of Party Organization, 1789–1801* (Chapel Hill: University of North Carolina Press, 1957), 259. See also Formisano, "Deferential-Participant Politics."

72. Robert J. Dinkin, *Voting in Revolutionary America: A Study of Elections in the Original Thirteen States, 1776–1789* (Westport, CT: Greenwood Press, 1982), 57.

73. Dinkin, *Voting in Revolutionary America*, 60.

74. Harvey Strum, “Property Qualifications and Voting Behavior in New York, 1807–1816,” *Journal of the Early Republic* 1, no. 4 (Winter 1981): 347–371.

75. Strum, “Property Qualifications,” 370–371.

76. Aric Gooch and Jay Dow, “Congressional Nominations and Party Emergence, 1788–1808,” *Social Science Quarterly* 102, no. 6 (2022): 2836–2848.

77. *Carlisle Gazette*, September 21, 1804.

78. Hoadley, *Origins of American Political Parties*, 38.

79. Donald J. Ratcliffe, “The Right to Vote and the Rise of Democracy, 1787–1828,” *Journal of the Early Republic* 33 no. 2 (Summer 2013): 221–230. Further, some states did enfranchise women and free African Americans. From 1776 until 1807 New Jersey enfranchised unmarried women possessing property. See Judith Apter Klinghoffer and Lois Elkins, “‘The Petticoat Electors’: Women’s Suffrage in New Jersey, 1776–1807,” *Journal of the Early Republic* 12, no. 2 (Summer 1992): 159–193. See also Rosemarie Zagarri, *Revolutionary Backlash: Women and Politics in the Early American Republic* (Philadelphia: University of Pennsylvania Press, 2007), 30–37.

80. Parliament, House of Commons, The History of the Parliamentary Franchise, March 1, 2013, https://commonslibrary.parliament.uk/research-briefings/rp13-14/.

81. Chilton Williamson, *American Suffrage: From Property to Democracy, 1760–1860* (Princeton, NJ: Princeton University Press, 1960), 136.

82. Ratcliffe, “The Right to Vote,” 221, 230.

83. Ratcliffe, “The Right to Vote.”

84. Alexander Keyssar, *The Right to Vote: The Contested History of Democracy in the United States*, rev. ed. (New York: Basic Books, 2000). 9. See also *Oxford English Dictionary*.

85. Williamson, *American Suffrage*, 62. See also Keyssar, *The Right to Vote*, 11–12.

86. Quoted in Williamson, *American Suffrage*, 11.

87. Williamson, *American Suffrage*, 11.

88. Williamson, *American Suffrage*, 160.

89. Williamson, *American Suffrage*, 160.

90. Williamson, *American Suffrage*, 122.

91. Ratcliffe, *The Right to Vote*, 220.

92. Keyssar, *The Right to Vote*, 5.

93. These included Pennsylvania, North Carolina, and South Carolina.

94. Keyssar, *The Right to Vote*, 13.

95. Keyssar, *The Right to Vote*, 13.

96. Williamson, *American Suffrage*, 136.

97. Keyssar, *The Right to Vote*, table A.1. Note that New York and some other states maintained a two-tiered franchise requirement with a higher threshold required to vote for the state senate and governor. Also, Quakers were required to take an oath of allegiance to the state.

98. Ratcliffe, *The Right to Vote*, 221.

99. Ratcliffe, *The Right to Vote*, 225–226.

100. Ratcliffe, *The Right to Vote*, 224.

101. Ratcliffe, *The Right to Vote*, 225. In the colonial period small freeholds were sometimes created by dividing property and transferring title specifically for the purpose of enfranchising sympathetic voters. This practice largely ceased by the late eighteenth century. Williamson, *American Suffrage*, 50.

102. Ratcliffe, *The Right to Vote*, 228.

103. John A. Munroe, *Federalist Delaware 1775–1815* (New Brunswick, NJ: Rutgers University Press, 1954), 195–196.

104. Ratcliffe, *The Right to Vote*, 229.

105. Williamson, *American Suffrage*, 139.

106. Williamson, *American Suffrage*, 98. See also Ratcliffe, *The Right to Vote*, 226.

107. Apter, Klinghoffer, and Elkins, "The Petticoat Electors," esp. 159–160.

108. Van Gosse, *The First Reconstruction: Black Politics in America from the Revolution to the Civil War* (Chapel Hill: University of North Carolina Press, 2021), tables 3.1, 8.1.

109. Gosse *The First Reconstruction*. See also Paul J. Polgar, "'Whenever They Judge It Expedient': The Politics of Partisanship and Free Black Voting Rights in Early National New York," *American Nineteenth Century History* 12, no. 1 (March 2011): 1–23. For a more cautious assessment, see Ratcliffe, "The Right to Vote," 229–230.

110. See, for example, Dinkin, *Voting in Revolutionary America*, chap. 5; Robertson, "Voting Rites and Voting Acts."

111. Robertson, "Voting Rites and Voting Acts."

112. Alan Taylor, "The Art of Hook & Snivey": Political Culture in Upstate New York During the 1790s," *Journal of American History* 79, no. 4 (March 1993): 1371–1396.

113. Taylor, "Hook & Snivey," 1372.

114. Dinkin, *Voting in Revolutionary America*, 84.

115. Robertson, *The Language of Democracy*, 23; Dinkin, *Voting in Revolutionary America*, 73.

116. Robertson, "Voting Rites and Voting Acts," 61.

117. Robertson, *The Language of Democracy*, 60.

118. Robertson, *The Language of Democracy*, 60–63.

119. Dinkin, *Voting in Revolutionary America*, 81.

120. Robertson, *The Language of Democracy*, 60.

121. Robertson, *The Language of Democracy*, 60. See also Taylor. "Hook & Snivey," 1387.

122. Taylor, "Hook & Snivey," 1387.

123. Dinkin, *Voting in Revolutionary America*, 82–83.

124. David Waldstreicher, *In the Midst of Perpetual Fetes: The Making of American Nationalism, 1776–1820* (Chapel Hill: University of North Carolina Press, 1997), 196–197.

125. Dinkin, *Voting in Revolutionary America*, 89.

126. Zagarri, *Revolutionary Backlash*, 46–47, 68–75.

127. Waldstreicher, *In the Midst of Perpetual Fetes*, 186.

128. Pasley, "The Cheese and the Words."

129. Waldstreicher, *In the Midst of Perpetual Fetes*, 186.

130. A New Nation Votes. https://elections.lib.tufts.edu/catalog/tufts:va.uscongress.13.1799, accessed July 15, 2018. A special election in the Virginia Thirteenth District the following year saw a total of 1,206 votes cast.

131. The election was tied in Henrico County, where Clopton and Marshall observed the voting. The candidates, of course, would have no idea how the voting was progressing in Charles City, Hanover, James City, and New Kent Counties, which formed the balance of the district.

132. Jean Edward Smith, *John Marshall: Definer of a Nation* (New York: Henry Holt, 1996), 249–250.

133. Quoted in Smith, *John Marshall*, 243.

134. Smith, *John Marshall*, 242.

135. Smith, *John Marshall*, 243.

136. Smith, *John Marshall*, 246.

137. Robertson, *The Language of Democracy*, 43.

138. Dinkin, *Voting in Revolutionary America*, 85.

139. Dinkin, *Voting in Revolutionary America*, 85.

140. Robertson, *The Language of Democracy*, 43.

141. Dinkin, *Voting in Revolutionary America*, 86.

142. Robertson, *The Language of Democracy*, 64.

143. Waldstreicher, *Perpetual Fetes*, 9, 203. Quoted text from Zagari, "Festive Nationalism," 508.

144. Waldstreicher, *Perpetual Fetes*, 203.

145. Robertson, *The Language of Democracy*, 44.

146. Robertson, *The Language of Democracy*, 44.

147. Dinkin, *Voting in Revolutionary America*, 79.

148. Waldstreicher, *Perpetual Fetes*, 181.

149. Waldstreicher, *Perpetual Fetes*, 13.

150. Dinkin, *Voting in Revolutionary America*, 77, 81, 87–88.

151. Dinkin, *Voting in Revolutionary America*, 87.

152. Waldstreicher, *Perpetual Fetes*, 196–197.

153. Waldstreicher, *Perpetual Fetes*, 200–201.

154. Waldstreicher, *Perpetual Fetes*, 198.

155. Waldstreicher, *Perpetual Fetes*, 180.

156. Albrecht Koschnik, "Political Conflict and Public Contest: Rituals of National Celebration in Philadelphia, 1788–1815," *Pennsylvania Magazine of History & Biography* 118, no. 3 (July 1994): 209–248.

157. Waldstreicher, *Perpetual Fetes*, 192.

158. Waldstreicher, *Perpetual Fetes*, 187.

159. Waldstreicher, *Perpetual Fetes*, 196.

160. Waldstreicher, *Perpetual Fetes*, 193.

161. Len Travers, *Celebrating the Fourth: Independence Day and the Rites of Nationalism in the Early Republic* (Amherst: University of Massachusetts Press, 1997), 226. Quoted in Zagarri, *Revolutionary Backlash*, 505.

162. Bohmer, "The Maryland Electorate," 173.
163. Dinkin, *Voting in Revolutionary America,* 88.
164. Dinkin, *Voting in Revolutionary America,* 78.
165. Waldstreicher, *Perpetual Fetes,* 184–185.
166. Zagarri, *Revolutionary Backlash,* 116, 140–147.
167. Zagarri, *Revolutionary Backlash,* 140–147.
168. Robertson, *The Language of Democracy,* 50–51.

3. *The Middle Atlantic States*

1. Quoted in Tinkcom, *The Republicans and Federalists,* 144.
2. Tinkcom, *The Republicans and Federalists,* 153.
3. McCormick, *The History of Voting in New Jersey,* 87.
4. McCormick. *The History of Voting in New Jersey,* 87.
5. Tinkcom, *The Republicans and Federalists,* 179.
6. Tinkcom, *The Republicans and Federalists,* 175.
7. McCormick, *The History of Voting in New Jersey,* 88.
8. John L. Brooke, *Columbia Rising: Civil Life on the Upper Hudson from the Revolution to the Age of Jackson* (Chapel Hill: University of North Carolina Press, 2010), 300.
9. Edward Countryman, "The Empire State and the Albany Regency," in *The Empire State: A History of New York,* ed. Milton M. Klein (Ithaca, NY: Cornell University Press, 2001), 300. For a discussion of the Quids and their importance in early Pennsylvania politics, see Andrew Shankman, *Crucible of Democracy: The Struggle to Fuse Egalitarianism and Capitalism in Jeffersonian Pennsylvania* (Lawrence: University Press of Kansas, 2004), chap. 3.
10. Countryman, "The Empire State," 297.
11. Edward Countryman, "A Large and Valuable Canal," in *The Empire State: A History of New York,* ed. Milton M. Klein (Ithaca, NY: Cornell University Press, 2001), 275.
12. For a discussion of the rise of DeWitt Clinton and the Clintonians, see Hofstadter, *The Idea of a Party System,* 219–223.
13. Hofstadter, *The Idea of a Party System,* 223.
14. Rosemarie Zagarri, "New Jersey," A New Nation Votes, accessed August 13, 2019, https://elections.lib.tufts.edu/.
15. In this table and corresponding tables in the following chapters, I label columns by congresses rather than years because there was no standard election calendar. Some states elected representatives to the upcoming Congress in the year in which the Congress convened.
16. Gosse, *The First Reconstruction,* chap. 3 and 8.
17. Gosse, *The First Reconstruction,* chap. 3 and 8. See also Klinghoffer and Elkins, "'The Petticoat Electors"; McCormick, *The History of Voting in New Jersey,* 98–99.
18. Burnham, *Voting in American Elections,* table 2.1.

19. The general ticket elects representatives at-large. Electors receive as many noncumulative votes as there are seats to be selected. See Dow, *Electing the House,* chap. 4, for a discussion of its use in early House elections.

20. New Jersey highlights some of the challenges of studying early general-ticket elections. The Federalists only seriously contested House seats in eight cycles. These are 1797, 1798, 1800, 1806, 1808, 1812, 1813, and 1814. The county-level returns from noncontested elections are not informative. Finally, sometimes a district return is complete when one or more of its constituent county returns is missing. However, this is seldom the case in the Middle Atlantic region.

21. I calculate the corresponding figures for multimember districts similarly.

22. These "Quids" are identified as Constitutionalist Party candidates. This "party" attracted candidates that ran under both Democratic-Republican and Federalist labels. This is true for these candidates, both of whom at different points in their political careers sought election as a Democratic-Republican and as a Federalist. The "Constitutionalists" were Quids as the term was used in Pennsylvania. See Cunningham, "Who Were the Quids?"

23. After 1816 many candidates ceased competing under the Federalist label. Here I just consider elections contested by Democratic-Republican and Federalist candidates.

24. In 1804 New York allowed those who rented tenements costing $25 or who met the 1777 requirements to vote. New York dropped it property requirement for whites in 1821 but retained them for "men of color." New Jersey added a tax-based franchise in 1807. See Keyssar, *The Right to Vote,* app. A2.

25. These are slight *underestimates* of the number of voters and turnout rates in 1796, 1804, 1806, and 1818 because of the few missing districts in these years.

26. In 1808, after an unsuccessful attempt to impeach Democratic-Republican governor Thomas McKean, the liberal wing of the party successfully nominated Simon Snyder, who defeated Federalist James Ross with a 61 percent majority. In 1820 Democratic-Republican governor William Findlay's financial improprieties contributed to his defeat by Federalist Joseph Hiester. Sanford W. Higginbotham, *The Keystone in the Democratic Arch: Pennsylvania Politics, 1800–1816* (Philadelphia: Pennsylvania Historical and Museum Commission, 1952), 154–155. Hiester was also supported by "Old School Republicans."

27. The Federalists and "Quids" also experienced significant internal divisions in this election. Historian Sanford W. Higginbotham writes that "The Federalists and Quids were unable to reach any [nomination] agreement. In a Constitutionalist caucus at Lancaster on January 29, 1808, the Quids proposed Joseph Heister and John Spayd as candidates for Governor. The former's name was later withdrawn; and they united behind Spayd. . . . The Federalists for the most part backed James Ross. . . . he Quids refused the Federalist proposal for a nominating convention, and the latter walked out of the caucus rather than be bound by the nomination of Spayd. The Quids then adjourned their meeting to March 23, 1808, when they made formal announcement of their nominees.

They included Spayd as candidate for Governor." In the gubernatorial contest Spayd received 4,006 votes, or 3.5 percent of the vote. Higginbotham, *The Keystone in the Democratic Arch,* 154–155.

28. For presentation purposes I label the horizontal axis by year even though the election years in these states do not match evenly. Each symbol corresponds to elections to the Fifth–Nineteenth Congresses in order.

29. By way of comparison, US election turnout since 1980 has averaged about 57 percent in presidential years and 40 percent in off-year elections. See Michael P. McDonald, United States Election Project, accessed September 23, 2019, http://www.electproject.org/.

30. See, for example, Pole, *Political Representation in England,* 149–150; Richard P. McCormick, "New Perspectives on Jacksonian Politics," *American Historical Review* 65, no. 2 (January 1960): 288–301; and Peart, *Era of Experimentation,* app. A.1.2.

31. Nearly a quarter of these candidates previously sought office as a Democratic-Republican or as a Federalist.

32. This requirement dates from 1797. McCormick, *The History of Voting,* 79–80, 91–96.

33. New Jersey Election Law of 1797. McCormick, *The History of Voting,* 104.

34. The Ninth District.

35. The Second was a dual-member district. The Seventh was single-member district until the Eighteenth Congress, when it elected two representatives. The Fourteenth District elected one representative.

36. These analyses require the districts to have four contested elections in the apportionment cycles. In the 1802–1810 period the districts are First, Third, Sixth, and Eleventh. In 1812–1820 the districts are First, Second, Third, Fifth, Seventh, Eleventh, and Fourteenth.

37. Census-identified counties, 1800, 1810, and 1820. See also Long, John Hamilton, ed., *Atlas of Historical County Boundaries* (Chicago: Newberry Library, Dr. William M. Scholl Center for American History and Culture, 2012), https://www.loc.gov/item/2018487899/.

38. Long, *Atlas of Historical County Boundaries.*

39. The Federalists did not receive votes in Mongomery County in 1804 or 1806, and neither the Republicans nor Federalists received votes in 1824.

40. These are the Sixth–Tenth Districts.

41. New Jersey added Warren County in 1824 by dividing Sussex County. This has no implications for this analysis.

42. As in Pennsylvania, the Federalist success rate was closer to 50 percent, while that for Republican incumbents was over 70 percent.

43. There were 108 district elections featuring incumbents, but some of these were multimember districts featuring more than one incumbent. In addition, an incumbent may seek election multiple times. Fifty-nine unique incumbents ran in these elections.

44. Southard served in the Seventh to Eleventh Congresses, and then again in the Fourteenth through Sixteenth Congresses.

45. An important exception to this pattern is the aforementioned and

immensely competitive four-member district centered on Philadelphia and Delaware Counties. Here the Federalists won three of five elections between 1812 and 1820. Importantly, the Federalists showed strongest at the end of the era, winning the district in both 1818 and 1820. The Pennsylvania First District elected four representatives each cycle between 1812 and 1820. Of these twenty representatives, thirteen were Federalists, six were Republicans, and one was supported by both parties.

46. Griffith, *The Rise and Development of the Gerrymander*, 58.

47. This apportionment changed slightly over the years. For example, Essex County's representation increased to four in 1803. In addition, Cumberland, Morris, and Monmouth Counties received an additional Assembly member between 1815 and 1818. This again reflects the advantageous use of rules as New Jersey Republicans recognized that a more proportional representation of counties based on population would benefit them in the long run. They were able to make some adjustments in this direction over the objections of southern New Jersey Federalists. See McCormick, *The History of Voting in New Jersey*, 101–102.

48. Dubin, *Party Affiliations in the State Legislatures*, 126.

4. *The Border States*

1. Munroe, *Federalist Delaware*, 122.

2. Paul Goodman, "The First American Party System," in *The American Party Systems: Stages of Political Development*, ed. William Nisbet Chambers and Walter Dean Burnham (New York: Oxford University Press, 1975), 67.

3. John H. Fenton, *Politics in the Border States* (New Orleans: Hauser Press, 1957), 191–192.

4. McCormick, *The Second American Party System*, 154–155.

5. McCormick, *The Second American Party System*, 158–159.

6. Keyssar, *The Right to Vote*, table A2. See also J. R. Pole, "Suffrage and Representation in Maryland from 1776 to 1810: A Statistical Note and Some Reflections," *Journal of Southern History* 24, no. 2 (May 1958): 218–255.

7. Maryland Election Law of 1805.

8. Nobel E. Cunningham Jr., *The Jeffersonian Republicans in Power: Party Operations, 1801—1809* (Chapel Hill: University of North Carolina Press, 1963), 276.

9. McCormick, *The Second American Party System*, 158.

10. Herbert was a powerful Maryland lawyer and politician who served in a variety of offices including Speaker of the Maryland House of Delegates and as a representative in the Fourteenth and Fifteenth Congresses. Fischer, *The Revolution of American Conservatism*, 102.

11. *Alexandria Herald*, August 16, 1816.

12. Munroe, *Federalist Delaware*, 123.

13. Munroe, *Federalist Delaware*, 120.

14. Munroe, *Federalist Delaware*, 287.

15. The northern Delaware Quaker vote differs from in that neighboring

Pennsylvania, where Quakers generally voted Federalist. Not unlike Quaker support for the Democratic-Republicans in the north, southern Delaware slaveholding is intriguing because one would expect this would foster greater Democratic-Republican support.

16. There was a slight boundary adjustment to Calvert County, but this had no electoral importance.

17. As before, I update the population and electorate figures throughout the apportionment cycle.

18. McCormick, *The Second American Party System*, 150–151. See also Fischer, *The Revolution of American Conservatism*, 75.

19. McCormick, *The Second American Party System*, 157.

20. McCormick, *The Second American Party System*, 157. See also Fischer, *The Revolution of American Conservatism*, 68–71.

Cunningham, *The Jeffersonian Republicans in Power*, 176–177.

21. Cunningham, *The Jeffersonian Republicans in Power*, 176–177.

22. Cunningham, *The Jeffersonian Republicans in Power*, 177.

23. Fischer, *The Revolution of American Conservatism*, 68–71.

24. Endorsing documents including letters, pamphlets, and broadsheets were common. For an example of a coordinating document in a more complex electoral setting, see "Address of the District Delegates to the Democratic Citizens of the County of Philadelphia" (Philadelphia, 1810), which endorsed six Democratic House of Representatives candidates. Reprinted by American Antiquarian Society, Worcester, Massachusetts, 2018.

25. Cunningham, *The Jeffersonian Republicans in Power*, 176–177.

26. Cunningham, *The Jeffersonian Republicans in Power*, 149.

27. Pole, "Suffrage and Representation in Maryland from 1776 to 1810," 222.

28. Delaware and Maryland turnout is only modestly correlated. This is primarily because turnout in both states was consistently high. There was not a lot of movement in these figures, either up or down.

29. The Maryland decline is more difficult to explain. Pole records the same pattern in his data.

30. Bohmer, "The Maryland Electorate and the Concept of a Party System in the Early National Period,", esp. table 4.4 and 169.

31. These counties had stable boundaries throughout the era, with the minor exceptions of Montgomery and Prince Georges Counties, which each lost a small amount of territory to Washington, DC, in 1801. I begin this series in 1800 to ensure sufficient observed elections for meaningful analysis.

32. See Fischer, *The Revolution of American Conservatism*, 159–160, 166–177. Fischer points to the difficulty of correlating areas of agricultural practices and slavery with party support, 212.

33. Paul E. Johnson, *The Early American Republic, 1789—1829* (New York: Oxford University Press, 2007), 86–88.

34. Archer was identified as a "Quid."

35. Griffith, *The Rise and Development of the Gerrymander*, 92–94.

36. Griffith, The Rise and Development of the Gerrymander, 92–94.

37. Goodman, "The First American Party System," 67.

5. *New England*

1. As in other states, electors received as many noncumulative votes as seats available to elect. Rhode Island used two separate ballots to elect each of its representatives between 1796 and 1800. Beginning in 1802 it adopted the standard general ticket to elect both representatives. It maintained this system for the rest of the era.

2. New Hampshire required runoffs in 1796, 1810, 1822, and 1824 to select a handful of representatives that were not elected in the first round. Rhode Island elections required multiple rounds in 1800, 1806, and 1825. However, most of these were one-party affairs where more candidates received votes than the apportionment would support. Only New Hampshire's 1810 election required a second ballot, because both parties were equally matched and votes so close that candidates from both parties were elected on the second ballot.

3. Cunningham, *The Jeffersonian Republicans in Power*, 137–142.

4. Jonathan D. Sassi, "The First Party Competition and Southern New England's Public Christianity," *Journal of the Early Republic* 21, no. 2 (Summer 2001): 276.

5. Fischer, *The Revolution of American Conservatism*, 98.

6. Fischer, *The Revolution in American Conservatism*, 97.

7. Richard J. Purcell, *Connecticut in Transition, 1775–1818* (Middletown, CT: Wesleyan University Press, 1963), 187.

8. C. Edward Skeen, "'Vox Populi, Vox Dei': The Compensation Act of 1816 and the Rise of Popular Politics," *Journal of the Early Republic* 6, no. 3 (Autumn 1986): 257–274.

9. Bianco, Spence, and Wilkerson, "The Electoral Connection in the Early Congress."

10. Purcell, *Connecticut in Transition*, 147.

11. Purcell, *Connecticut in Transition*, 206.

12. Purcell, *Connecticut in Transition*, 137.

13. Purcell, *Connecticut in Transition*, 138.

14. Purcell, *Connecticut in Transition*, 151.

15. Purcell, *Connecticut in Transition*, 161.

16. Purcell, *Connecticut in Transition*, 151–152.

17. Cheshire, New Hampshire, *Political Observatory*, October 13, 1804.

18. Sassi, "The First Party Competition."

19. Andrew R. L. Clayton, "The Fragmentation of a 'Great Family': The Panic of 1819 and the Rise of the Midding Interest in Boston, 1818–1822," *Journal of the Early Republic* 2 (Summer 1982): 143–167; Peart, *Era of Experimentation*, 21–22.

20. Massachusetts elected twenty representatives to the Thirteenth through the Sixteenth Congresses. Beginning with the Seventeenth Congress and the admission of Maine and Missouri to the Union, Massachusetts apportionment decreased to thirteen, where it remained through the Nineteenth Congress.

21. Between 1797 and 1822 Massachusetts made several changes to county boundaries, but most of these were minor and have few electoral implications.

22. Merrimack County was created in 1824 and is not included in this analysis.

23. Gooch and Dow, "Congressional Nominations and Party Emergence," 75.

24. *Courier of New Hampshire*, May 16, 1804; *New-Hampshire Gazette*, August 7, 1804.

25. Fischer, *Revolution in American Conservatism*, 62.

26. Cunningham, *The Jeffersonian Republicans in Power*, 133–138; Fischer, *Revolution in American Conservatism*, 60.

27. Cunningham, *The Jeffersonian Republicans in Power*, 127.

28. Cunningham, *The Jeffersonian Republicans in Power*, 146–147.

29. Cunningham, *The Jeffersonian Republicans in Power*, 146–147.

30. Cunningham, *The Jeffersonian Republicans in Power*, 129.

31. There are complete nomination election returns from 1798 to 1818. The missing general election returns are for elections contested in 1806, 1808, and 1814. Since there are no tickets in a nomination election, and only Federalist candidates stand in the general election, I calculate the number of voters as the sum of total votes divided by eighteen. Each elector received this number of noncumulative votes. For the same reason, in the general election I calculate turnout by dividing the total votes by the apportionment. So, for example, Connecticut's 1812 voting-eligible population was 57,162 and its apportionment was 7. In the general election, electors cast 72,937 noncumulative votes. Assuming complete ballots, this returns 10,420 electors and a turnout rate of 18.2 percent. This was high for Connecticut. The 1812 nomination election turnout rate was about half this figure.

32. The election years for which there are both complete nomination returns and complete general election returns are 1798, 1800, 1802, 1804, 1810, 1812, 1816, and 1818.

33. V.O. Key Jr., *Southern Politics in State and Nation* (New York: Knopf, 1949), 409.

34. The Republicans won elections here in 1802, 1804, and 1808.

35. In 1820 Massachusetts had twenty-one counties including the seven that would shortly become part of Maine.

36. Following is information on county-level party strength:

Republican Counties	*Elections/ Wins*	*Region*	*Federalist Counties*	*Elections/ Wins*	*Region*
Berkshire	15/11	Northwest	Cumberland	15/11	Maine
Kennebec	13/12	Maine	Essex	15/12	Northeast
Middlesex	15/13	Northeast	Hampshire	15/13	Northwest
Nantucket	15/11	Southeast	Suffolk	15/13	Northeast
Norfolk	15/12	Northeast	Washington	14/10	South-central
			Worcester	15/13	North-central

37. This district included the towns of Andover, Ipswich, and Newburyport.

38. In Maine's Hancock County the Republican vote is noticeably more stable than the Federalist vote. The Republicans typically enjoyed support ranging from 50 to 66 percent while Federalist support ranged from roughly 29 percent to 52 percent.

39. These are nearly complete. New Hampshire's Coos County was created in 1803.

40. The Federalists swept the elections of 1802, 1804, 1808, 1812, and 1814. The Republicans swept the 1806, 1816, and 1819 elections. In 1810 Republicans won four seats to the single Federalist seat. The partisanship of the 1820 candidates is unclear.

41. Geography provides scant insight on the Connecticut vote. This is because of Connecticut's primary system.

42. In first-round elections.

43. Kittridge sought election from the district center on Essex County, which changed boundaries and names during the period. Most of his efforts were centered in the Essex North district. In some directories his last name is spelled Kittredge.

44. Foster was initially elected in 1794, but given the time frame of this study, I treat his and all similarly situated candidates' initial election as 1796.

45. These men averaged well under two wins.

46. Specifically, eighty-nine elections included an incumbent, and the incumbent won sixty-nine of these contests.

47. *Salem Gazette*, November 5, 1816. The spelling of some words changed to modern conventions.

48. One nonaffiliated incumbent also lost.

49. Griffith, *The Rise and Development of the Gerrymander*, 73–74.

50. *Columbia* (Massachusetts) *Centinel*, a Federalist publication, December 16, 1812. This is certainly one of the first times a newspaper referenced "Gerrymander" to explain districting effects.

51. Griffith, *The Rise and Development of the Gerrymander*, 89.

52. Goodman, "The First American Party System," 81.

53. Connecticut towns typically elected two assemblymen, each requiring a majority. This often produced multi-round elections.

54. The 1820 populations of the counties were thus: Cheshire (45,376), Coos (5,549), Grafton (32,989), Hillsborough (53,884), Rockingham (55,246), and Strafford (51,117).

6. *The South*

1. Lee Soltow, *Distribution of Wealth and Income in the United States in 1798* (Pittsburgh: University of Pittsburgh Press, 1989), 41–42.

2. Throughout the period the only "large" southern city was Charleston, South Carolina. Its 1810 population, for example, was 25,000. Campbell Gibson, "Population of the 100 Largest Cities and Other Urban Places in the

United States: 1790 to 1990," Working Paper Number POP-WP027 (Washington, DC: Census Bureau, 1998).

3. Rusk, *A Statistical History of the American Electorate*, table 4–1. Beginning in 1800 Virginia used statewide elections to selected presidential electors whereas North Carolina primarily elected presidential electors at the district level until 1812, after which it selected presidential electors statewide.

4. Lampi, "The Federalist Party Resurgence."

5. The essay was reprinted in the Democratic-Republican *Baltimore Whig*.

6. This refers to Federalist William Loughton Smith, who served in Congress 1789–1787. Loughton was a close congressional ally of Treasury Secretary Alexander Hamilton and later served as minister to Portugal.

7. Charleston *City Gazette*, September 12, 1808.

8. Gray's partisanship is misidentified in the NNV returns. He is identified as a Federalist. He was a Democratic-Republican. This has few implications for the subsequent analyses.

9. Virginia held its elections in March, after the start of the congressional session.

10. Cunningham, "The Jeffersonian Republicans in Power," 189–191; Fischer, *The Revolution of American Conservatism*, 70.

11. Fischer, *The Revolution in American Conservatism*, 202.

12. To balance these divisions, South Carolina, for example, moved its capital from Charleson to Columbia in 1786.

13. Griffith, *The Rise and Development of the Gerrymander*, 82–83.

14. Ira Berlin, *Many Thousands Gone: The First Two Centuries of Slavery in North America* (Cambridge, MA: Belknap Press of Harvard University Press, 1998), table 1, 369–370.

15. Keyssar, *The Right to Vote*, tables A.2–A.4. Keyssar records that Georgia had no explicit racial restriction on voting, but all evidence indicates that free African Americans were excluded from the suffrage. The same is true for North Carolina, Virginia, and South Carolina, all of which explicitly denied franchise to African Americans.

16. South Carolina's missing county returns is exacerbated by the state's use of parishes and other territorial units for reporting votes. South Carolina's subdistrict reporting units cannot be matched to a census FIPS code.

17. Chambers, *Political Parties in a New Nation*; George Daniel Luetscher, *Early Political Machinery in the United States* (Philadelphia: University of Pennsylvania, 1903).

18. *Farmer's Repository*, February 15, 1811. The county is now in West Virginia.

19. Now Charleston, West Virginia.

20. This makes little difference in Georgia, which had universal white male franchise.

21. Virginia's counties increased from eighty-eight at the election of the Eighth Congress to 108 counties twenty years later.

22. Virginia required a freehold of fifty acres, or twenty-five acres and an improved dwelling from 1762 to 1804. Thereafter, the statute simply required

the ownership of property. There was no tax-paying requirement. North Carolina had no freehold requirement for House elections but did have a tax-paying requirement. Keyssar, *The Right to Vote*, app. A.2. As noted, these requirements were not always rigorously enforced.

23. Only the 1808 election to the Eleventh Congress is missing.

24. Georgia counties remained largely stable from 1800 to 1817, but the state created three new counties in 1818. Overall, the counties remain largely the same in the period, giving confidence that the county figures accurately capture political participation at this level. Georgia did, however, significantly increase the number of counties after 1820.

25. *Alexandria* (Virginia) *Daily Gazette, Commercial and Political*, April 17, 1811.

26. The residual vote elected two nonaffiliated candidates.

27. Other affiliated candidates won the remaining counties.

28. Nonaffiliated and other party candidates received only a trivial number of votes, so the Federalist vote share also captures the Democratic-Republican vote.

29. This figure includes the 1810 election, which the Federalists conceded without a fight.

30. I do not attribute party to candidates, but if one were to do so, arguably, four Republicans were elected to the Tenth Congress. Rusk, *A Statistical History of the American Electorate*, tables 5–9.

31. In 1821 the lower Chesapeake's Mathews County saw the combined votes of the Federalists equal that of the Republican candidate, who won 109 county votes. One of the Federalists was a spoiler who received only three votes, but this was enough for the combined Federalist tally to equal that of the Republican tally.

32. The vote medians and their deviations are calculated using contested elections.

33. These counties are Accomack, Berkeley, Hampshire, Hardy, Loudoun, Monongalia, and Northampton. Northampton County presents a significant outlier to this pattern, with 47 percent of its population enslaved.

34. Incumbents are not present in the surviving post-1820 South Carolina returns.

35. Griffith, *The Rise and Development of the Gerrymander*, 83–84.

36. These counties are Elizabeth City, Gloucester, James City, Matthews, Middlesex, Warwick, City of Williamsburg, and York.

37. Griffith, *The Rise and Development of the Gerrymander*, discusses this district as well, but suggests another rearrangement of counties—Middlesex placed in the Twelfth District—that would achieve similar objectives. Both rearrangements of counties would rebalance district populations while maintaining contiguous districts. That neither option was pursued further suggests that they were purposely overlooked by the Democratic-Republicans.

7. *National Electoral Development and Party Systems*

1. There is evidence that citizens engaged representatives to the early Congresses. See Cunningham, *The Process of Government Under Jefferson,* 300.

2. Formisano, "Deferential-Participant Politics," 483, emphasis added.

3. Purcell, *Connecticut in Transition,* 193–194.

4. Purcell, *Connecticut in Transition,* 194.

5. Zagarri. *Revolutionary Backlash,* 157.

6. Reeve Huston, "Rethinking the Origins of Partisan Democracy in the United States, 1795–1840," in *Practicing Democracy: Popular Politics in the United States from the Constitution to the Civil War,* ed. A. I. P. Smith and Daniel Peart (Charlottesville: University of Virginia Press, 2014), 54.

7. Kenneth Owen, "Legitimacy, Localism and the First Party System," in *Practicing Democracy: Popular Politics in the United States from the Constitution to the Civil War,* ed. A. I. P. Smith and Daniel Peart (Charlottesville: University of Virginia Press, 2014), 175, 190.

8. Cohen et al., *The Party Decides,* 26–29.

9. Joel H. Silby, *The American Political Nation, 1838–1893* (Stanford, CA: Stanford University Press, 1991), 15.

10. Donald J. Ratcliffe, *Party Spirit in a Frontier Republic: Democratic Politics in Ohio 1793–1821* (Columbus: Ohio State University Press, 1998), 85.

11. Ratcliffe, *Party Spirit in a Frontier Republic,* 83–84.

12. Richard S. Katz, *Democracy and Elections* (Oxford: Oxford University Press, 1997), 243.

13. Peart, *Era of Experimentation,* 7.

14. Michael Lewis-Beck et al., *The American Voter Revisited* (Ann Arbor: University of Michigan Press, 2008), 89–97.

15. The seminal theoretical discussion is found in Anthony Downs, *An Economic Theory of Democracy* (New York: Harper & Row, 1957). For an overview of the empirical literature, see Benny Geys, "Explaining Voter Turnout: A Review of Aggregate-Level Research," *Electoral Studies* 25, no. 4 (December 2006): 637–663.

16. Williamson, *American Suffrage,* 133.

17. Ratcliffe, *Party Spirit in a Frontier Republic,* 2–5.

18. See Dow, *Electing the House,* figure 8.1.

19. Rusk, *A Statistical History of the American Electorate,* 204.

20. This total does not include a couple of seats that were not immediately awarded because of a special election, and other circumstances not clear from the raw returns.

21. New Jersey *Centinel of Freedom,* November 3, 1812.

22. Polsby, "The Institutionalization of the US House of Representatives."

23. *Albany Advertiser,* March 23, 1816.

24. Claggett, Flanigan, and Zingale, "Nationalization of the American Electorate."

25. Elmer E. Schattschneider, *The Semisovereign People: A Realist's View of Democracy in America* (Fort Worth, TX: Harcourt Brace Jovanovich, 1975), 90–91.

26. New Jersey used three dual-member districts in 1813. In 1824 one New Hampshire Federalist contested the election, but the party did not field a slate. Beginning in 1821 a few Connecticut Federalists won votes in the general election, but the party presented no organized opposition. In Georgia candidates stood and secured votes in 1798, 1802, and 1808, but there was little or no organized Federalist opposition in the era.

27. Combined, in 1810 these states count 2,874,534 persons, which is roughly 40 percent of the total US population. These numbers must be interpreted while recognizing the large numbers of enslaved persons in Virginia and Maryland.

28. For a discussion of the tensions in Connecticut political culture and the efforts to sustain the Standing Order, see Sassi, "The First Party Competition."

29. Zagarri, *Revolutionary Backlash*, 36.

30. James W. Ceaser, *Presidential Selection: Theory and Development* (Princeton, NJ: Princeton University Press, 1979), 123.

31. Ceaser, *Presidential Selection*, 127–153.

32. Ceaser, *Presidential Selection*, 135.

33. Ceaser, *Presidential Selection*, 153.

34. James Madison, "For the *National Gazette*, 22 September 1792," Founders Online, National Archives, https://founders.archives.gov/documents/Madison/01-14-02-0334.

35. Stanley Elkins and Eric McKitrick, *The Age of Federalism: The Early American Republic, 1788—1800* (New York: Oxford University Press, 1993), esp. chap. 7.

36. Hofstadter, *The Idea of a Party System*, 212–231.

37. Fischer, *The Revolution of American Conservatism*, 57–72.

38. Huston, "Rethinking the Origins of Partisan Democracy in the United States," 47.

Bibliography

"Address of the District Delegates to the Democratic Citizens of the County of Philadelphia." 1810. Reprinted by American Antiquarian Society, Worchester, MA: 2018.

Aldrich, John H. *Why Parties? The Origin and Transformation of Party Politics in America.* Chicago: University of Chicago Press, 1995.

Aldrich, John H., and Ruth W. Grant. "The Antifederalists, the First Congress, and the First Parties." *Journal of Politics* 55, no. 2 (May 1993): 295–326.

Ball, Burgess. "Letter from Burgess Ball to James Madison, 8 December 1788." In *The Documentary of the First Federal Elections: 1788–1790, Vol. II,* edited by Gordon DenBoer. Madison: University of Wisconsin Press, 1984.

Beneke, Chris. "Review: The New, New Political History." *Reviews in American History* 33, no. 3 (September 2005): 314–324.

Berlin, Ira. *Many Thousands Gone: The First Two Centuries of Slavery in North America.* Cambridge, MA: Belknap Press of Harvard University Press, 1998.

Bianco, William T., David B. Spence, and John D. Wilkerson. "The Electoral Connection in the Early Congress: The Compensation Act of 1816." *American Journal of Political Science* 40, no. 1 (February 1996): 145–171.

Bohmer, David A. "The Maryland Electorate and the Concept of a Party System in the Early National Period." In *The History of American Electoral Behavior,* edited by Joel H. Silbey, Alland G. Bogue, and William H. Flanigan. Princeton, NJ: Princeton University Press, 1978.

Brooke, John L. *Columbia Rising: Civil Life on the Upper Hudson from the Revolution to the Age of Jackson.* Chapel Hill: University of North Carolina Press, 2010.

Broussard, James H. *The Southern Federalist, 1800–1816.* Baton Rouge: Louisiana State University Press, 1979.

Brown, Robert E. *Middle-Class Democracy and the Revolution in Massachusetts, 1691–1780.* Ithaca, NY: Cornell University Press, 1955.

Brown, Robert E., and B. Katherine Brown. *Virginia 1705–1786: Democracy or Aristocracy.* East Lansing: Michigan State University Press, 1964.

Burke, Edmund. "Letter to Langriche from Edmund Burke." In *The Concept of Representation,* edited by Hanna Pitkin. Berkeley: University of California Press, 1967.

Burnham, Walter Dean. "The Changing Shape of the American Political Universe." *American Political Science Review* 59, no. 1 (March 1965): 7–28.

———. "Elections as Democratic Institutions." In *Elections in America,* edited by Kay Lehman Schlozman. Boston: Allen & Unwin, 1987.

———. *Voting in American Elections: The Shaping of the American Political Universe Since 1788.* Bethesda, MD: Academica Press, 2010.

Carrington, Edward. "Letter from Edward Carrington to James Madison, 30 December 1788." In *The Documentary History of the First Federal Elections: 1788–1790, Vol. II*, edited by Gordon DenBoer. Madison: University of Wisconsin Press, 1984.

Carson, Jamie L., and Erik J. Engstrom. "Assessing the Electoral Connection: Evidence from the Early United States." *American Journal of Political Science* 49, no. 4 (October 2005): 746–757.

Carson, Jamie L., and Jeffrey A. Jenkins. "Examining the Electoral Connection Across Time." *Annual Review of Political Science* 14 (2011): 25–46.

Ceaser, James W. *Presidential Selection: Theory and Development.* Princeton, NJ: Princeton University Press, 1979.

Census Bureau. Working Paper POP-WP027, Washington, DC, 1998.

Chambers, William Nisbet. "Party Development and the American Mainstream," in *The American Party System: Stages of Political Development*, 2nd[d] ed., ed. William Nisbet Chambers, Walter Dean Burnham, and Frank J. Sorauf. New York: Oxford University Press, 1975.

———. *Political Parties in a New Nation: The American Experience, 1776–1809.* New York: Oxford University Press, 1963.

Chambers, William Nisbet, Walter Dean Burnham, and Frank J. Sorauf, eds. *The American Party System: Stages of Political Development*, 2nd ed. New York: Oxford University Press, 1975.

Chhibber, Pradeep, and Ken Kollman. "Party Aggregation and the Number of Parties in India and the United States." *American Political Science Review* 92, no. 2 (June 1998): 329–342.

Claggett, William, William Flanigan, and Nancy Zingale. "Nationalization of the American Electorate." *American Political Science Review* 78, no. 1 (1984): 77–91.

Clayton, Andrew R. L. "The Fragmentation of a 'Great Family': The Panic of 1819 and the Rise of the Midding Interest in Boston, 1818–1822." *Journal of the Early Republic* 2 (Summer 1982): 143–167.

Cohen, Marty, David Karol, Hans Noel, and John Zaller. *The Party Decides: Presidential Nominations Before and After Reform.* Chicago: University of Chicago Press, 2008.

Countryman, Edward. "The Empire State and the Albany Regency." In *The Empire State: A History of New York*, edited by Milton M. Klein. Ithaca, NY: Cornell University Press, 2001.

———. "A Large and Valuable Canal." In *The Empire State: A History of New York*, edited by Milton M. Klein. Ithaca, NY: Cornell University Press, 2001.

Cox, Gary W. *The Efficient Secret: The Cabinet and the Development of Political Parties in Victorian England.* New York: Cambridge University Press, 1987.

———. "Electoral Rules and Electoral Connection." *Annual Review of Political Science* 2 (1999): 145–161.

———. *Making Votes Count: Strategic Coordination in the World's Electoral Systems.* New York: Cambridge University Press, 1997.

Cox, Gary W., and Mathew McCubbins. "The Institutional Determinants of Policy Outcomes." In *Presidents, Parliaments, and Policy*, edited by Stephan Haggard and Mathew D. McCubbins. Cambridge: Cambridge University Press, 2001.

Cunningham, Nobel E., Jr. *The Jeffersonian Republicans: The Formation of Party Organization, 1789–1801*. Chapel Hill: University of North Carolina Press, 1957.

———. *The Jeffersonian Republicans in Power: Party Operations, 1801–1809*. Chapel Hill: University of North Carolina Press, 1963.

———. *The Process of Government Under Jefferson*. Princeton, NJ: Princeton University Press, 1978.

———. "Who Were the Quids?" *Mississippi Valley Historical Review* 50, no. 2 (September 1963): 252–263.

DenBoer, Gordon, ed. *The Documentary History of the First Federal Elections: 1788–1790*, vol. 2. Madison: University of Wisconsin Press, 1984.

Dinkin, Robert J. *Voting in Revolutionary America: A Study of Elections in the Original Thirteen States, 1776–1789*. Westport, CT: Greenwood Press, 1982.

Dow, Jay K. *Electing the House: The Adoption and Performance of the US Single-Member District Electoral System*. Lawrence: University Press of Kansas, 2017.

Downs, Anthony. *An Economic Theory of Democracy*. New York: Harper & Row, 1957.

Dubin, Michael J. *Party Affiliations in the State Legislatures: A Year by Year Summary, 1796–2006*. Jefferson, NC: McFarland, 2007.

Elkins, Stanley, and Eric McKitrick. *The Age of Federalism: The Early American Republic, 1788–1800*. New York: Oxford University Press, 1993.

Fenton, John H. *Politics in the Border States*. New Orleans: Hauser Press, 1957.

Finocchiaro, Charles J., and Jeffery A. Jenkins. "Distributive Politics, the Electoral Connection, and the Antebellum US Congress: The Case of Military Service Pensions." *Journal of Theoretical Politics* 28, no. 2 (April 2016): 192–224.

Fischer, David Hackett. *The Revolution of American Conservatism: The Federalist Party in the Era of Jeffersonian Democracy*. New York: Harper & Row, 1965.

Formisano, Ronald P. "Deferential-Participant Politics: The Early Republic's Political Culture: 1789–1840." *American Political Science Review* 68, no. 2 (June 1974): 473–487.

———. "Federalists and Republicans: Parties, Yes—System, No." In *The Evolution of American Electoral Systems*, edited by Paul Kleppner, Walter Dean Burham, Ronald P. Formisano, Samuel P. Hays, Richard Jensen, and William G. Shade. Westport, CT: Greenwood Press, 1981.

Geys, Benny. "Explaining Voter Turnout: A Review of Aggregate-Level Research." *Electoral Studies* 25, no. 4 (December 2006): 637–663.

Gibson, Campbell. *Population of the 100 Largest Cities and Other Urban Places in the United States: 1790 to 1990*. Working Paper POP-WP027. Washington, DC: Census Bureau, 1998.

Gooch, Aric, and Jay Dow. "Congressional Nominations and Party Emergence, 1788–1808." *Social Science Quarterly* 102, no. 6 (2022): 2836–2848.

Goodman, Paul. "The First American Party System." In *The American Party Systems: Stages of Political Development*, edited by W. N. Chambers and Walter Dean Burnham. New York: Oxford University Press, 1967.

Gosse, Van. *The First Reconstruction: Black Politics in America from the Revolution to the Civil War*. Chapel Hill: University of North Carolina Press, 2021.

Griffith, Elmer C. *The Rise and Development of the Gerrymander.* Chicago: Scott, Foreman, 1907.

Gross, Robert A., and Mary Kelly. *A History of the Book in America,* vol. 2. Chapel Hill: University of North Carolina Press, 2010.

Hacker, J. D. "Decennial Life Tables for the White Population of the United States, 1790–1900." *Historical Methods* 42, no. 2 (2010): 45–79.

Haines, Michael R., and Inter-university Consortium for Political and Social Research. *Historical, Demographic, Economic, and Social Data: The United States, 1790–2002.* Hamilton, NY: Colgate University, 2010. https://doi.org/10.3886/ICPSR02896.v3.

Higginbotham, Sanford W. *The Keystone in the Democratic Arch: Pennsylvania Politics, 1800–1816.* Philadelphia: Pennsylvania Historical and Museum Commission, 1952.

Hoadley, James F. "The Emergence of Political Parties in Congress, 1789–1803." *American Political Science Review* 74, no. 3 (1980): 757–779.

———. *Origins of American Political Parties, 1789–1803.* Lexington: University Press of Kentucky, 1986.

Hofstadter, Richard. *The Idea of a Party System: The Rise of Legitimate Opposition in the United States, 1780–1840.* Berkeley: University of California Press, 1972.

Houpt, David W. "Contested Election Laws: Representation, Elections, and Party Building in Pennsylvania, 1788–1794." *Pennsylvania History: A Journal of Mid-Atlantic Studies* 79, no. 3 (Summer 2012): 257–283.

Hunter, Thomas Rogers. "The First Gerrymander? Patrick Henry, James Madison, James Monroe, and Virginia's 1788 Congressional Districting." *Early American Studies, An Interdisciplinary Journal* 9, no. 3 (Fall 2011): 781–820.

Huston, Reeve. *Rethinking the Origins of Partisan Democracy in the United States, 1795–1840.* In *Practicing Democracy: Popular Politics in the United States from the Constitution to the Civil War,* edited by A. I. P. Smith and D. Peart. Charlottesville: University of Virginia Press, 2014.

James, Scott C. "Patronage Regimes and American Party Development from 'The Age of Jackson' to the Progressive Era." *British Journal of Political Science* 36 (2006): 39–60.

Johnson, Paul E. *The Early American Republic, 1789–1829.* New York: Oxford University Press, 2007.

Katz, Richard S. *Democracy and Elections.* Oxford: Oxford University Press, 1997.

Kirby, John B. "Early American Politics—The Search for Ideology: An Historiographical Analysis and Critique of the Concept of "Deference." *Journal of Politics* 32, no. 4 (November 1970): 808–838.

Kernell, Samuel. "Toward Understanding 19th Century Congressional Careers: Ambition, Competition and Rotation." *American Journal of Political Science* 21, no. 4 (1997): 669–693.

Key, V. O., Jr. *Southern Politics in State and Nation.* New York: Knopf, 1949.

_____. "A Theory of Critical Elections." *Journal of Politics* 17, no. 1 (1955): 3–18.

Keyssar, Alexander. *The Right to Vote: The Contested History of Democracy in the United States,* rev. ed. New York: Basic Books, 2000.

Kim, Jae-On, John R. Petrocik, and Stephen N. Enokson. "Voter Turnout

Among the American States: Systemic and Individual Components." *American Political Science Review* 69, no. 1 (1975): 107–123.

Kirby, John B. "Early American Politics—The Search for Ideology: An Historiographical Analysis and Critique of the Concept of 'Deference.'" *Journal of Politics* 32, no. 4 (1970): 808–838.

Klinghoffer, Judith Apter, and Lois Elkins. "'The Petticoat Electors': Women's Suffrage in New Jersey, 1776–1807." *Journal of the Early Republic* 12, no. 2 (1992): 159–193.

Koschnik, Albrecht. "Political Conflict and Public Contest: Ritual of National Celebration in Philadelphia, 1788–1815." *Pennsylvania Magazine of History and Biography* 118, no. 3 (1994): 209–248.

Labunski, Richard. *James Madison and the Struggle for the Bill of Rights.* New York: Oxford University Press, 2006.

Lampi, Phillip J. "The Federalist Party Resurgence, 1808–1816: Evidence from the New Nation Votes Database." *Journal of the Early Republic* 33, no. 2 (2013): 255–281.

———. A New Nation Votes: American Election Returns, 1787–1825. American Antiquarian Society, 2007. https://elections.lib.tufts.edu/.

Leonard, Gerald, and Saul Cornell. *The Partisan Republic: Democracy, Exclusion and the Fall of the Founders' Constitution, 1780s-1830s.* New York: Cambridge University Press, 2019.

"Letter to the Freeholders of the Several Religious Denominations . . . ," *Virginia Herald* (Fredericksburg), January 15, 1789. Reprinted in Gordon DenBoer, ed., *The Documentary History of the First Federal Elections: 1788–1790, Vol. II* (Madison: University of Wisconsin Press, 1984.

Lewis-Beck, Michael S., Helmut Norpoth, William G. Jacoby, and Herbert F. Weisberg. *The American Voter Revisited.* Ann Arbor: University of Michigan Press, 2008.

Lockridge, Kenneth. *Literacy in Colonial New England.* New York: W. W. Norton, 1975.

Long, John Hamilton, ed. *Atlas of Historical County Boundaries.* Chicago: Newberry Library, Dr. William M. Scholl Center for American History and Culture, 2012. https://www.loc.gov/item/2018487899/.

Luetscher, George Daniel. *Early Political Machinery in the United States.* Philadelphia: University of Pennsylvania, 1903.

Madison, James. *Federalist,* no. 39, "Conformity of the Plan to Republican Principles." *Independent Journal,* January 16, 1788. http://www.constitution.org/fed/federa39.htm.

———. "For the *National Gazette,* 22 September 1792." Founders Online, National Archives, https://founders.archives.gov/documents/Madison/01-14-02-0334.

———. "Letter from James Madison to Thomas Jefferson, 8 December 1788." In *The Documentary of the First Federal Elections: 1788–1790, Vol. II,* edited by Gordon DenBoer. Madison: University of Wisconsin Press, 1984.

———. "Letter to the Freeholders of the Several Religious Denominations in the *Virginia Herald* (Fredericksburg) 15 January 1789." In *The Documentary*

History of the First Federal Elections: 1788–1790, Vol. II, edited by Gordon DenBoer. Madison: University of Wisconsin Press, 1984.

Martis, Kenneth C. *The Historical Atlas of Political Parties in the United States Congress, 1789–1989.* New York: Macmillan, 1989.

McCormick, Richard P. *The History of Voting in New Jersey: A Study of the Development of Election Machinery, 1664–1911.* New Brunswick, NJ: Rutgers University Press, 1953.

———. "New Perspectives on Jacksonian Politics." *American Historical Review* 65, no. 2 (January 1960): 288–301.

———. "The Party Period and Public Policy: An Exploratory Hypothesis." *Journal of American History* 66, no. 2 (1979): 279–298.

———. "Political Development and the Second Party Systems: Stages of Political Development." New York: Oxford University Press, 1975.

———. *The Second American Party System: Party Formation in the Jacksonian Era.* Chapel Hill: University of North Carolina Press, 1966.

McDonald, Michael P. United States Election Project. Accessed September 23, 2019. http://www.electproject.org.

Morgenstern, Scott, Stephen M., Swindel, and Andrea Castagnola. "Nationalization and Institutions." *Journal of Politics* 71, no. 4 (2009): 1322–1341.

Munroe, John A. *Federalist Delaware 1775–1815.* New Brunswick, NJ: Rutgers University Press, 1954.

Owen, Kenneth. "Legitimacy, Localism and the First Party System." In *Practicing Democracy: Popular Politics in the United States from the Constitution to the Civil War,* edited by A. I. P. Smith and D. Peart. Charlottesville: University of Virginia Press, 2015.

Pasley, Jeffrey L. "The Cheese and the Words: Popular Political Culture and Participatory Democracy in the Early American Republic." In *Beyond the Founders: New Approaches to the Political History of the Early American Republic,* edited by Jeffrey L. Pasley, Andrew Whitmore Robertson, and David Waldstreicher. Chapel Hill: University of North Carolina Press, 2004.

———. *The First Presidential Contest: 1796 and the Founding of American Democracy.* Lawrence: University Press of Kansas, 2013.

———. *The Tyranny of Printers: Newspaper Politics in the Early American Republic.* Charlottesville: University of Virginia Press, 2001.

Patterson, Samuel C., and Gregory A. Caldeira. "Getting Out the Vote: Participation in Gubernatorial Elections." *American Political Science Review* 77, no. 3 (1983): 675–689.

Peart, Daniel. *Era of Experimentation: American Political Practices in the Early Republic.* Charlottesville: University of Virginia Press, 2014.

Peart, Daniel, and Adam I. P. Smith. *Practicing Democracy: Popular Politics in the United States from the Constitution to the Civil War.* Charlottesville: University of Virginia Press, 2015.

Pitkin, Hanna Fenichel. *The Concept of Representation.* Berkeley: University of California Press, 1967.

Pole, J. R. *Political Representation in England and the Origins of the American Republic.* Berkeley: University of California Press, 1966.

———. "Suffrage and Representation in Maryland from 1776 to 1810: A Statistical Note and Some Reflections." *Journal of Southern History* 24, no. 2 (May 1958): 218–225.

Polgar, Paul J. "'Whenever They Judge It Expedient': The Politics of Partisanship and Free Black Voting Rights in Early National New York." *American Nineteenth Century History* 12 (2011): 1–23.

Polsby, Nelson W. "The Institutionalization of the US House of Representatives." *American Political Science Review* 62, no. 1 (1968): 144–168.

Purcell, Richard J. *Connecticut in Transition 1775–1818*. Middletown, CT: Wesleyan University Press, 1963.

Ratcliffe, Donald J. *Party Spirit in a Frontier Republic*. Columbus: Ohio State University Press, 1998.

———. "The Right to Vote and the Rise of Democracy, 1787–1828." *Journal of the Early Republic* 33 (Summer 2013): 221–230.

Reardon, John J. "Religious and Other Factors in the Defeat of the 'Standing Order' in Connecticut, 1800–1818." *Historical Magazine of the Protestant Episcopal Church* 30, no. 2 (1961): 93–110.

Robertson, Andrew W. "Afterword: Reconceptualizing Jeffersonian Democracy." *Journal of the Early Republic* 33, no. 2 (2013): 317–334.

———. "Jeffersonian Parties, Politics, and Participation." In *Practicing Democracy: Popular Politics in the United States from the Constitution to the Civil War*, edited by Daniel Peart and Adam I. P. Smith. Charlottesville: University of Virginia Press, 2015.

———. *The Language of Democracy: Political Rhetoric in the United States and Britain, 1790–1900*. Charlottesville: University of Virginia Press, 1995.

———. "Voting Rites and Voting Acts: Electioneering Ritual, 1790–1820." In *Beyond the Founders: New Approaches to the Political History of the Early American Republic*, edited by Jeffrey L. Pasley, Andrew W. Robertson, and David Waldstreicher. Chapel Hill: University of North Carolina Press, 2004.

Ross, Robert E. *The Framers' Intentions: The Myth of the Nonpartisan Constitution*. South Bend, IN: Notre Dame Press, 2019.

Rusk, Jerrold G. *A Statistical History of the American Electorate*. Washington, DC: CQ Press, 2001.

Sassi, Johnathan D. "The First Party Competition and Southern New England's Public Christianity." *Journal of the Early Republic* 21, no. 2 (2001): 261–299.

Schattschneider, Elmer E. *The Semisovereign People: A Realist's View of Democracy in America* Fort Worth, TX: Harcourt Brace Jovanovich, 1975.

Schlesinger, A. "Political Party Organization." In *Handbook of Organizations*, edited by James G. March. Chicago: Rand McNally, 1965.

Selinger, Jeffrey S. "Rethinking the Development of Legitimate Party Opposition in the United States, 1793–1828." *Political Science Quarterly* 127, no. 2 (2012): 263–287.

Shade, William G. "Political Pluralism and Party Development: The Creation of a Modern Party System: 1815–1852." In *The Evolution of American Electoral Systems*, edited by Paul Kleppner. Westport, CT: Greenwood Press, 1981.

Shankman, Andrew. *Crucible of American Democracy: The Struggle to Fuse Egalitari-*

anism and Capitalism in Jeffersonian Pennsylvania. Lawrence: University Press of Kansas, 2004.

Silbey, Joel H. *The American Political Nation, 1838–1893.* Stanford, CA: Stanford University Press, 1991.

———. "Beyond Realignment and Realignment Theory: American Political Eras, 1789–1989." In *The End of Realignment? Reinterpreting American Electoral Eras,* edited by Byron E. Schafer. Madison: University of Wisconsin Press, 1991.

———. "The Incomplete World of American Politics, 1815–1829: Presidents, Parties and Politics in the 'Era of Good Feelings.'" *Congress and the Presidency* (March 1984): 1–17.

———. "The Origins and Development of U.S. Political Parties, 1790–1861." In *Guide to U.S. Political Parties,* edited by Marjorie Randon Hershey. Washington, DC: CQ Press. 2014.

Skeen, C. Edward. "'Vox Populi, Vox Dei': The Compensation Act of 1816 and the Rise of Popular Politics." *Journal of the Early Republic* 6, no. 3 (Autumn 1986): 257–274.

Sloan, William David. "The Party Press: The Newspaper Role in National Politics, 1789–1816." PhD diss., University of Texas at Austin, 1981.

Sloat, Caroline F. "A New Nation Votes and the Study of American Politics, 1789–1824." *Journal of the Early Republic* 33, no. 2 (Summer 2013): 183–186.

Smith, Jean Edward. *John Marshall: Definer of a Nation.* New York: Henry Holt, 1996.

Soltow, Lee. *Distribution of Wealth and Income in the United States in 1798.* Pittsburgh: University of Pittsburgh Press, 1989.

Stokes, Donald E. "Parties and the Nationalization of Electoral Forces." In *The American Party Systems: Stages of Political Development,* edited by W. N. Chambers and Walter Dean Burnham. New York: Oxford University Press, 1967.

Strum, Harvey. "Property Qualifications and Voting Behavior in New York, 1807–1816." *Journal of the Early Republic* 1, no. 4 (Winter 1981): 347–371.

Sundquist, James L. *Dynamics of the Party System: Alignment and Realignment of Political Parties in the United States.* Washington, DC: Brookings Institution, 1973.

Taylor, Alan. "'The Art of Hook & Snivey': Political Culture in Upstate New York During the 1790s." *Journal of American History,* 79, no. 4 (1993): 1371–1396.

Tinkcom, Harry Marlin. "The Republicans and Federalists in Pennsylvania, 1790–1801." Harrisburg: Pennsylvania Historical and Museum Commission, 1950.

Travers, Len. *Celebrating the Fourth: Independence Day and the Rites of Nationalism in the Early Republic.* Amherst: University of Massachusetts Press, 1997.

Tuberville, George L. "Letter from George Lee Tuberville to James Madison, 14–16 December 1788." In *The Documentary of the First Federal Elections: 1788–1790, Vol. II,* edited by Gordon DenBoer. Madison: University of Wisconsin Press, 1984.

Waldstreicher, David. *In the Midst of Perpetual Fetes: The Making of American Nationalism, 1776–1820.* Chapel Hill: University of North Carolina Press, 1997.

Washington, George. "On Recruiting and Maintaining an Army." In *The Writings of George Washington*. Vol. 4, *1776*, edited by Worthington Chauncey Ford. New York: G. P. Putnam's Sons, 1889. http://oll.libertyfuld.org/titles/2402/.

Williamson, Chilton. *American Suffrage: From Property to Democracy, 1760–1860*. Princeton, NJ: Princeton University Press, 1960.

Wood, Gordon S. *The Idea of America: Reflections on the Birth of the United States*. New York: Penguin Press, 2011.

Young, James Sterling. *The Washington Community: 1800–1828*. New York: Columbia University Press, 1966.

Zagarri, Rosemarie. "Festive Nationalism and Antiparty Partyism." *Reviews in American History* 26, no. 3 (1998): 504–509.

———. "New Jersey." A New Nation Votes. Accessed August 13, 2019. https://elections.lib.tufts.edu/.

______. *The Politics of Size: Representation in the United States, 1776-1850*. Ithaca, New York: Cornell University Press, 1987.

———. *Revolutionary Backlash: Women and Politics in the Early American Republic*. Philadelphia: University of Pennsylvania Press, 2007.

Index

Page references in *italics* indicate a figure; page references in **bold** indicate a table.

www.ingramcontent.com/pod-product-compliance
Lightning Source LLC
LaVergne TN
LVHW091124080826
845145LV00008B/2040

* 9 7 8 0 7 0 0 6 4 3 8 8 2 *